AIR FORCE FOLLOW-ON REVIEW
PROTECTING THE FORCE: LESSONS FROM FORT HOOD

PREVENTING VIOLENCE ...
ENHANCING RESPONSE

EVERY AIRMAN A WINGMAN

AIR FORCE FOLLOW-ON REVIEW
PROTECTING THE FORCE: LESSONS FROM FORT HOOD

Secretary of the Air Force
The Honorable Michael B. Donley

Chief of Staff of the Air Force
Gen Norton A. Schwartz

Chair
Gen Stephen Lorenz

Vice-Chair
Lt Gen Richard Newton

Executive Director
Brig Gen Sharon Dunbar

Director of Staff
Col Joan Garbutt

Headquarters Air Force Representatives

AF/A1	Brig Gen Sharon Dunbar
AF/A2	Maj Gen Jim Poss
AF/A2	Mr. Mark Tapper
AF/A3/5	Mr. Harry Disbrow
AF/A4/7	Ms. Trish Young
AF/A4/7	Mr. David Beecroft
AF/A9	Mr. Kevin Williams
AF/A10	Billy Mullins, PhD
AF/RE	Brig Gen Maryanne Miller
AF/SE	Maj Gen Fred Roggero
AF/SG	Brig Gen Michael Miller
AF/HC	Chap (Maj Gen) Cecil Richardson
AF/HO	Timothy Keck, PhD
AF/JA	Mr. Conrad Von Wald
SAF/AQ	Maj Gen Mike Skinner
SAF/PA	Col Donald Snyder
SAF/GC	Mr. W. Kipling At Lee Jr.
SAF/XC	Mr. Bobby Smart
SAF/IG	Col Kevin Jacobsen
SAF/MR	Ms. Sheila Earle
NGB	Brig Gen Allyson Solomon

Major Command Vice-Commanders and Direct Reporting Unit Commanders

AMC	Lt Gen Vern Findley
AFRC	Lt Gen Charles Stenner
USAFA	Lt Gen Michael Gould
ACC	Lt Gen William Rew
AFMC	Lt Gen Janet Wolfenbarger
AFSOC	Maj Gen Kurt Cichowski
AFOTEC	Maj Gen Stephen Sargeant
AETC	Maj Gen James Whitmore
USAFE	Maj Gen William Chambers
AFSPC	Maj Gen Michael Basla
NGB	Maj Gen Patrick Moisio
AFGSC	Maj Gen James Kowalski
AFDW	Maj Gen Darrell Jones
PACAF	Maj Gen Douglas Owens

Headquarters Air Force Team Leads

Col Elizabeth Arledge
Col Dan Charchian
Col Andy Huff
Col Jim Miner
Col Keith Givens
Col Michael Hafer
Mr. Tom Kelly

Major Command and Direct Reporting Unit Team Leads

AETC	Col Bruce Lovely
PACAF	Col James Strickler
NGB	Col Ronald Gionta
AFSOC	Col Brady Reitz
USAFE	Col Carla Gammon
AMC	Col Frank Jones
AFSPC	Col Gerald Curry
AFGSC	Col Peter Ellis
ACC	Col Robert LaBrutta
AFRC	Col Joseph Vivori
USAFE	Col Gus Green
AFSPC	Col William Hampton
AFOTEC	Col Edgar Vaughan
AFDW	Mr. Steve Doss
AFMC	Mr. Dave Taylor
USAFA	Mr. Paul Ceciliani

Council of Colonels

AF/A1	Col Jim Miner	AF/RE	Col Michael Ricci	SAF/AQ	Col Becky Weirick
AF/A2	Ms. Connie Wright	AF/SE	Col Earle Thompson	SAF/PA	Col Donald Snyder
AF/A3/5	Col Michael Hafer	AF/SG	Col Angela Thompson	SAF/XC	Col Brian Pierson
AF/A4/7	Col Elizabeth Arledge	AF/HC	Chap (Col) Jerry Pitts	SAF/IG	Col Keith Givens
AF/A9	Col Dan Charchian	AF/HO	Timothy Keck, PhD	NGB	Col Ronald Gionta
AF/A10	Lt Col Mark Formica	AF/JA	Mr. Gregory Girard		

Contents

Executive Summary

On 5 November 2009, a tragic shooting allegedly carried out by a military member at Fort Hood, Texas, left 13 dead and 43 wounded or injured.[1] Secretary of Defense Robert M. Gates subsequently established the Department of Defense Independent Review Related to Fort Hood and appointed former Secretary of the Army Togo D. West, Jr., and former Chief of Naval Operations Adm Vern Clark to lead that effort. The review identified possible deficiencies and provided recommendations regarding Department of Defense (DoD) policies, programs, and procedures related to force protection, personnel policies, mass casualty response, and sufficiency of care for the health care providers in-

volved in such events. Key concerns included developing a credible process for identifying individuals who pose a potential threat to themselves or others, providing time-critical information to the right people, employing appropriate force protection measures, and planning for and responding to incidents. The report, *Protecting the Force: Lessons from Fort Hood*, was delivered to Secretary Gates on 15 January 2010.[2] It concluded force protection measures focused solely on external threats are no longer sufficient. Force protection measures must now also consider internal threats—"disaffected individuals within the force motivated to violence against the force and the nation."[3]

The DoD report recommended that each of the Services conduct in-depth follow-on reviews. In response, Secretary of the Air Force Michael B. Donley issued Terms of Reference on 25 January 2010 and directed Gen Stephen R. Lorenz, Commander of Air Education and Training Command, to chair an in-depth Air Force Follow-on Review (Air Force FOR) to identify and resolve policy, program, and procedural gaps that could create vulnerabilities to the health and safety of Air Force personnel, other supported personnel, and their families.[4] The Office of the Secretary of Defense (OSD) and other Services likewise initiated reviews based on the DoD report findings and recommendations.

Air Force Follow-on Review

Unit leaders must collect isolated bits of information—like disparate points of light— to concentrate into a single beam focused on preventing violence affecting Air Force personnel and installations.

Although the Air Force review emerged as a result of the shootings at Fort Hood in November 2009, the study expanded its focus beyond traditional force protection measures by addressing a broader range of violent physical threats and the potential precursors or indicators of violence. This attention to indicators sets the conditions for moving toward preventing violence rather than relying on response in its aftermath. This more expansive approach emphasizes integrating existing programs not normally identified within the force protection agenda. For example, the terms *resiliency* and *Wingman* appear throughout our report as desired effects of improving prevention and protection measures.

A New Awareness—Violent Internal Threats

Our review addressed three fundamental force protection shortfalls identified in the DoD report related to the internal threat challenge. First, there is no commonly accepted list of indicators concerning potential violence. Second, outside the medical field, there is no centralized process for assessing an individual's potential for violence. Third, there is no effective means for sharing information about those with a history of violence or those who may become violent. Our team confirmed the DoD findings and concluded that the current means available to unit leaders regarding internal threats are incomplete and may hinder prevention and response efforts. Removing this hindrance requires creating a new force protection culture that incorporates preventive measures aimed at internal threats.

Identifying threats from internal sources is not an exact science—behavioral indicators for different types of violence do exist, but no single set of criteria is sufficient. Specialists are researching and developing

> There is no commonly accepted list of indicators concerning potential violence.

techniques for detecting these indicators. Distinguishing those personnel for whom these indicators are precursors of violence from those who cope effectively with life challenges defines the essence of the problem confronting our leaders at all levels.

Commander's Intent: Preventing Violence through Vigilant Wingmen

Our team found that mental health professionals who specialize in treating violent disorders are best prepared to detect and intervene with at-risk individuals. However, these professionals are not always available or accessible to individuals and unit leaders before the potential for violence becomes reality. To mitigate this, all Air Force members should be trained to understand relevant indicators and apply that knowledge in assessing situations. As Wingmen, Air Force members can help guide troubled or potentially violent individuals more effectively toward the care they need. The overall goal is to move toward an institutional emphasis on preventing violence through trained and vigilant Wingmen.

Situational Awareness—Sharing Information about Indicators

Indicators of potentially violent behavior reside among numerous sources. Organizations like the Community Action Information Board (CAIB) and the Threat Working Group (TWG) focus on specific kinds of information that may help leaders more effectively address trends of concern. Security Forces and the Office of Special Investigations have distinct missions, responsibilities, and restrictions governing the information they can collect, record, and make available to unit leaders. Federal, state, and local agencies may also have information that could help commanders and supervisors prevent an escalation toward violence. At present, however, there is no universally accessible process for sharing information. Further, unless risky or violent behaviors are documented, subsequent commanders and supervisors may not be aware of the potential for violent behaviors. Consequently, the initiative often rests with commanders and supervisors to ask the right questions of the right people, analyze the information, and discern trends toward violent behavior. Routine sharing of information among various organizations and individuals is a prerequisite for more effective force protection against threats, particularly internal threats. We believe that addressing these fundamental challenges is essential to preventing violence that may affect our personnel, our installations, and our community.

Methodology

Our review team conducted simultaneous top-down and bottom-up assessments. Major commands (MAJCOM), direct reporting units (DRU), the Air National Guard (ANG), and the Air Force Reserve Command (AFRC) provided inputs and reviews. Representatives from across the Headquarters Air Force (HAF) staff formed six cross-functional teams—Risk Assessment and Prevention, Sharing Information, Preparing the Force, Developing the Force, Leading the Force, and Responding and Recovering. The HAF also drew upon the DoD findings and recommendations as a baseline from which to assess relevant Air Force policies, programs, procedures, and practices. A full team roster is provided at appendix D.

More than 2,000 Total Force commanders and civilian directors provided insight into practices related to information sharing, training, recognition of internal threats, force protection, and mass casualty response and recovery through a survey conducted by the Air Force Manpower Agency (AFMA). Selected survey results are integrated throughout the report and provided at appendix C.

The team reviewed 160 Air Force publications comprised of 11,386 pages, 111 DoD documents totaling 3,827 pages, 40 publications from other Services totaling 1,565 pages, 33 federal laws and regulations totaling 946 pages, 12 executive orders at 99 pages, and 233 other documents totaling 2,719 pages. In sum, the team evaluated 589 documents comprising 20,542 pages.

Our review developed 118 findings and 151 recommendations focused on preventing violence and enhancing response. A summary of our recommendations appears at appendix E. The terms of reference for both the DoD and the Air Force reviews requested notation of best practices to be shared across the DoD. Those identified during our review are provided in appendix B.

Preventing Violence

The desired effect of our review is to help our leaders anticipate, prevent, and respond to violence. Preventing violence from internal threats requires aligning policies, programs, procedures, and practices. The following chapters recommend ways to augment traditional force protection measures with processes to counter emerging internal threats.

Risk Assessment and Prevention

Risk Assessment and Prevention focuses on identifying indicators of violent behavior, refining guidance on prohibited activities, standardizing tools that address prohibited body markings, assessing the potential for violence, clarifying firearms policies, and promoting consistent application of policies related to workplace violence and religious issues.

Preventing violence is preferable to responding to, and recovering from, tragedies and requires the ability to assess indicators of violent behaviors. Traditional threat assessments do not focus on internal threats that might arise from military personnel, DoD civilians, contractors, and family members. Our team found the *Air Force Leader's Guide for Managing Personal Distress* an available reference tool for assessing potentially violent behavior, but its use is not widespread.

Mental health professionals have requisite knowledge and experience to assist with violence risk assessments; however, traditional clinical roles do not foster close working relationships among mental health

professionals, commanders, unit leaders, and supervisors. Accordingly, our team developed recommendations for policies, programs, and procedures to facilitate regular consultancy between credentialed mental health providers and unit leaders to discuss difficult personnel issues, exchange information, and develop trust.

Our review confirmed the DoD report finding that ambiguities exist in policies governing prohibited activities (e.g.,

association with gangs and subversive groups). Current policies are not sufficient to provide unit leaders adequate guidance for acting on potential internal threats to good order and discipline. The DoD *Interim Recommendations of the Fort Hood Follow-on Review* tasked the Under Secretary of Defense for Personnel and Readiness to ensure guidance on prohibited activities is actionable, includes examples of inappropriate behavior, describes how to respond to uncertain situations, and updates DoD policies as appropriate.[5] We recommend close coordination with DoD to accomplish this review and update applicable Air Force instructions consistent with forthcoming policy changes.

The DoD report and the *Interim Recommendations* identified deficiencies in pre- and post-deployment health assessments as a potential source of vulnerability.[6] We found that Air Force policies removed requirements for personal interviews during post-deployment health assessments. We recommend reinstituting these interviews with credentialed mental health care providers to help redeploying Airmen develop healthy coping strategies for stress. Interviews with trained and experienced personnel should be routine practice to develop resilient Airmen and address self-reported violence risk factors. Coupling post-deployment interviews with partnerships between unit leaders and mental health providers should assist commanders with early intervention of the compounded effects of stress.

The DoD report recommended evaluating the need for a DoD policy on privately owned weapons to align Service policies.[7] Our review discovered a gap in Air Force policy and recommends updating Air Force instructions to comply with the Lautenberg Amendment (18 USC 922), which prohibits possession of firearms by persons convicted of domestic violence offenses.

Sharing Information

Sharing Information addresses force protection-related policies, programs, and procedures concerning commander support forums, background investigations, storing and transferring information, threat reporting systems, protected health information, and information sharing related to cyber activities. A key theme of our review is the need for greater information sharing from the national level to the installation level.

Within the Air Force, several organizations are responsible for elements of the force protection mission. Consolidating these elements under one force protection focal point at the HAF will enable unity of effort from HAF to installation levels. We also examined how organizations support unit leaders as they assess the potential for internal threats at the installation level. Venues like the Community Action Information Board (CAIB) and the Threat Working Group (TWG) inform leaders about specific types of information and threats. Engaging to assist individuals at risk for potentially violent behavior requires a different focus and membership than those found in either the current CAIB or TWG.

We recommend establishing a new installation-level forum called the Status of Health and Airmen Resiliency Exchange (SHARE). Linked to the CAIB, this forum will better support commanders as they address those who experience difficulties. The CAIB can then propose strategies to promote a more resilient Air Force community. Establishing a full-time installation-level position to serve as the executive director of the CAIB and SHARE coordinator will enhance integration across community programs.

In line with DoD report recommendations, we reviewed information-sharing-related issues to ensure the Air Force will be postured to support forthcoming changes to DoD policies. The DoD *Interim Recommendations* highlighted two areas for prompt action: establishing a consolidated law enforcement database and adopting a common threat-reporting system.[8] Our recommendations emphasize close coordination with the ongoing DoD efforts.

While constructive engagement is important to preventing violence from those who experience difficulty coping with stress, we acknowledge the existence of subversive and dangerous threats. We recommend partnering with other Services, DoD, and other government agencies to share information—in appropriate and legal ways—to protect the force from internal threats. Forging closer relationships with agencies that have access to information could better inform unit leaders' decisions.

Our review team found that current background checks may be insufficient to disclose risk factors associated with non-US citizen accessions. Therefore, we recommend more stringent background checks. Other Services have enhanced their screening of alien accessions through the DoD Military Accessions Vital to National Interests (MAVNI) program. This program expands basic background checks to include National/Intelligence Agency checks, a Single Scope Background Investigation, and Automated Continuous Evaluation System. We recommend the Air Force participate in the DoD MAVNI program.

> In order to make informed decisions, a commander needs all the relevant information in a case, which means more data from care providers to build a whole-person picture.
>
> —Survey comment, squadron commander

Preparing the Force

Preparing the Force focuses on organizing for force protection, providing tools for unit leaders to detect and prevent violence, operational reporting procedures, interagency coordination, and joint basing. The Air Force does not have an organizational focal point for integrating force protection policy and guidance. Measures to prepare the force to counter internal threats involve a shift from prevention toward active response. Preparation measures involve engaging with appropriate command and control, notification, and response agencies. Timely notification and warning procedures ensure that US Northern Command (USNORTHCOM) and its Air Force component command (AFNORTH) can assess the threat and coordinate response measures as necessary.

The Air Force should ensure that tenant units and joint partners are included in host installation force protection and emergency management exercises and inspections. Some installations include joint partners and tenant units in exercises and inspections, but involvement is inconsistent. Conversely, Air Force units located on other Service installations must actively participate in exercises and inspections to prepare their personnel for both internal and external threats. Our team recommends coordinating with DoD and the other Services to establish policies, programs, and procedures to close this gap.

A critical element of preparation involves establishing relationships and the ability to share vital information with other Services and agencies in bodies like the Joint Terrorism Task Force (JTTF) and National Counterterrorism Center (NCTC). Both the DoD report and the DoD *Interim Recommendations* noted the importance of representation within the JTTF.[9] We recommend continuing to fill available billets on the JTTF and expanding Air Force participation in the JTTF and the NCTC should additional opportunities become available.

Developing the Force

Developing the Force recommends integrating force protection concepts into the continuum of learning that frames force development for all Air Force personnel. Total Force training and education programs are among the Air Force's most effective tools for improving awareness and influencing behaviors. Several MAJCOMs and DRUs reported examples of the value of Air Force training in saving lives in both military and civilian settings.

Violence from internal threats has many faces, including radicalization, harassment, sexual assault, domestic violence, workplace violence, and suicide.[10] Despite overlapping risk factors, current Air Force training and education programs address most of these topics separately. We recommend synchronizing these training programs to develop awareness of common risk factors and appropriate intervention strategies.

Our review confirmed the DoD report finding that the Air Force rescinded all requirements for workplace violence training in 2008. AF/A1 has initiated action to reinstitute this training to comply with Air Force policy and to improve general awareness of workplace violence indicators and response procedures.

The Air Force is just beginning to define and develop concepts and initiatives to strengthen the resiliency of Airmen and our Air Force community. The new Tiered Airman Resiliency Program supports Airmen returning from deployments by providing services based on specific groups' risks of developing post-traumatic stress symptoms, depression, anxiety, suicidal thoughts, or other potentially adverse conditions.[11] To facilitate early identification of vulnerabilities and awareness of coping tools to manage stressors, we recommend emphasizing resiliency and self-care concepts early and throughout specialty training and continuing education. This much-needed focus will also enhance force readiness.

Care providers—chaplains, medical personnel, mental health providers, and family support personnel—often witness signs indicating a progression toward violent behavior. We recommend including care providers who have special insights and expertise in violence prevention into the continuum of learning to improve the resiliency of the force.

Leading the Force

Individuals who feel isolated or disconnected from their unit, mission, or community may be more prone to violent behaviors or may become more vulnerable or sympathetic to radical or extremist groups. There have been instances when military personnel became violent after being ostracized, harassed, ridiculed, or isolated.[12] This kind of treatment is unacceptable.

> Violence from internal threats has many faces, including radicalization, harassment, sexual assault, domestic violence, workplace violence, and suicide.

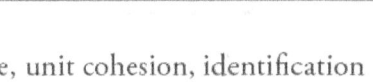

Leaders at all levels must foster good order and discipline, unit cohesion, identification with the Air Force, and a shared sense of community.

Leading the Force recommends improving interaction between unit leaders and their subordinates through engaged interaction with Airmen in transition, Wingman initiatives, feedback processes, support for health care providers, and support for Airmen meeting medical and physical evaluation boards. Because unit leaders are often the first and most visible line of support for their subordinates, they also need support to cope with the stress inherent in leadership responsibilities.

Frequent engagement by leaders at all levels is essential for early intervention to prevent risky and violent behaviors. Our team developed several recommendations to enhance such engagement. Bolstering existing sponsor programs can foster a greater sense of inclusion as Air Force members transition to new assignments. The Air Force can further instill a Wingman culture by improving Wingman Day agendas. Adding force protection strategic messages, themes, activities, and training templates that address potentially violent behavior will raise awareness and enhance prevention. Also, revising current feedback processes should facilitate interaction and achieve a higher level of familiarity between supervisors and subordinates. Increasing the frequency and quality of interpersonal exchanges allows leaders to learn and share information that may better help them support their personnel and the mission.[13]

Providing high-quality health care for the force requires recruiting, caring for, and retaining qualified professionals. The DoD *Interim Recommendations* directed the Under Secretary of Defense for Personnel and Readiness to review and update policies to sustain high-quality care and issue a DoD instruction to reverse stigma associated with medical providers seeking mental health support.[14] Our review confirmed the need for such guidance and developed a parallel finding and recommendation to coordinate with DoD in bolstering care provider resiliency initiatives.

Responding and Recovering

Responding and Recovering addresses lead agent responsibilities for emergency-response and exercise-evaluation teams, emergency management systems at all levels, including emergency communications and common operating picture, high-risk response scenarios, mutual aid agreements, and casualty assistance.

Preventing violence is always preferable to responding to its aftermath. Despite the best efforts of engaged commanders, unit leaders, supervisors, and Airmen, some violent acts will occur. Fortunately, many Air Force emergency preparedness and response policies, programs, procedures, and practices are well designed and implemented. However, we found opportunities to improve installation emergency management programs, notification systems, and on-scene command procedures. The Fort Hood tragedy focused attention on the importance of active shooter response, but the equally effective actions taken by police, emergency services, medical, and casualty affairs personnel helped shooting victims, survivors, and families take the first steps on the road toward recovery.

Executive Summary

Although the DoD report emphasized the strength of some Air Force emergency management programs, we found aspects of our emergency-response program that are not institutionalized. At present, there is no HAF-level office of primary responsibility (OPR) to oversee the Exercise Evaluation Team (EET) program. For installations to be considered fully prepared, exercises should be multifunctional, include tenant units and incidental personnel, and involve off-base organizations to the greatest extent possible. We recommend identifying an OPR to focus and coordinate efforts at the HAF level to ensure MAJCOMs, DRUs, and installations appropriately resource, exercise, and inspect vital emergency preparation and response programs.

The ability to notify personnel of an incident through mass notification and provide updates is essential to timely and effective response and recovery operations. The DoD report determined that the Services do not consistently have mass notification system (MNS) capabilities. We confirmed this finding applies to the Air Force, as MNS capabilities vary from installation to installation. Additionally, DoD and Air Force guidance have not defined clear standards for installation MNS capabilities. The lack of clear guidance, combined with implementation costs, complicates installations' abilities to meet this need. Accordingly, we recommend establishing a formal acquisition program for MNS capabilities, including procurement, sustainment support, and milestones for reaching full operational capability.

An efficient and effective dispatch function is central to getting responders to the scene of an incident. The Air Force has not issued policy to ensure effective routing of emergency calls, to include Enhanced 9-1-1 (E 9-1-1). Accordingly, we recommend designating a single HAF OPR for developing emergency dispatch and response policy.

A common operational picture (COP) information-sharing system should be inherent to an installation's emergency-response capabilities. The Air Force has studied and defined system requirements for sharing common information at both the tactical and strategic levels. The efforts of this research are in the final stages. In the interim, we recommend leveraging existing Web-based systems to close short-term gaps.

Conclusion: Preventing Violence...Enhancing Response

Military, civilians, contractors, and family members experience many of the same sources of stress. Stressors may lead to violence that affects the entire community. All Air Force members must care for those around them and offer support to those who may feel isolated or disassociated. In our research, the team members were reminded time and again of the importance of engaged leadership at all levels. Unit leaders must instill confidence that they are engaged and accessible to their people. Creating more effective and resilient communities, capable of preventing violence from internal and external threats, is essential to meeting the complex and evolving force protection challenge leaders face today.

The recommendations that follow are intended to strengthen the Air Force community through processes that better care for our people, prevent violence, and ultimately protect the force from both internal and external threats. We recommend taking the steps contained in this report as soon as practical.

STEPHEN R. LORENZ
General, USAF

RICHARD Y. NEWTON III
Lieutenant General, USAF

Notes

1. Department of Defense, *Protecting the Force: Lessons from Fort Hood: Report of the DoD Independent Review* (Washington, DC: Department of Defense, January 2010), http://www.defense.gov/pubs/pdfs/DOD-ProtectingTheForce-Web_Security_HR_13Jan10.pdf, 1.

2. Referred to throughout as the DoD report or the DoD IR.

3. *Protecting the Force.*

4. Full text of Terms of Reference is shown at appendix A.

5. Secretary of Defense Memorandum, *Interim Recommendations of the Ft Hood Follow-on Review*, 12 April 2010, 4–5.

6. Ibid., 3.

7. *Protecting the Force.*

8. *Interim Recommendations*, 4–6.

9. Ibid., 5.

10. "The process of adopting or promoting an extremist belief system for the purpose of facilitating ideologically based violence to advance political, religious, or social change." HR 1955, Violent Radicalization and Homegrown Terrorism Prevention Act of 2007, http://www.govtrack.us/congress/billtext.xpd?bill-h110-1955.

11. Lt Gen Bruce Green, USAF, "Tiered, Targeted and Tracked Interventions," presentation, 22 February 2010.

12. For example, an Army sergeant was convicted in 2005 for killing two individuals and wounding 14 others during the opening days of the Iraq war. See "Akbar Convicted of Murder," 22 April 2005, available at http://www.foxnews.com/story/0,2933,154220,00.html.

13. The Air Force Sponsor, Feedback, and Wingman programs share a common goal of fostering personal and professional success for all Airmen. The three separate programs are not connected to a larger Air Force program but could be readily incorporated into the Airman and Family Support pillar in the Year of the Air Force Family program.

14. Ibid., 9.

Cross Reference to DoD Report

Finding 2.1 ✦ **pages 1, 17, 84, 86**

DoD programs, policies, processes, and procedures that address identification of indicators for violence are outdated, incomplete, and fail to include key indicators of potentially violent behaviors.

Finding 2.2 ✦ **pages 29, 32, 84, 86**

Background checks on personnel entering the DoD workforce or gaining access to installations may be incomplete, too limited in scope, or not conducted at all.

Finding 2.3 ✦ **page 20**

DoD standards for denying requests for recognition as an ecclesiastical endorser of chaplains may be inadequate.

Finding 2.4 ✦ **pages 30, 31**

DoD has limited ability to investigate Foreign National DoD military and civilian personnel who require access to DoD information systems and facilities in the US and abroad.

Finding 2.5 ✦ **page 9**

The policies and procedures governing assessment for pre- and post-deployment medical risks do not provide a comprehensive assessment of violence indicators.

Finding 2.6 ✦ **pages 12, 14**

The Services have programs and policies to address prevention and intervention for suicide, sexual assault, and family violence, but guidance concerning workplace violence and potential self-radicalization is insufficient.

Finding 2.7 ✦ **page 18**

DoD policy regarding religious accommodation lacks the clarity necessary to help commanders distinguish appropriate religious practices from those that might indicate a potential for violence or self-radicalization.

Finding 2.8 ✦ **page 37**

DoD Instruction 5240.6, *Counterintelligence (CI) Awareness, Briefing, and Reporting Programs*, does not thoroughly address emerging threats, including self-radicalization, which may contribute to an individual's potential to commit violence.

Finding 2.9 ✦ **pages 34, 36**

DoD and Service guidance does not provide for maintaining and transferring all relevant information about contributing factors and behavioral indicators throughout Service members' careers.

Finding 2.10 ✦ page 37

There is no consolidated criminal investigation database available to all DoD law enforcement criminal investigation organizations.

Finding 2.11 ✦ page 124

DoD guidance on establishing information-sharing agreements with Federal, State, and local law enforcement and criminal investigation organizations does not mandate action or provide clear standards.

Finding 2.12 ✦ pages 46, 75

Policies governing communicating protected health information to other persons or agencies are adequate at the DoD-level, though they currently exist only as interim guidance. The Services, however, have not updated their policies to reflect this guidance.

Finding 2.13 ✦ pages 43, 45

Commanders and military health care providers do not have visibility on risk indicators of Service members who seek care from civilian medical entities.

Finding 2.14 ✦ page 49

DoD does not have a comprehensive and coordinated policy for counterintelligence activities in cyberspace. There are numerous DoD and interagency organizations and offices involved in defense cyber activities.

Finding 2.15 ✦ page 4

DoD policy governing prohibited activities is unclear and does not provide commanders and supervisors the guidance and authority to act on potential threats to good order and discipline.

Finding 2.16 ✦ pages 14, 16

Authorities governing civilian personnel are insufficient to support commanders and supervisors as they attempt to identify indicators of violence or take actions to prevent violence.

Finding 3.1 ✦ pages 57, 59, 62

- DoD has not issued an integrating force protection policy.
- Senior DoD officials have issued DoD policy in several force protection-related subject areas such as antiterrorism but these policies are not well integrated.

Finding 3.2 ✦ pages 27, 61

DoD force protection programs and policies are not focused on internal threats.

Cross Reference to DoD Report

Finding 3.3 ✦ page 68

DoD's commitment to support JTTFs is inadequate.

Finding 3.4 ✦ page 63

There is no formal guidance standardizing how to share Force Protection threat information across the Services or the Combatant Commands.

Finding 3.5 ✦ pages 37, 39, 59

DoD does not have direct access to a force protection threat reporting system for suspicious incident activity reports.

Finding 3.6 ✦ pages 65, 66, 67

There are no force protection processes or procedures to share real-time event information among commands, installations, and components.

Finding 3.7 ✦ pages 39, 40

DoD installation access control systems and processes do not incorporate behavioral screening strategies and capabilities, and are not configured to detect an insider threat.

Finding 3.8 ✦ pages 8, 9

DoD does not have a policy governing privately owned weapons.

Finding 3.9 ✦ page 41

Services cannot share information on personnel and vehicles registered on installations, installation debarment lists, and other relevant information required to screen personnel and vehicles, and grant access.

Finding 4.1 ✦ page 112

Services are not fully interoperable with all military and civilian emergency management stakeholders.

Finding 4.2 ✦ pages 113, 114, 115, 116

There is no DoD policy implementing public law for a 911 capability on DoD installations. Failure to implement policy will deny the military community the same level of emergency response as those communities off base.

Finding 4.3 ✦ pages 119, 120, 122

DoD policy does not currently take advantage of successful models for active shooter response for civilian and military law enforcement on DoD installations and facilities.

Finding 4.4 ◆ pages 108, 113

Based on Joint Staff Integrated Vulnerability Assessments, many DoD installations lack mass notification capabilities.

Finding 4.5 ◆ pages 111, 117, 118

Services have not widely deployed or integrated a Common Operational Picture capability into Installation Emergency Operations Centers per DoD direction.

Finding 4.6 ◆ page 107

Stakeholders in the DoD Installation Emergency Management program, including the Under Secretary of Defense for Policy; Under Secretary of Defense for Personnel and Readiness; Under Secretary of Defense for Intelligence; Under Secretary of Defense for Acquisition, Technology & Logistics; Assistant Secretary of Defense for Public Affairs; and Assistant Secretary of Defense for Networks and Information Integration/Chief Information Officer, have not yet synchronized their applicable programs, policies, processes, and procedures.

Finding 4.7 ◆ page 123

Mutual Aid Agreements (MAAs) between DoD and civilian support agencies across the Services are not current.

Finding 4.8 ◆ page 125

DoD has not produced guidance to develop family assistance plans for mass casualty and crisis response. As a result, Service-level planning lacks consistency and specificity, which leads to variation in the delivery of victim and family care.

Finding 4.9 ◆ page 125

The lack of published guidance for religious support in mass casualty incidents hampers integration of religious support to installation emergency management plans.

Finding 4.10 ◆ pages 79, 80, 81

Inconsistencies among Service entry level chaplain training programs can result in inadequate preparation of new chaplains to provide religious support during a mass casualty incident.

Finding 4.11 ◆ pages 126

DoD has not yet published guidance regarding installation or unit memorial service entitlements based on new Congressional authorization to ensure uniform application throughout the Department.

Cross Reference to DoD Report

Finding 4.12 ✦ page 127

- DoD casualty affairs policy, Federal law, and DoD mortuary affairs guidance do not exist regarding injury or death of a private citizen with no DoD affiliation on a military installation within CONUS.

- There is no prescribed process to identify lead agencies for casualty notification and assistance or to provide care for the deceased, resulting in each case being handled in an ad-hoc manner.

Finding 5.1 ✦ pages 128, 129

- DoD installations are not consistent in adequately planning for mental health support for domestic mass casualty incidents to meet needs of victims and families.

- At Fort Hood, advanced treatment protocols developed at our universities and centers were not available to the commander prior to the incident.

- Fort Hood developed a Behavioral Health plan that incorporated current practices including a "whole community" approach, and a strategy for long-term behavioral health care not reflected in any DoD policy.

Finding 5.2 ✦ pages 82, 83, 84

- DoD does not have comprehensive policies that recognize, define, integrate, and synchronize monitoring and intervention efforts to assess and build health care provider readiness.

- DoD does not have readiness sustainment models, with requisite resources, for the health provider force that are similar to readiness sustainment models for combat and combat support forces.

- The demand for support for caregivers in general, and from mental health care providers in particular, is increasing and appears likely to continue to increase due to the stress on military personnel and their families from our high operational tempo and repeated assignments in combat areas.

Finding 5.3 ✦ pages 99, 100

The lack of a readiness sustainment model for the health provider force, the unique stressors that health care providers experience, and the increasing demand for support combine to undermine force readiness—care for both warriors and health care providers.

Finding 5.4 ✦ page 101

Senior caregivers are not consistently functioning as clinical peers and mentors to junior caregivers.

Chapter 1 ◆ Risk Assessment and Prevention

Military risk assessments have traditionally focused on external threats. The DoD report, however, addressed the need to also encompass internal threats; now is the time to devote more attention to preventing violence while enhancing our response capabilities. Sensing whether a person may become violent begins with understanding how to assess indicators and knowing how to intervene appropriately as a Wingman.

The Air Force has access to useful tools for assessing internal threats, but knowledge of their existence is not widespread, and there is no policy outlining their use. Mental health professionals have the knowledge and experience to help with risk assessment for violence; however, traditional clinical roles do not foster close working relationships between mental health professionals and unit leaders. A strong mental health consultancy program could help unit leaders access collateral workplace information if they have concerns about an Airman's attitude or behavior. Finally, resiliency training and multidimensional fitness may decrease overall violence risk by helping Air Force members become more adaptive to stress at work and home. Assessing risk and preventing acts of violence are not easy. Developing appropriate tools such as acceptable indicators of violence is an essential first step.

> … now is the time to devote more attention to preventing violence while enhancing our response capabilities.

Risk Indicators

Finding 1

(This refers to DoD report Finding/Recommendation 2.1.)

- There is no commonly accepted list of indicators for violence among military personnel.

- Current academic research does not concentrate on, and therefore does not address, potential indicators of violence among military personnel.

- The Air Force has an existing internal risk-assessment resource designed for Air Force leaders; however, Air Force policy does not address it, and awareness of its existence is limited.

- The Army's Criminal Investigation Command and the FBI's Behavioral Science Unit are cooperating to identify motivations and behavioral indicators of violence specific to the military population.

Discussion

Research on long-term indicators of violence in the military community is limited compared to similar research addressing other populations.[1] Developing long-term behavioral indicators in Air Force populations may yield better insight toward progressive indicators of violence and inform modifications to the behavioral screening process. This research may also reveal that indicators leading to violence differ across the Air Force community. According to our survey of unit leaders, negative behaviors regularly documented by unit supervisors differed by Air Force affiliation (active duty, Guard, Reserve, civilian, contractor).[2] Specifically, military leaders were most likely to indicate that supervisors regularly documented financial problems and alcohol abuse, whereas civilian directors were most likely to report documentation of harassing statements, threats of violence, displays of violence, and verbal outbursts.[3] Associations with groups that advocate violence or extremist ideologies were among the least likely behaviors regularly documented.

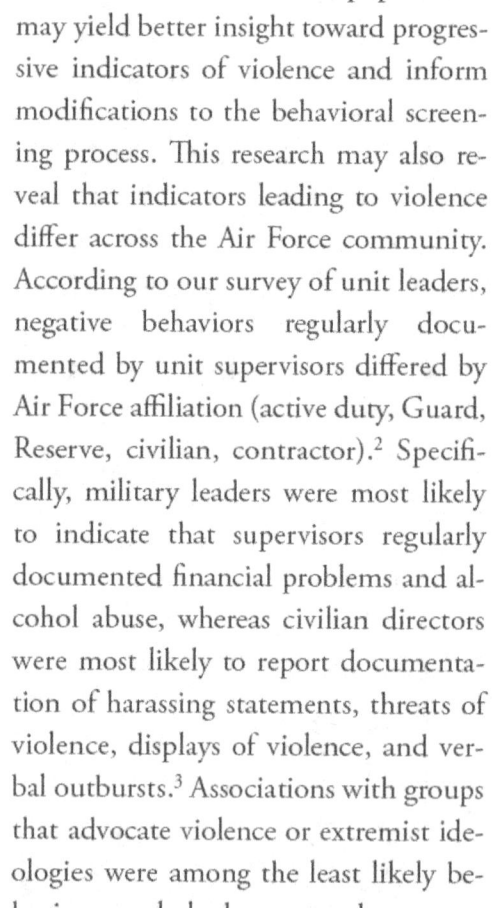

Developing long-term behavioral indicators in Air Force populations may yield better insight toward progressive indicators of violence …

The FBI Behavioral Science Unit's new Comprehensive Analysis of Military Offenders (CAMO) project is designed to apply well-tested methodologies such as the perpetrator-motive research design (for understanding violent criminals in the US population) to the military population.[4] The FBI has offered to assist DoD efforts to develop immediate tactical deliverables (training and consultation) as well as long-term strategic deliverables (predictive analysis). In turn, Air Force participation would help improve FBI interview protocols by including Air Force issues of concern while improving the quality of research.

The DoD report recommended that DoD develop a risk assessment tool. At present, the Air Force provides limited information to help Air Force members detect signs of potential harm. Instruction on other signs of internal threats is directed primarily at organizations that manage risk as a part of their profession (e.g., law enforcement, mental health professionals, and clergy). Although these professionals are trained to address the complexities involved in identifying and preventing potential violence, providing useful and relevant information to all Air Force personnel will better prepare them to identify indicators and alert unit leaders (or support agencies) about behaviors of concern.

Uncertainty about the seriousness of risk factors may be a barrier to reporting concerns. Unit leaders surveyed indicated the most common reason they might be hesitant to report personnel concerns was "not sure there's anything worth reporting" (45 percent). When asked why people in their unit might be hesitant to report possible risk factors for violence, more than 60 percent chose "not sure there's anything worth reporting," and just under 60 percent chose "concern that they might be over-reacting," and/or "concern that they might be wrong."[5]

One available Air Force resource is *The Air Force Leader's Guide for Managing Personnel in Distress*, an online resource to help leaders identify and respond to Air Force members who may pose a risk to themselves or others.[6] Developed by the Air Force Medical Service (AFMS) as a guide for Air Force leaders, this tool contains material related to risks associated with many forms of violence, including terrorism and workplace violence, typically managed by other communities. Sections of this tool were updated in 2009 to address new challenges. Further expansion of this resource—to include guidance specific to contractors, members of other Services, National Guard members, and Reservists—would markedly increase its utility. Air University's *Guidelines for Command* references the AFMS's leadership guide, but it is not referenced in official Air Force policy, and promotion of its use remains limited.[7]

The Air Force must routinely update risk assessment tools in response to changes in the threat environment, advances in behavioral research, and revisions to Air Force, other Service, and DoD policy.

Recommendations

1.1　Develop Air Force policy addressing how risk assessment tools can be used to improve care and overall force protection for Air Force members. (OPR: SAF/IG)

1.2　Develop a risk assessment reference available for all Air Force members. (OPR: AF/SG)

1.3　Partner with the FBI's Comprehensive Analysis of Military Offenders project to ensure that its research approach reflects Air Force concerns and its products are applicable to Air Force populations. (OPR: SAF/IG)

1.4　Continue to update assessment tools as the state of knowledge and policy develop and include appropriate courses of action and resources for active-duty, National Guard, Air Force Reserve, civilians, contractors, and dependents. (OPR: SAF/IG)

1.5　Sponsor research to develop long-term behavioral indicators that may point to progressive indicators of violence among Air Force personnel. (OPR: SAF/IG)

Prohibited Activities

Finding 2

(This refers to DoD report Finding/Recommendation 2.15.)

- Department of Defense Instruction (DoDI) 1325.06, *Handling Dissident and Protest Activities among Members of the Armed Forces*, does not provide clear guidance on extremist and prohibited activities.

- Unit leaders need sufficient guidance to act on potential threats to good order and discipline.

- DoD and the Air Force do not have adequate training tools to support official guidance regarding extremist and other prohibited activities.

Discussion

Organizations, networks, and individuals who advocate hatred and violence present a dynamic challenge for leaders. Only half of the Air Force military leaders and 30 percent of civilian directors surveyed believe they have the means to verify whether groups and/or networks their personnel are associated with pose a threat to the Air Force community.[8]

Chapter 1 ◆ Risk Assessment and Prevention

DoDI 1325.06 is the overarching publication pertaining to prohibited activities.[9] It defines prohibited activities, discusses active participation, and outlines corrective actions for commanders to address such concerns. Commanders have broad authority to employ the full range of administrative and disciplinary actions in addressing active participation in prohibited activities or association with extremist organizations.[10]

Although DoDI 1325.06 governs policies on prohibited activities, it does not clearly define "extremism" and "supremacist," explain what constitutes active participation in extremist organizations, or provide indicators of such involvement. Coordinating with DoD to address these issues in the instruction will enhance Service policies and procedures on identifying extremist and supremacist individuals or organizations.

Air Force Instruction (AFI) 51-903, *Dissident and Protest Activities*, is the overarching Air Force policy regarding prohibited activities for military personnel.[11] It prescribes policy on detecting individuals who engage in supremacist behaviors as outlined in DoDI 1325.06, *Handling Dissident and Protest Activities among Members of the Armed Forces*.[12] A comparison with corresponding Navy, Marine Corps, and Army policies reveals areas for potential improvement to AFI 51-903, including:

- definitions of supremacist and extremist individuals and groups,

- a definition of active participation,

- guidelines for commanders with respect to addressing Air Force members' participation in such groups,

- a list of potential indicators of violent behavior, and

- Total Force training responsibilities.

Our team drafted these changes to AFI 51-903 into a proposed Air Force Guidance Memorandum, currently pending Air Force Judge Advocate (AF/JA) and General Counsel (SAF/GC) review.

The Department of the Army published Pamphlet (DA PAM) 600-15, *Extremist Activities*, to provide guidance for Soldiers, commanders, and others in implementing Army policy on extremist activities and organizations.[13] The pamphlet explains general societal influences affecting members of the Army and underscores that countering extremism is every Soldier's responsibility. It describes supremacist and extremist activities, clarifies rules governing active participation by members with such individuals or groups, and provides commanders, Soldiers, and Army leaders with a training tool to address and educate others on related behaviors. It also lists proactive steps for unit leaders to evaluate and prevent extremist activities and provides instructions for commanders to address extremist behaviors in accordance with Army Regulation (AR) 600-20, *Army Command Policy*.[14] In concert with proposed changes to AFI 51-903, publishing a related AF pamphlet would provide Total Force leaders with an accessible reference from which to train, identify, mitigate, and address behaviors or activities of concern.[15]

Recommendations

2.1   Coordinate with the Under Secretary of Defense for Personnel and Readiness to review and update DoDI 1325.06, *Handling Dissident and Protest Activities among Members of the Armed Forces*, to ensure guidance is actionable and includes behavior examples as well as guidance on how to respond to uncertain situations, and revise AFI 51-903 accordingly. (OPR: AF/JA, SAF/GC)

2.2   Revise AFI 51-903, via an Air Force Guidance Memorandum, to improve identification of potential threats and clarify how commanders may determine which activities, including group participation, are disruptive to good order and discipline. (OPR: AF/JA, SAF/GC)

2.3   Update *The Military Commander and the Law* by adding resources on addressing extremist behaviors, including information or actions that indicate personnel may be engaged in extremist or other prohibited activities. (OPR: AF/JA)

2.4   Ensure unit leaders are aware of DA PAM 600-15, *Extremist Activities*, and consider publishing a similar Air Force document and associated training material to improve current awareness of extremist and prohibited activities. (OPR: AF/JA, SAF/IG)

Prohibited Markings

Finding 3

- DoD and Service programs, policies, processes, and procedures are insufficient to address the full range of prohibited markings, including tattoos, that may indicate affiliation with groups or organizations prone to violence or radicalization.

Discussion

Permanent body markings such as tattoos, branding, and piercings are becoming increasingly common. One 2006 survey found that 36 percent of Americans between 18 and 29 have at least one tattoo, more than twice as many as 40- to 50-year-olds (15 percent).[16] Body art can signify commitment to a group or set of beliefs and therefore can be an important indicator of an individual's evolving belief systems. Specific types of body art may indicate to unit leaders a propensity or potential for violence.[17]

Although DoD and the Services prohibit certain types of body markings, the limits and sanctions vary based on recruiting needs, demographic changes, and other factors. AFI 36-2903, *Dress and Personal Appearance of Air Force Personnel*, addresses Air Force policy on body markings and specifically prohibits tattoos and brands that are obscene; advocate sexual, racial, ethnic, or religious discrimination; are commonly associated with gang affiliations; or are "prejudicial to good order and discipline."[18] The Army, Navy, and Marine Corps policies explicitly prohibit tattoos that are "extremist," although governing policies do not define the term.[19] Those involved in the accessions

process, commanders, and supervisors have wide latitude to determine which markings may exceed standards but do not have a readily accessible tool to provide current information on markings that signify extremist beliefs.

Revising AFI 36-2903 is a major step toward providing guidance on tattoos for the Total Force. While additional tools like an online tattoo database will take more time, revising the instruction and distributing the Air Force Office of Special Investigation's (AFOSI) Criminal Intelligence Bulletin "Visual Iconography: Gang and Right-Wing Hate Group Affiliated Symbols and Body Art" to unit leaders should clarify and standardize identifying and handling tattoos within the Air Force.[20] Additionally, unit leaders need a centralized means of tracking previously approved body markings to inform their decisions.

Recommendations

3.1   Update AFI 36-2903, *Dress and Personal Appearance of Air Force Personnel*, to address prohibited tattoos, brands, and body art and to reference acceptable tools for unit leaders and other Airmen to identify prohibited markings. (OPR: AF/A1)

3.2 Disseminate AFOSI's "Visual Iconography: Gang and Right-Wing Hate Group Affiliated Symbols and Body Art" to commanders as an initial reference tool, followed by the AFI update. (OPR: SAF/IG)

3.3 Establish a comprehensive reference tool of prohibited body markings for recruiters, trainers, commanders, and supervisors. (OPR: SAF/IG)

3.4 Develop a centralized tracking tool to inform commander decisions of previously approved body markings. (OPR: AF/A1)

Firearms Policies

Finding 4

(This refers to DoD report Finding/Recommendation 3.8.)

- Air Force policies and procedures with respect to privately owned weapons are current and consistent with other Service policies but do not address policies for transporting firearms, for personal firearms storage in privatized housing on Air Force installations, or disseminating notice of policies.

Discussion

AFI 31-101, *Integrated Defense,* does not outline firearm policy for occupants of privatized housing. To correct this deficiency, paragraph 8.2.4.2 should be amended to read:

> Use AF Form 1314, *Firearms Registration*, to register privately owned firearms maintained in a government facility or in military family housing (to include public/private venture [PPV] or privatized housing) with the installation security forces.

Forthcoming DoD guidance will also specify minimum procedures for registering, transporting, using, and storing privately owned weapons on DoD installations as well as guidance on communicating policy to installation personnel to include employees, residents, and visitors.[21]

Recommendations

4.1 Amend current Air Force policy and procedures contained in AFI 31-101, *Integrated Defense*, to govern privately owned weapons in all Air Force housing. In doing so, consider whether effective as well as constructive notice is provided to individuals who enter installations but do not live on them. (OPR: AF/A4/7)

4.2   Coordinate with the Under Secretary of Defense for Intelligence to prepare a department-wide interim guidance message and interim guidance that will be incorporated into a revision of DoD 5200.08-R, *Physical Security Program*. (OPR: AF/A4/7)

Finding 5

(This refers to DoD report Finding/Recommendation 3.8.)

- AFI 31-101, *Integrated Defense*, does not require individuals who register privately owned weapons on Air Force installations to certify they have not been convicted of domestic violence in accordance with the provisions of the Lautenberg Amendment (18 USC 922).

Discussion

Current Air Force policy does not require compliance with the Lautenberg Amendment to the 1968 Gun Control Act (18 USC 922).[22] The amendment makes it a felony for those convicted of misdemeanor crimes of domestic violence, including members of the Armed Forces, to ship, transport, possess, or receive firearms or ammunition. DoDI 6400.06, *Domestic Abuse by DoD Military Members and Other Designated Persons*, specifies DD Form 2760, *Qualification to Possess Firearms or Ammunition*, for Service members to certify they have not been convicted of an applicable offense.[23] A requirement to complete DD Form 2760 when registering firearms on base is not codified in Air Force instructions.

Recommendation

5.1   Revise AFI 31-101, *Integrated Defense*, to require individuals to sign DD Form 2760, *Qualification to Possess Firearms or Ammunition*, when firearms are registered in accordance with DoDI 6400.06 and 18 USC 922. (OPR: AF/A4/7)

Assessing the Potential for Violence

Finding 6

(This refers to DoD report Finding/Recommendation 2.5.)

- Post-deployment interviews with properly trained and experienced health care professionals to detect risk for violence are no longer required unless an Airman indicates a problem on his or her post-deployment health reassessment (PDHRA) survey.

- Personal behavioral screenings are not required before deployment. Specifically, Airmen with current periodic health assessments (PHA) and no subsequent duty-limiting conditions are presumed fit to deploy unless otherwise noted in their medical or personnel records.

- Current methods for assessing pre- and post-deployment risk rely extensively on self-reported concerns without the benefit of collateral information from coworkers, immediate supervisors, or family members.

Discussion

The Air Force primarily relies on Airmen self-reporting their pre- and post-deployment health concerns through various questionnaires prescribed by DoD. Individual interviews supplement the post-deployment health assessment (PDHA), and originally were included in a PDHRA six months later.[24]

In late 2009, the Air Force requested a waiver to the policy of including interviews for PDHRAs in which Airmen didn't identify health concerns. The acting Deputy Assistant Secretary of Defense for Force Health Protection and Readiness granted this temporary waiver. Interviews are, however, a clinical standard in violence risk assessment. A closer working relationship between unit leaders and mental health professionals may be an avenue for unit leaders to relay additional pre- or post-deployment behavioral or health concerns to mental health staff. This information flow may include direct observations from coworkers and supervisors. The Fort Lewis Soldier Wellness Assessment Program sets a higher standard for clinical assessment by including personal interviews by a credentialed mental health provider for all redeploying personnel.[25] The use of only credentialed mental health professionals distinguishes the Fort Lewis program from other behavioral PDHA and PDHRA interviews. This initiative emphasizes assessment and preventive care over more traditional mental health clinic-based treatment. Finally, the Air Force should promote greater awareness and acceptance of Airmen raising pre- and post-deployment behavioral concerns to unit leaders. Doing so would be consistent with initiatives to develop resilient Airmen.[26]

Recommendations

6.1   Train health care providers who conduct pre- or post-deployment interviews to assess non-mental-health-related risks for violence (e.g., potential for radicalization, gang involvement). (OPR: AF/SG)

6.2   Expand deployment risk assessment methods to include reliable, accessible collateral information. (OPR: AF/SG)

6.3   Encourage Airmen to share with leadership or support service providers pre- and post-deployment concerns about themselves as well as others. (OPR: AF/SG)

6.4   Consider adopting a program similar to the Fort Lewis Soldier Wellness Assessment Program, which requires all deploying personnel to meet personally with credentialed mental health providers. (OPR: AF/SG)

Finding 7

- Mental health professionals do not, as a matter of routine, serve as expert advisors for commanders and supervisors as they evaluate concerns with personnel or situations in their chain of command.

Discussion

Mental health factors are significant to identifying risk for many types of violence. Ready access and direct consultations with mental health professionals would help commanders and supervisors gain perspective on stress levels and other potential concerns affecting their personnel and ensure they receive timely, expert advice on possible courses of action.

Aligning mental health providers to units in manners similar to chaplains or flight surgeons could facilitate more frequent interaction and help identify concerns. Mental health providers could help unit leaders identify disconcerting behavior or signs of distress and recommend whether evaluation or intervention is warranted. They could also provide commanders with on-site monthly to quarterly consultations to maintain lines of communication, foster discussion of behavioral and leadership issues, and provide an avenue for mental health providers to address unit challenges through training and broader discussions with unit personnel.

Recommendation

7.1   Develop appropriate changes to policy, programs, and procedures to establish mental health consultancy to help unit leaders more effectively address the risks for violence, similar to the manner in which unit leaders consult with chaplains. (OPR: AF/SG)

Workplace Violence

Finding 8

(This refers to DoD report Finding/Recommendation 2.6.)

- There is no overarching DoD policy governing workplace violence prevention and response.

Discussion

The Occupational Safety and Health Administration (OSHA) promotes a set of voluntary guidelines to underpin voluntary workplace violence prevention. The Office of Personnel Management (OPM) also recommends all employees know how to report incidents of violent, intimidating, threatening, or other disruptive behavior.[27] Without overarching DoD policy guidance, the Services and DoD may not be addressing workplace violence sufficiently, effectively, or consistently. The Air Force should work with DoD to develop policy addressing workplace violence.

Recommendation

8.1   Coordinate with DoD to develop workplace violence and internal threat prevention and response policies, programs, and procedures. (OPR: AF/A4/7)

Finding 9

(This refers to DoD report Finding/Recommendation 2.6.)

- Air Force policy addressing violence in the workplace or potential for self-radicalization is inadequate.

Discussion

Effectively addressing workplace violence requires sufficient focus on prevention, training, and response. Prevention efforts should focus on eliminating circumstances associated with workplace violence, such as abuse or marginalization by unit members. Personnel must also be trained to understand indicators of workplace-specific violence and proper reporting of indicators to appropriate agencies. Should prevention efforts fail, swift and appropriate response is paramount to limit the trauma that accompanies violent attacks. Current Air Force workplace violence policy lacks enforcement mechanisms similar to those outlined in AFI 36-2706, *Military Equal Opportunity (MEO) Program*, which requires immediate response to unacceptable behavior.[28]

Although chapter 6 in Air Force Manual (AFMAN) 31-201, vol. 4, *High-Risk Response*, focuses on workplace violence, its two paragraphs on this subject include vague and outdated information.[29] These gaps could result in insufficient workplace violence prevention programs. As a minimum, AFMAN 31-201, vol. 4, should be revised to emphasize engaging unit leaders, contacting Security Forces or OSI for concerns involving workplace violence or potential criminal conduct, or contacting the Equal Employment Opportunity (EEO) Program office for concerns involving discrimination. Additionally, the manual should be revised to reference AFI 44-154, *Suicide and Violence Prevention Education and Training*, as the primary policy document on training and prevention, with reference to OPM violence prevention materials as an additional resource.

The Air Force is currently developing a chapter for inclusion in AFMAN 31-201, vol. 4, on active shooter response based on lessons learned from the Columbine and Virginia Tech shootings.[30] This new material is timely and should support established guidance on countering high-risk threats.

Recommendations

9.1   Revise AFMAN 31-201, vol. 4, *High Risk Response*, to establish policy and procedures on reporting indicators of violence and enable swift and appropriate response to prevent escalation. (OPR: AF/A4/7)

9.2   Update AFI 44-154, *Suicide and Violence Prevention Education and Training*, to include internal threat exercise requirements. (OPR: AF/SG)

Finding 10

(This refers to DoD report Finding/Recommendation 2.6.)

- Air Force policies, programs, and procedures do not address comprehensive workplace violence prevention and response.

Discussion

The DoD report identified a shortfall in policies and programs governing preventing and responding to workplace violence.[31] According to OSHA, workplace violence is violence or the threat of violence against workers, occurring at or outside the workplace; it can range from threats and verbal abuse to physical assaults and homicide.[32] The Air Force derives prevention and response policies and programs from this broad definition. For example, AFI 44-154, *Suicide and Violence Prevention Education and Training*, establishes the Suicide and Violence Prevention and Education Program; AFI 40-301, *Family Advocacy*, establishes the program for family advocacy and domestic violence prevention; and AFI 36-6001, *Sexual Assault Prevention and Response (SAPR) Program*, establishes the SAPR Program.[33]

Currently, separate Air Force functional communities manage policies and programs addressing specific subsets of violence. But they do not identify or link the subset to an overarching focus toward more effective violence prevention and response. Without integrating policies addressing the full spectrum of violence education and training, the Air Force may miss important opportunities to link and reinforce violence prevention, detection, and response capabilities. The same concern exists with current DoD policies.[34] Creating DoD bridge policy similar to that proposed for the Air Force should reduce gaps inherent in separate, functionally managed policies and programs.[35]

Recommendation

10.1   Coordinate with DoD to draft an instruction, followed by a 90- or 40-series AFI integrating the full spectrum of violence into a comprehensive prevention and response program. (OPR: AF/A1)

Finding 11

(This refers to DoD report Finding/Recommendation 2.16.)

- DoD and Air Force contract language do not fully address inappropriate contractor behavior and potential indicators of violence.

Chapter 1 ◆ Risk Assessment and Prevention

Discussion

The Air Force holds contractors responsible for the conduct of their employees. Under current legal and regulatory frameworks, the Air Force can enhance indicator visibility and flexibility for action for contractor behaviors off base only under specific authorities such as determining suitability for access to classified information.

Many contractors sit side by side with members of the Air Force workforce, and they should be held to the same standards. Behavior accountability can be added to current contract language. There is a contract clause addressing business conduct which applies to contracts over $5 million and performance periods of 120 days or greater. However, this does not produce a standard result as each company provides a plan with the language applying to its workforce.[36] For lesser-value contracts, there is no requirement for a clause to address business conduct. A requirement could be drafted and included in the performance of work statement requiring each contractor to submit an employee mitigation plan (code of conduct) detailing how the contractor will handle problem employees if a need arises.[37]

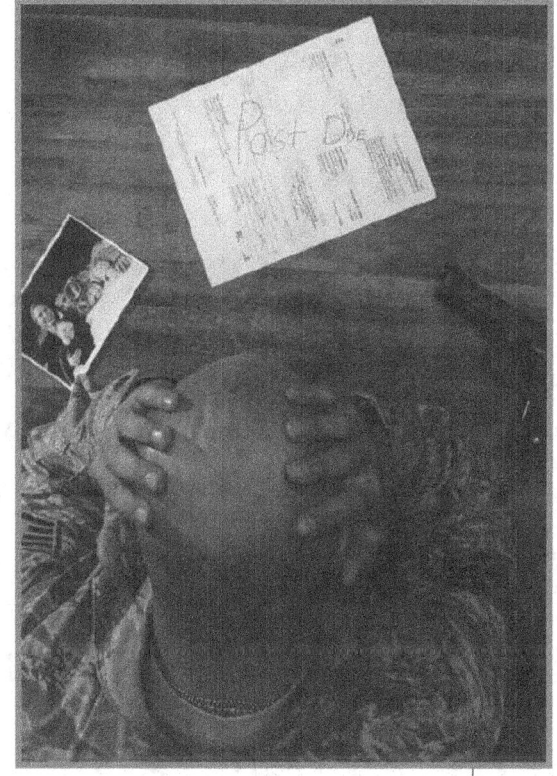

Defense acquisition regulations could be changed to include a standard behavior clause in contracts to address the behavior of contractors who work in government facilities. The intent should be to ensure the government can take appropriate action if contract employees exhibit violent or potentially violent behavior or are found to be engaging in prohibited activities such as associating with hate groups. DoD must develop associated legal justification to effect changes to defense acquisition regulations.

Recommendation

11.1   Coordinate with DoD to establish standard contract language regarding prohibited activities, inappropriate or high risk behavior related to violence in the DoD workplace. If feasible, the standard language should be required for inclusion in all DoD contracts and should parallel standards set for government civilian employees on potential indicators of violence in the workplace. (OPR: SAF/AQ)

Finding 12

(This refers to DoD report Finding/Recommendation 2.16.)

- Air Force policies regarding civilian behaviors do not address all potential indicators of violence in the workplace.

Discussion

Supervisors of civilian employees are expected to act when they perceive indicators of potentially violent behavior or receive a report of such an indicator. Appropriate response may be as basic as showing concern and helping the individual find assistance, or as complex as contacting law enforcement or investigative agencies for threat assessment or intervention. Authority for acting on potential indicators is predicated on requirements such as ensuring a safe and healthy workplace and proper personnel management.[38]

AFI 36-703, *Civilian Conduct and Responsibility*, provides little guidance on violent behavior indicators.[39] Disciplinary and adverse actions could apply for behaviors exhibited at work, off-duty behaviors having a connection to official duties, or actions falling into the category of egregious off-duty misconduct.[40] The basic framework for addressing inappropriate behaviors is sound even though AFI 36-704, *Discipline and Adverse Actions*, was cited in the DoD report as an example of Service guidance being inadequate for addressing civilian behaviors that may be associated with violence in a timely manner.[41] We found, however, that AFI 36-704 provides administrative procedures allowing supervisors to take appropriate action to protect the safety and well being of employees. In cases of imminent threat, the employee can immediately be removed from the

> Authority for acting on potential indicators is predicated on requirements such as ensuring a safe and healthy workplace …

work site; the person would remain in a pay status according to his or her work schedule—but not be physically present at work until the matter is investigated and appropriately resolved.

Further clarification regarding workplace violence in AFI 36-703 should clearly address violent behavior indicators, but it will not be available until administrative staffing, including AF/JA and SAF/GC review, is complete. Federal labor-management relations requirements, including union involvement in the pre-decisional phase, also apply.[42]

Recommendation

12.1   Revise AFI 36-703, *Civilian Conduct and Responsibility*, to more clearly address violence in the workplace. (OPR: AF/A1)

Finding 13

(This refers to DoD report Finding/Recommendation 2.1.)

- The Air Force has no risk assessment tool or program to identify personal risk factors, recommended courses of action, and associated support resources.

Discussion

Formalized resiliency programs could encourage personnel to discuss work, family, and life concerns, as well as improve awareness and access to support resources. The resiliency training developed for medics, security forces, and explosive ordnance disposal personnel could serve as a model. Another model may be the Comprehensive Airman Fitness (CAF) Program, which Air Mobility Command and Air Combat Command are currently testing.[43]

Recommendation

13.1   Address personal resiliency and risk management through formalized programs that provide an overarching approach to identifying and managing stressors. (OPR: AF/A1)

Finding 14

- Current Integrated Delivery System (IDS) community outreach and prevention programs do not integrate information on detecting and preventing internal threats.

Discussion

AFI 90-501, *Community Action Information Board (CAIB) and Integrated Delivery System (IDS)*, requires a comprehensive, coordinated plan for integrating and implementing community outreach and prevention programs (e.g., violence awareness, intervention, and prevention; sexual assault, suicide, and domestic violence prevention).[44] These programs are vital to reaching all personnel and providing persistent violence awareness messages throughout the year.

When surveyed, commanders and directors identified threats from disgruntled personnel, alcohol abuse, and mass casualty incidents involving firearms among their top five internal concerns.[45] These internal threats affect safety, security, force readiness, and quality of life for the entire base community; the CAIB is the primary forum for addressing these issues and their impacts.[46] The IDS allows commanders to focus awareness campaigns as necessary, based on the specific climate and culture at the installation. An integrated program for preventing and responding to the full range of violence, including internal and external threats, strengthens overall force protection, readiness, and quality of life.[47]

Recommendation

14.1   Integrate information on internal threats and workplace violence into IDS community outreach and prevention programs. (OPR: AF/A1)

Religious Issues

Finding 15

(This refers to DoD report Finding/Recommendation 2.7.)

- The lack of consolidated Air Force policy concerning religious accommodation complicates consistent application by unit leaders.

Discussion

The Air Force is committed to recognizing and accommodating religious practices in accordance with the standards provided in the Religious Freedom Restoration Act of 1993. DoDI 1300.17, *Accommodation of Religious Practices within the Military Services*, specifies that decisions related to religious accommodation will reside with military commanders.[48] Accommodation requests are approved by commanders based on review of the duty and mission impact, safety, unit location, and other relevant factors. Although requests are considered on an individual basis, consistent accommodation of religious practices can reduce perceptions of inequities. Consistent application can be difficult to achieve; commanders must refer to several Air Force policies to evaluate whether to grant an accommodation and may not be aware of their option to consult with chaplains and judge advocates general for advice.[49] An AFI consolidating collective guidance on religious accommodation would provide commanders consistent guidance to address issues related to religious accommodation in a fair and informed manner.

Training on religious accommodation should also be consistent and comprehensive. This training is not currently formalized across the Air Force, which may diminish awareness of policies, programs, and procedures as well as consistency in their application. Prospective Air Force wing and group commanders receive training on religious accommodation at their respective pre-command courses at Air University.[50]

Squadron commander course content is developed by each MAJCOM. There is no standardized curriculum addressing religious accommodation policies and procedures or the particular challenges of religious accommodation in joint locations where other Service policies and practices may differ. Although not a specific curriculum item, religious accommodation is generally discussed during the MAJCOM chaplain's module.[51] To ensure clarity and consistency in training, the Air Force Chief of Chaplains, Plans and Programs Division has agreed to annually review, validate, and disseminate to MAJCOMs religious accommodation training resources presented in the wing and group pre-command courses.

Inconsistent responses to requests for religious accommodation may be perceived as discriminatory. In addition, religious-based threats, harassment, jokes or slurs, marginalization, and exclusionary behaviors are other actions that may cause individuals to isolate themselves from the Air Force community. Those individuals may lose their sense of belonging within the organization and build resentment toward those they believe responsible. Air Force personnel may even become violent because of perceptions that they have been treated unfairly based on their religious beliefs or practices. Greater transparency about how accommodation requests are evaluated may help allay concerns of inequity over requests granted in one set of circumstances but denied in another.

Effective in late 2010, all Air Force personnel will be required biennially to complete Total Force awareness computer-based training (CBT) on free exercise of religion as approved by the Secretary of the Air Force.[52] A five-minute supervisory module will supplement the standard 15-minute training. This standardized training will improve overall awareness of policies, programs, and appropriate procedures related to religious practice.

Recommendations

15.1   Consolidate guidance related to religious accommodation (e.g., dress, religious observance, immunization) in a single 52-series AFI. (OPR: AF/HC)

15.2   Revise policy to recommend leaders consult chaplains and legal counsel when making decisions about religious accommodation requests and to guide leaders on the challenges of such decisions in joint environments. (OPR: AF/HC)

15.3   Revise AFI 52-101, *Planning and Organizing*, to include procedures for religious accommodation. After AFPD 52-1 coordination is complete, ensure that the prevention, identification, and response to religious-based disrespect, harassment, and discrimination are sufficiently addressed in relevant training (e.g., equal opportunity training, free exercise of religion training, Wingman training, and commander courses). (OPR: AF/HC)

Finding 16

(This refers to DoD report Finding/Recommendation 2.3.)

- DoD and Air Force policies do not address approving or removing religious organizations as ecclesiastical endorsers of chaplains or processes for investigative bodies that become privy to adverse information on religious organizations and their endorsing agents.

Discussion

The Armed Forces Chaplains Board (AFCB) must have the ability to make informed recommendations to the Under Secretary of Defense for Personnel and Readiness (USD[P&R]) to approve or remove ecclesiastical endorsers of military chaplains. DoDI 1304.28, *Guidance for Appointment of Chaplains for the Military Departments*, requires

Chapter 1 ♦ Risk Assessment and Prevention

military chaplains to be sponsored by an authorized endorsing agent of a recognized religious organization.[53] Endorsing agents certify that prospective military chaplains are professionally qualified to perform all offices, functions, sacraments, ordinances, and ceremonies required of a DoD chaplain for a particular religious organization and are capable and authorized to counsel as required within a pluralistic environment.[54]

DoDI 1304.28 requires religious organizations (e.g., the Roman Catholic Church, the American Muslim Armed Forces and Veterans Affairs Council, the Central Conference of American Rabbis) to provide background information on the authorized endorsing agent they wish to act on their behalf.[55] If approved by USD(P&R), the authorized endorsing agent can represent the religious organization and has authority to grant or withdraw ecclesiastical endorsements of military chaplains on the organization's behalf.

DoDI 1304.28 requires that USD(P&R) take appropriate steps to verify with DoD components and other federal agencies that religious organizations comply with stated requirements such as not engaging in practices that are illegal or contrary to defined public policy.[56] However, DoD and other federal agency information is generally not available to the AFCB in determining whether to recommend approval or removal of religious organization endorsing agents.

There is no requirement for security checks of endorsing agents (e.g., national agency check with local agency check [NACLC], special background investigation [SBI]).[57] Since religious organizations with malicious intent are unlikely to select an endorsing agent easily identified by adverse information in a background check, the Air Force Judge Advocate General and Chief of Chaplains see little value in conducting background checks on endorsing agents. Instead, potential concerns with adverse ecclesiastical endorser background and influence can be more effectively and affordably mitigated by requiring DoD investigative agencies to share adverse information with the AFCB via the Deputy Under Secretary of Defense for Military Personnel Policy (DUSD[MPP]).

Should investigative functions verify a threat or criminal activity, sharing this information with the DUSD(MPP) will enable DoD to take appropriate action. Although some members of these investigative bodies may already share information in practice, it is not specifically required by DoD or Air Force policies. Air Force Policy Directive (AFPD) 52-1, *Chaplain Service*, should therefore be revised to incorporate forthcoming changes to DoDI 1304.28 addressing ecclesiastical endorsers.

Recommendations

16.1   Coordinate with the DUSD(MPP) to develop procedures for investigative bodies to convey pertinent information to the Armed Forces Chaplains Board on religious organizations and their endorsing agents that may affect their status to endorse military chaplains. (OPR: AF/HC)

16.2   Following revisions to DoD policy, update AFPD 52-1, *Chaplain Service*, to reflect any revised roles and responsibilities of the Air Force Chief of Chaplains. (OPR: AF/HC)

Notes

1. Jeffrey W. Swanson et al., "Violence and Psychiatric Disorder in the Community: Evidence from the Epidemiologic Catchment Area Surveys," *Hospital Community Psychiatry* 41 (July 1990): 761–70; Henry J. Steadman et al., "Violence by People Discharged from Acute Psychiatric Inpatient Facilities and by Others in the Same Neighborhoods," *Archives of General Psychiatry* 55, no. 5 (May 1998): 393–401; and Randy Borum, "Improving the Clinical Practice of Violence Risk Assessment: Technology, Guidelines, and Training," *American Psychologist* 51, no. 9 (September 1996): 945–56.

2. AFMA Survey, appendix C.

3. Ibid., 20.

4. Laura Miller, PhD, interviewed by Gregory M. Vecchi, PhD (Chief, Behavioral Science Unit, FBI Academy, Quantico, VA), December 2009.

5. AFMA Survey, appendix C.

6. The document provides overviews on the types of problems, information on resiliency, checklists of behavioral indicators of distress, and advisable leadership courses of action (including care, additional inquiry, referrals, disciplinary action, and follow-up). Air Force and DoD policy related to those problems, responses, and corresponding resources (e.g., the Family Advocacy Program and the Web site for the National Institute of Mental Health) are also included. Air Force Medical Service, *Air Force Leader's Guide for Managing Personnel in Distress*, http://airforcemedicine.afms.mil/leadersguide.

7. Air University (AU)-2, *Guidelines for Command* (Maxwell AFB, AL: Air University Press, February 2008), 216, 227, 232–33, 235–38.

8. AFMA Survey, appendix C.

9. DoDI 1325.06, *Handling Dissident and Protest Activities among Members of the Armed Forces*, 27 November 2009.

10. AFI 51-903 defines such organizations as those that advocate supremacist doctrine, ideology, or causes; attempt to create illegal discrimination based on race, creed, color, sex, religion, ethnicity, or national origin; advocate the use of force, violence, or criminal activity; or otherwise engage in efforts to deprive individuals of their civil rights. AFI 51-903, *Dissident and Protest Activities*, 1 February 1998.

11. AFI 51-903, *Dissident and Protest Activities*, 1 February 1998.

12. DoDI 1325.06, *Handling Dissident and Protest Activities among Members of the Armed Forces*.

13. DA PAM 600-15, *Extremist Activities*, 1 June 2000.

14. AR 600-20, *Army Command Policy*, 30 November 2009.

15. AFI 51-903, *Dissident and Protest Activities*.

16. Elizabeth Crown, "Tattoos and Piercings Go Mainstream, but Risks Continue," *Northwestern University NewsCenter*, 12 June 2006, http://www.northwestern.edu/newscenter/stories/2006/06/tattoos.html.

17. Air Force Office of Special Investigations (AFOSI), Criminal Intelligence Bulletin, "Visual Iconography: Gang and Right-Wing Hate Group Affiliated Symbols and Body Art" (U), AFOSI Criminal Analysis Special Report, 5 March 2010, 2.

18. AFI 36-2903, *Dress and Personal Appearance of Air Force Personnel*, 6 August 2007, 86–88.

19. Marine Corps Order (MCO) P1020.34G, *Marine Corps Uniform Regulations*, 31 March 2003, 1–6; Marine Administrative Message (MARADMIN) 198/07, *Announcement of Changes to the Marine Corps Tattoo Policy*, 19 March 2007; Navy Administrative Message (NAVADMIN) 110/06, *Navy Uniforms*, 21 April 2006, 1; AR 670-1, *Wear and Appearance of Army Uniforms and Insignia*, 3 February 2005, 5–6; and All Army Activities Message (ALARACT) 017/2006, *Wear and Appearance of Army Uniforms and Insignia*, 25 January 2006.

20. AFOSI, Criminal Intelligence Bulletin, "Visual Iconography: Gang and Right-Wing Hate Group Affiliated Symbols and Body Art" (U), AFOSI Criminal Analysis Special Report, 5 March 2010.

21. Secretary of Defense, to all DoD activities, draft memorandum, subject: Privately Owned Weapons, 25 March 2010.

22. *Omnibus Consolidated Appropriations Act*, 1997, Public Law 104-208, 104th Cong., 2d sess., 30 September 2006, 369–72.

23. DoDI 6400.06, *Domestic Abuse Involving DoD Military and Certain Affiliated Personnel*, 21 August 2007, 10.

24. Air Force, *Post-Deployment Health Reassessment Application Users Guide*, http://www.pdhealth.mil/dcs/downloads/PDHRA_AUG.pdf.

25. Gregory A. Gahm et al., "History and Implementation of the Fort Lewis Soldier Wellness Assessment Program," *Military Medicine* 174, no. 7 (July 2009): 721–27.

26. AFI 10-403, *Deployment Planning and Execution*, 13 January 2008, 133–41; AFI 44-153, *Traumatic Stress Response*, 13 March 2006, 4; Col John Forbes, USAF, "Airmen Resiliency Training" (presentation, 22 February 2010); and Lt Gen Bruce Green, USAF, "Tiered, Targeted and Tracked Interventions" (presentation, 22 February 2010).

27. Office of Personnel Management, *Dealing with Workplace Violence: A Guide for Agency Planners*, OWR-09, February 1998, 19.

28. AFI 36-2706, *Military Equal Opportunity (MEO) Program*, certified current 17 February 2009, 40, 60.

29. AFMAN 31-201, *Security*, vol. 4, *High-Risk Response*, 20 March 2002, 37.

30. Draft AFMAN 31-201, *Security*, vol. 4, *High-Risk Response*.

31. Department of Defense, *Protecting the Force: Lessons from Fort Hood: Report of the DoD Independent Review* (Washington, DC: Department of Defense, January 2010), http://www.defense.gov/pubs/pdfs/DOD-ProtectingTheForce-Web_Security_HR_13Jan10.pdf, 15–16. (Subsequently referred to as *Protecting the Force*.)

32. OSHA, "OSHA Fact Sheet: Workplace Violence," US Department of Labor, http://www.osha.gov/OshDoc/data_General_Facts/factsheet-workplace-violence.pdf.

33. AFI 44-154, *Suicide and Violence Prevention Education and Training*, 3 January 2003; AFI 36-6001, *Sexual Assault Prevention and Response (SAPR) Program*, 29 September 2008; and AFI 40-301, *Family Advocacy*, 30 November 2009.

34. For example, Department of Defense Directive (DoDD) 6495.01, *Sexual Assault Prevention and Response (SAPR) Program*, 6 October 2005, establishes guidance for the SAPR, and DoDD 6400.1, *Family Advocacy Program*, 23 August 2004, establishes guidance for the family advocacy program, but there is no current policy directive on suicide prevention.

35. AFI 44-154, *Suicide and Violence Prevention Education and Training*, 3 January 2003; AFI 36-6001, *Sexual Assault Prevention and Response (SAPR) Program*, 29 September 2008; AFI 40-301, *Family Advocacy*, 30 November 2009; Air National Guard Instruction (ANGI) 52-154, *Suicide Prevention and Violence Awareness Education and Training*, 28 July 2003; Air Force Pamphlet (AFPAM) 44-160, *The Air Force Suicide Prevention Program*, April 2001; AFI 10-245, *Antiterrorism (AT)*, 30 March 2009; AFI 90-501, *Community Action Information Board and Integrated Delivery System*, 31 August 2006; and AFI 91-301, *Air Force Occupational and Environmental Safety, Fire Protection, and Health (AFOSH) Program*, 1 June 1996.

36. Federal Acquisition Regulation (FAR) 52.203-13, *Contractor Code of Business Ethics and Conduct*, December 2008.

37. Ibid.

38. *Occupational Safety and Health Act of 1970*, Public Law 91-596, 91st Cong., 29 December 1970; and *Delegation of Authority, US Code*, vol. 5, sec. 302.

39. AFI 36-703, *Civilian Conduct and Responsibility*, 17 February 2009.

40. *Cause and Procedure, US Code*, vol. 5, sec. 7513; and Peter Broida, *Guide to Merit System Protection Board Law and Practice*, 26th ed. (Arlington, VA: Dewey, 2009).

41. *Protecting the Force*, 23.

42. *Labor-Management Relations, US Code*, vol. 5, secs. 7101-7135; and Executive Order 13522, Creating Labor-Management Forums to Improve Delivery of Government Services, 9 December 2009. Sample language for the change in AFI 36-703, *Civilian Conduct and Responsibility*, as a new Section E—Violence in the Workplace, follows:

> 9. **Supervisors**. Violent behavior is not acceptable in the Air Force workplace. Supervisors manage their work centers in a way that promotes good order, implement a violence response plan in their work area, and make sure staff members are familiar with the plan.
>
> > 9.1. When a supervisor receives a report of an indicator of potential violence, he or she will assess the situation and take appropriate action. The supervisor will receive the support of Security Forces, the Civilian Personnel Office, the Legal Office, and base medical staff, as appropriate.
>
> 10. **Employees**. While supervisors play a key role in recognizing potentially violent situations and taking proactive measures to reduce the negative impact of these situations, employees can contribute to maintaining a safe work place. If employees observe any of the following indicators, or sense that something is not right, they will report the concern to their supervisor or other appropriate authority identified at their work location.

A list of indicators will be developed by OSD and incorporated into Air Force instructions.

43. Developed after the Army's comprehensive Soldier fitness initiative, CAF is an approach that targets four pillars of physical, social, mental, and spiritual health of our Airmen. The overarching CAF philosophy is to care for people based on the "five Cs": care, connect, communicate, commit, and celebrate. See US Army, *Comprehensive Soldier Fitness*, http://www.army.mil/csf/.

44. AFI 90-501, *Community Action Information Board and Integrated Delivery System*, 31 August 2006, 3.

45. AFMA Survey, appendix C.

46. AFI 90-501, *Community Action Information Board and Integrated Delivery System*, 31 August 2006, 2.

47. Ibid., 3–6.

48. DoDI 1300.17, *Accommodation of Religious Practices within the Military Services*, 10 February 2009, 4.

49. AFPD 52-1, *Chaplain Service*, addresses the rights of Air Force members to observe the tenets of their respective religions and the role of chaplains to assist and advise commanders regarding such observations. This directive is being updated; estimated completion date is 1 July 2010 (AFPD 52-1, *Chaplain Service*, 2 October 2006, 1–2). AFI 52-101, *Planning and Organizing*, provides guidance for accommodating religious practices, including the role of chaplains in religious accommodation (and further recognition of chaplains as leadership advisors in such matters). AFI 52-101 will be revised following the update to AFPD 52-1 (anticipated date of revision and coordination for AFI 52-101 is 1 October 2010) (AFI 52-101, *Planning and Organizing*, 14 March 2008, 6, 8). AFPD 36-29, *Military Standards*, outlines policies regarding uniform standards and presentation (AFPD 36-29, *Military Standards*, 29 October 2009, 2). AFI 36-2903, *Dress and Appearance of Air Force Personnel*, addresses specific procedures regarding religious apparel and items (AFI 36-2903, *Dress and Appearance of Air Force Personnel*, 6 August 2007, 89–91, 93). AFPD 36-27, *Equal Opportunity (EO)*, covers issues of equal opportunity, including protections from discrimination and harassment based on religion and the resolution of related complaints (AFPD 36-27, *Equal Opportunity [EO]*, 22 May

2009). AFI 36-2706, *Military Equal Opportunity (MEO) Program*, further outlines general guidelines and procedures for religious accommodation (AFI 36-2706, *Military Equal Opportunity [MEO] Program*, 17 February 2009, 69–70). Air Force Joint Instruction (AFJI) 48-110, *Immunizations and Chemoprophylaxis*, addresses exemptions from immunization requirements to accommodate doctrinal religious belief (AFJI 48-110, *Immunizations and Chemoprophylaxis*, 29 September 2006, 3–4).

50. Commanders' Professional Development School, Wing Commanders' Seminar, http://www.au.af.mil/au/ecpd/cpds/Wing_CC_Curriculum.html.

51. Chaplains generally explain the role of the base chaplain in relation to day-to-day wing activities and the expeditionary environment and summarize current religious guidelines, initiatives, and policy changes.

52. The 15-minute training module will include scenarios and address various religious issues including religious accommodation, public prayer outside worship settings, individual sharing of religious faith, and good order and discipline. Thomas Mahoney, program manager, Air Force Equal Opportunity (presentation, Air Force Learning Committee Working Group, 17 March 2010).

53. DoDI 1304.28, *Guidance for Appointment of Chaplains for the Military Departments*, 7 August 2007, 3–4.

54. Ibid., 11.

55. Ibid., 13. DoDI 1304.28 requires that the religious organization provide the name, title, mailing address, telephone number, electronic contact, employer identification number as assigned by the Internal Revenue Service, and the telephone number of the representative it is authorizing to represent it. To avoid any conflict of interest, endorsing agent candidates are not permitted to be serving as a military chaplain (i.e., active duty, National Guard, Reserve).

56. Ibid., 12–13.

57. The Air Force general counsel advised against pursuing security checks of endorsing agents because attorney-general policy does not authorize non–law enforcement officials, such as the DUSD(MPP) or the AFCB, to request and obtain information concerning ongoing investigations of nongovernment officials. See also, DoD Inspector General, *Evaluation Report on the DoD Chaplain Program*, Report No. IE-2004-001, 10 November 2004.

Sharing information is one of the pivotal issues discussed within the DoD report. As Secretary West and Admiral Clark testified before the House Armed Services Committee, "Robust information sharing is essential, along with the accompanying command and

control structures converting active information gathered by different agencies into decisions and actions, to include disseminating the analysis and assessments to the appropriate levels of command."[1] Our review identified several interagency, DoD, and Air Force processes that, if better connected, could improve the overall capability of leaders to protect personnel. Forging these relationships is critical.

Better coordination with organizations outside the Air Force could improve a number of processes designed to identify personnel who may pose a threat to themselves or others. Likewise, internal to the Air Force, information sharing must be improved; for example, unit leaders, care providers, law enforcement, and investigative services should communicate on a regular basis.

Information-Sharing Forums

Finding 17

(This refers to DoD report Finding/Recommendation 3.2.)

- The Air Force lacks integrated policy, programs, and procedures to ensure installation commanders have a comprehensive means to identify and assist Airmen and members of the Air Force community who may exhibit behaviors of concern.

Discussion

Tragedies like the incident at Fort Hood are reminders of the need to remain aware of indicators of concern and prepare to respond to threats within the Air Force community. Left unaddressed, seemingly innocuous indicators could become precursors of potentially violent behavior. Unit leaders are responsible for supporting their personnel but have no formally established forum within which to discuss personnel concerns, share information and support options, and determine best courses of action.

Several existing forums partially address issues of concern that affect Air Force personnel, the most comprehensive being the Community Action Information Board (CAIB), a venue for cross-organizational discussions of quality of life, health and readiness, good order and discipline, morale, and climate issues experienced by individuals, organizations, and families.[2] A threat of immediate and serious harm to family members activates the High Risk for Violence Response Team (HRVRT), which provides support.[3] Additionally, the Threat Working Group (TWG) meets to assess internal and external threats to the Air Force community and provide installation leaders with proactive threat assessments.[4] None of these organizations have a charter that encourages routine discussions among unit leaders about individuals' behavior that may or may not rise to the level of requiring immediate action.

Unit leaders would benefit from an opportunity to share relevant information in a forum that could improve their ability to assess issues more holistically and to mobilize professional and unit support appropriately, thereby averting additional concerns. By better understanding issues affecting their personnel, care provided, and availability of additional support, unit leaders can develop more effective support strategies. Early engagement with professional care providers is essential. Capitalizing on existing capabilities resident in the CAIB, HRVRT, and TWG could bolster individual resiliency and enhance force protection measures.[5]

Headquarters Air Force (HAF), major command (MAJCOM), and direct reporting unit representatives expressed a need for an information-sharing forum linked to the CAIB.[6] Since the installation commander chairs the CAIB, executive sessions of the board would provide an opportunity to conduct a more individually focused executive forum named Status of Health and Airmen Resiliency Exchange (SHARE).[7] Primary SHARE attendees would include the wing commander, vice-commander, command chief, or senior enlisted adviser; staff judge advocate (SJA); group, squadron, and detachment commanders; chaplain; health care providers; mental health personnel; and TWG members. Others may be invited to attend as the installation commander deems necessary, based on current installation composition, issues, resources, and personnel.

The SHARE forum would offer commanders an opportunity to discuss potential at-risk members and seek assistance and feedback. It also would foster sharing of information between commanders and other support professionals outside of the SHARE forum to more effectively address concerns. Furthermore, the forum would benefit from a full-time civilian community support director position at each installation. This director would continuously monitor community wellness through the CAIB and individual wellness through SHARE. In doing so, the director would integrate community, family, and resiliency programs. Specific duties would include leading the installation resiliency program, serving as the permanent CAIB executive director, integrating information in support of monthly SHARE meetings, developing and executing the Community Action Plan, and administering the Integrated Delivery System. Establishing a full-time position to direct installation CAIB and resiliency efforts would add permanence and procedures to program efforts that currently have no dedicated staff but remain vital to the Air Force community. Air Force Instruction (AFI) 90-501, *Community Action Information Board and Integrated Delivery System*, will need revision to reflect these changes.

Recommendations

(Relevant best practices are identified in appendix B.)

17.1   Revise AFI 90-501, *Community Action Information Board and Integrated Delivery System*, to incorporate a forum geared to support Air Force members who need assistance or intervention to preclude more serious issues. (OPR: AF/A1)

17.2   Fund a full-time, installation-level civilian position to oversee and integrate community, family, individual support, and resiliency programs. (OPR: AF/A1)

Background Checks

Finding 18

(This refers to DoD report Finding/Recommendation 2.2.)

   •   Current background investigation policies and procedures provide adequate screening for granting access to classified material.

Discussion

Even the most stringent background investigations have, in some cases, failed to identify potential threats. The cost and time required to conduct in-depth background checks must be weighed against the risk that may be mitigated. Security clearance background checks validate information provided by respondents, with the ultimate goal of certifying a predetermined level of trust for handling classified information. The system is a risk-based model. Background checks for secret clearances average 64 days while those for top secret average 110 days.[8] Current investigative procedures are sufficient for evaluating an individual's eligibility for access to classified information.

AFI 31-501, *Personnel Security Program Management*, and DoD 5200.1R, *Information Security Program*, establish policy for background checks. Homeland Security Presidential

Directive–12, *Policy for a Common Identification Standard for Federal Employees and Contractors*, requires all employees to have a national agency check with inquiries for local area networks and unescorted access to federal installations.[9] These instructions result in an annual average of 149,400 Air Force background checks.[10]

Background checks for higher levels of security clearances include interviews with applicants, select coworkers, and acquaintances. Some checks also involve personal interviews with investigators and polygraph interviews. In-depth interviews may be impractical for the larger Air Force population. Adapting these techniques to validate potential risk indicators, when coupled with other available information sources, could provide unit leaders additional insight with which to make informed assessments.

Recommendation

18.1   Consider the feasibility of adapting current background investigation processes and techniques to improve identification of internal threats. (OPR: SAF/AA)

Finding 19

(This refers to DoD report Finding/Recommendation 2.4.)

- Department of State (DoS) and status of forces agreements (SOFA) determine clearance procedures for installations outside the continental United States (OCONUS).

Discussion

DoD has limited ability to investigate foreign national military and civilian personnel who require access to overseas DoD installations and information systems. Further, the Air Force has little control over procedures for granting clearances to foreign national military and civilian personnel who require access to OCONUS Air Force installations. DoS and SOFAs govern clearance procedures for foreign national access to overseas installations.[11] The SOFA and the executive agency for each host nation enable access to military installations on foreign soil. Clearance requests are processed through host nation law enforcement, and US personnel do not have the ability to validate associated information. Combatant commands are ultimately responsible for force protection in their respective areas of responsibility and for coordination with supporting host nations.

Ensuring that host nations adequately assess individuals before granting access to OCONUS installations with Air Force personnel is key to overseas force protection. Coordination between combatant commands and host nations may help to increase host nation vigilance. Personal relationships between commanders and local military and law enforcement agencies may also aid in improving installation security. Ultimately, the Office of the Secretary of Defense (OSD) must work with the DoS to make permanent security improvements.

Recommendation

19.1   Coordinate with DoD, DoS, and combatant commands to ensure foreign nationals working on OCONUS installations are subject to stringent investigation standards and procedures. (OPR: SAF/IA)

Finding 20

(This refers to DoD report Finding/Recommendation 2.4.)

- Continental United States (CONUS) clearance procedures for foreign national visits are governed by the Department of Homeland Security's (DHS) passport and visa process and are administered by SAF/IA through Air Force instructions.

Discussion

Permanent exchange officers and visiting foreign nationals are currently cleared for access to CONUS facilities and information systems through reciprocal agreements executed through host nation embassies and DHS's passport and visa process.[12] The Air Force Assistant Secretary for International Affairs relies on the OSD Foreign Visit System for visit and clearance information. Foreign clearance information is provided through the host embassy with no additional DoD or Air Force checks. Improving coordination with DHS for foreign national clearance will help installation commanders balance the legitimate mission of hosting foreign nationals against the imperatives of force protection.

Recommendation

20.1   Coordinate with DHS to ensure that foreign nationals granted access to CONUS installations are subject to the most stringent investigation standards and procedures possible. (OPR: SAF/IA)

Finding 21

(This refers to DoD report Finding/Recommendation 2.2.)

- Background checks on foreign personnel who have been granted citizenship and security clearances are limited to immigration, Social Security, criminal, and national agency checks (law enforcement and credit).

Discussion

The DoD developed expedited processes for citizenship and clearances to fill operational requirements for linguists, interrogators, cultural advisors, and related specialties. Of the 1,399 registered immigrants accessed into the Air Force since 1971, 1,128 have entered since 2007.[13] Expedited processes for citizenship and clearances are currently limited to background checks related to immigration, Social Security, criminal, and national agency checks (law enforcement and credit).[14] However, these procedures may not disclose risk factors associated with non-US citizen accessions.

Air Force participation in the DoD Military Accessions Vital to National Interests (MAVNI) program would enable more stringent background checks on individuals who will have routine access to Air Force installations and personnel. The MAVNI program expands background checks for those qualifying under the expedited citizenship program.[15] These background checks include national/intelligence agency checks, a single scope background investigation (SSBI), and DHS automated continuous evaluation system (ACES) typically associated with top secret clearances.[16] The increased rigor involved in the higher-level security investigation process would help reduce the vulnerability inherent in current practices. The Army and Navy have both implemented pilot MAVNI programs.

The original MAVNI program was due to expire 31 December 2009, but was extended two months to 28 February 2010. It has subsequently been extended to 31 December 2010.

Recommendation

21.1   Adopt the DoD MAVNI program expanding background checks to include national/intelligence agency checks, SSBI (interviews), and automated continuous evaluation checks. (OPR: AF/A1)

Finding 22

- Air Force Reserve Command (AFRC) and Air National Guard (ANG) commanders have limited visibility over members' law enforcement information unless members voluntarily report the information.

Discussion

Unit leaders may be unaware of potentially violent indicators among their members. By monitoring criminal databases, ACES would identify potentially adverse incidents and report them to the appropriate military authority. ACES continuously monitors 40 criminal and financial databases for anomalies and reports of activity.[17] It can alert commanders of incidents which would not be officially reported to the military unless the individual voluntarily reports the information. For example, there is currently no official way for commanders to become aware of members who are arrested for a driving while intoxicated incident off base. They may learn of such incidents because of local news reports, court dates, or incarceration that cause an Airman to miss training, but these do not constitute official reports.

Recommendation

22.1   Examine the feasibility of implementing ACES checks on AFRC and ANG members. (OPR: AFRC, NGB)

Storing and Transferring Information

Finding 23

(This refers to DoD report Finding/Recommendation 2.9.)

- Commanders do not have consistent access to relevant information on personnel with potential for violent behavior.

- Air Force policies and procedures allow access to an Unfavorable Information File (UIF); however, contents of the UIF may be too limited in scope and duration and access to the UIF is limited.

Discussion

Air Force policies and procedures allow the use of a UIF to document administrative, judicial, or non-judicial censures concerning Airman performance, responsibility, and behavior. Despite mandatory documentation, the UIF contents may be too limited and each item or entry is only retained for two years.[18] These procedures also do not track adverse behaviors across assignments and thus may hinder a commander's ability to detect a potentially violent individual and possibly prevent violent acts.

> Additional research is required to determine and document potential indicators of violence.

Additional research is required to determine and document potential indicators of violence. Personnel must then be trained on how to use this information. This research is essential to inform future revisions to Air Force policies prescribing what information should follow personnel throughout their careers.

The Judge Advocate's Automated Military Justice Analysis and Management System (AMJAMS) is a tracking tool used to collect detailed information on offenses, processing timelines, and demographic information on judicial and nonjudicial punishment.[19] As such, it may represent one option for information storage and sharing.[20] Information entered into AMJAMS remains indefinitely. The system does not track personnel actions such as UIFs, Officer and Enlisted Performance Reports, control roster, selection record actions, etc., but it does contain copies of completed Article 15 actions and court-martial orders. Thus, we found that the system may represent a model upon which to base a more comprehensive tracking system. It would, however, need to track a wider range of behaviors documented by different sources across an Airman's career.

The Air Force owns the source code for AMJAMS, and it is currently maintained through a contract vehicle. The AMJAMS software could be modified to collect data of this nature, which could be a cheaper alternative than developing a new database. Resource requirements to modify AMJAMS would involve contract costs to modify the software and manpower support for entering and analyzing the data.[21]

Recommendations

23.1   Coordinate with the OSD Military Personnel Records Information Management Task Force (MPRIMTF) study that focuses on what information is appropriate to maintain in military personnel records over the course of a career. (OPR: AF/A1)

23.2   Develop procedures for storing and transferring information that includes possible indicators of violent behavior. (OPR: AF/A1)

23.3   Consider developing a system similar to the Air Force Judge Advocate's AMJAMS to track information that may indicate a potential for violent behavior. (OPR: AF/A1)

Finding 24

● Best practices for force protection and internal threat prevention and response are not being identified, maintained, or distributed.

Discussion

The Air Force best practice clearinghouse is a repository for documenting and accessing best practices that contribute to informing process improvements.[22]

Information sharing on best practices related to internal threat prevention and response is limited. Our review of the best practices database (1,791 total submissions) and the Air Force A9 internal review of joint lessons learned yielded only 42 indirectly related practices based on a search of 36 Fort Hood–related terms (e.g., "emergency response," "force protection," "deployment").[23] Making best practices a priority IG inspection item will help unit leaders and their personnel access the most effective practices for force protection.[24]

The Air Force does not disseminate details of force protection, internal threat, or suicide incidents. Unlike flight safety, there is no system for commands not directly involved to learn from the incident. When force protection incidents occur, details on lessons learned should be sent to MAJCOM and HAF OPRs for Air Force-wide dissemination.[25]

Recommendations

24.1   Revise AFI 90-201, *Inspector General Activities*, to make assessment of force protection, internal threat prevention, and response mandatory inspection items. (OPR: SAF/IG)

24.2   Develop a Force Protection Response Bulletin to disseminate best practices identified by IG inspections related to force protection, internal threats, and suicides. (OPR: SAF/IG)

Finding 25

(This refers to DoD report Finding/Recommendation 2.9.)

- There is no consolidated Air Force policy, program, or procedure to convey potentially adverse behavioral indicators between commanders during transitions (e.g., permanent change of station [PCS], deployments, training).

Discussion

AFI 36-2608, *Military Personnel Records System*, does not identify formal mechanisms for informing gaining commanders that members have potentially adverse behavioral indicators.[26] The stress of training, deployments, or PCS may exacerbate existing behaviors. DoD established the Military Personnel Records Information Management Task Force (MPRIMTF) to address "what additional or existing information should be maintained throughout Service members' careers as they change duty locations, deploy, and reenlist."[27] This includes examining DoD and Service guidance on collecting, maintaining, and transferring relevant information about contributing factors and behavioral indicators throughout a Service member's career. The Air Force has three representatives participating on the MPRIMTF; their report is due to the Secretary of Defense on 1 June 2010.

Recommendation

25.1   Review and incorporate findings of the ongoing MPRIMTF into Air Force policy. (OPR: AF/A1)

Finding 26

(This refers to DoD report Finding/Recommendation 2.10 and 3.5.)

- Air Force Office of Special Investigation's (AFOSI) Investigative Information Management System (I2MS) is a consolidated criminal and counterintelligence investigative case file database; however, this database is not linked with other military criminal investigative organizations (MCIO).

Discussion

DoD recognizes the need for a consolidated criminal investigation database available to all DoD law enforcement and criminal investigation elements.[28] As a result, in August 2008, the Secretary of Defense directed that the Defense Law Enforcement Exchange (D-DEx) be implemented. The D-DEx is based on an existing Naval Criminal Investigative Service (NCIS) system that includes the Department of Justice (DoJ) and DHS.[29] Each of the 13 DoD law enforcement agencies participates in D-DEx development and implementation.

All MCIO subjects are entered into the Defense Index of Investigations. This system only lists individuals who have been or are under investigation, but provides no further detail. Instead, it is incumbent upon investigators to contact the MCIO case file "owner" to obtain a more detailed report.

AFOSI, NCIS, Criminal Investigation Division, and Office of the Under Secretary of Defense for Personnel and Readiness have signed a MOU to cooperate on developing D-DEx with complete development, including funding requirements, due in FY2011.[30] AFOSI and NCIS will begin submitting data to the D-DEx as soon as it is operational.[31]

Recommendation

26.1 Integrate AFOSI I2MS case file database into D-DEx, the DoD consolidated criminal investigations database. (OPR: SAF/IG)

Threat Reporting

Finding 27

(This refers to DoD report Finding/Recommendation 2.8.)

- Current AFIs are consistent with DoD policies and directives on counterintelligence awareness.

- DoD Instruction (DoDI) 5240.6, *Counterintelligence (CI) Awareness, Briefing, and Reporting Programs*, does not thoroughly address emerging threats, including self-radicalization.

Discussion

Counterintelligence involves "information gathered and activity conducted to protect against espionage, other intelligence activities, sabotage, or assassinations conducted on behalf of foreign powers, organizations, persons, or international terrorist activities, but does not include personnel, physical, document, or communications security programs."[32] Current intelligence oversight policy restricts DoD counterintelligence agencies, such as AFOSI, from collecting information on behaviors not having a direct nexus to foreign intelligence or terrorist activities.[33] Current AFIs governing collection activities are consistent with DoD policies and directives on counterintelligence.[34]

Many indicators related to potential internal threats are behavioral-based (e.g., disassociation from friends and acquaintances, religious, or political affiliations).[35] These indicators cannot be collected or retained by AFOSI, either within its law enforcement authority (when there is no crime committed) or its counterintelligence authority (when there is no foreign nexus).[36] AFOSI can, however, collect information when movement of large sums of money or purchases of bomb-making material is indicated.[37]

The Under Secretary of Defense for Intelligence (USD[I]) is addressing this potential gap by coordinating procedural changes to address behaviors linking individuals to foreign terrorist organizations or activities.[38] These changes will specify procedures for coordinating between law enforcement, force protection, and command officials to ensure that appropriate authorities receive information reported to domestic intelligence elements.[39]

> Many indicators related to potential internal threats are behavioral-based …

Recommendation

27.1   Coordinate with the USD(I) to review DoDI 5240.6, *Counterintelligence (CI) Awareness, Briefing, and Reporting Programs.* (OPR: SAF/IG)

Finding 28

(This refers to DoD report Finding/Recommendation 3.5.)

- The DoD has not established a common threat reporting system.

Discussion

The DoD report identified the FBI's *eGuardian* system as a possible solution to the need for a single reporting system.[40] AFOSI successfully participated in field testing of *eGuardian* at four detachments. The only problem identified was access to the DoJ/FBI's *Law Enforcement On-line* which is required to establish an *eGuardian* account.[41] According to the DoD report:

> After two years of analysis and a successful pilot program completed in June 2009, the Department has selected the FBI's *eGuardian* system for DoD unclassified threat reporting. The *eGuardian system*, which is FBI-owned and maintained, provides an unclassified, secure Web-based, capability to report suspicious activity and will contribute to our overall force protection threat information structure. . . . The *eGuardian* system will appropriately safeguard civil liberties, while enabling information sharing among federal, state, local, and tribal law enforcement partners, including interagency fusion centers. By no later than 30 June 2010, the Under Secretary of Defense for Policy will establish a plan and issue policy and procedures for the implementation of the *eGuardian* system as DoD's unclassified suspicious activity reporting system. . . . Use of *eGuardian* will begin no later than September 2010.[42]

Recommendation

28.1   Coordinate with the DoD and the other Services to define requirements for a common threat reporting system similar to the DoJ/FBI *eGuardian* system. (OPR: SAF/IG)

Installation Access

Finding 29

(This refers to DoD report Finding/Recommendation 3.7.)

- The Air Force can benefit from ongoing research related to threat detection, assessment and management programs, processes, and technologies.

Discussion

The Technical Support Working Group (TSWG) of the Combating Terrorism Technical Support Office (CTTSO) is an effective forum for collaborating with other agencies on state-of-the-art threat prevention technologies and procedures. The CTTSO partners with more than 100 government agencies, state and local governments, law enforcement, and first responders to leverage technical expertise, operational objectives, and interagency sponsor funding for antiterrorism initiatives. The Air Force can remain informed about state-of-the-art access control procedures and technologies used within and across multiple organizations by engaging with the CTTSO.[43] Ongoing collaboration through the CTTSO will also provide an avenue to further inform, direct, update, and refine Air Force access control policies, programs, and technologies.

Recommendation

29.1   Continue participation in the TSWG of the CTTSO to collaborate with other Services, government agencies, academia, and civilian organizations on threat detection, prevention, and management efforts. (OPR: AF/A4/7)

Finding 30

(This refers to DoD report Finding/Recommendation 3.7.)

- Air Force participation in the Physical Security Equipment Action Group (PSEAG) provides a formalized means for evaluating leading-edge tools and technologies to augment physical inspections at entry control points.

Discussion

Installation access control points are critical defenses for deterring and detecting internal and external threats and should involve more than just credential checks. While current tactics, techniques, and procedures require personnel engaged in access control duties be trained in "verbal and behavioral assessments," no enterprise-wide program exists to develop this capability.[44] The Air Force has also not deployed technologies to augment verbal and behavioral assessments. Leveraging existing and evolving state-of-the-art access control procedures and technologies can reduce access control vulnerabilities at Air Force installations.

The Air Force, the PSEAG executive agent for access control, participates in and leads the Defense Installation Access Control (DIAC) working group (WG). The DIAC WG is tasked to standardize physical access control procedures to enhance security and protect personnel and resources by developing DoD-wide and federally interoperable access control capabilities.

The PSEAG and DIAC WG recently provided a $250,000 grant to study how behavior pattern recognition screening procedures and entry-point technologies can help detect persons motivated to deceive, conceal, or act with malicious intent. This study, will run from 1 May through 31 October 2010 to review and evaluate entry control point best practices and state-of-the-art entry control technologies, focusing on behavior pattern recognition screening.[45] Results from the PSEAG/DIAC WG study should inform Air Force decision making related to force protection systems by presenting options for developing and fielding leading-edge access control policies, programs, and technologies.

Recommendation

30.1   Continue participation in the PSEAG and the DIAC WG behavioral analysis study. (OPR: AF/A4/7)

Finding 31

(This refers to DoD report Finding/Recommendation 3.9.)

- Lack of information sharing on debarments from military installations may jeopardize force protection.

- The Air Force, like the other Services, lacks policies and programs for sharing information on personnel and vehicles registered on installations, contained on installation debarment lists, or other relevant information to thoroughly screen personnel and vehicles before granting installation access.

- The Defense Biometric Identification System (DBIDS) has the greatest potential for sharing vehicle registration, debarment lists, and other relevant information required to screen personnel and vehicles and grant access.

Discussion

Installation commanders require relevant information before granting individual requests for access to the installation. Current policies and supporting procedures do not include sharing all available information on Air Force or other Service registration, debarment lists, and vehicle information. Modifying the instructions followed by instituting supporting programs and procedures will increase the quantity and quality of information available to commanders.

DoDI 5200.08, *Security of DoD Installations and Resources*, establishes policy governing commanders' authority to bar individuals from military installations.[46] Air Force Manual 31-201, vol. 7, *Security Forces Administration and Reports*, provides further guidance on debarment actions.[47]

AFI 31-201, *Security Forces Standards and Procedures*, addresses sharing law enforcement data but does not adequately discuss sharing debarment information.[48] Debarment actions only apply to the issuing installation and do not preclude a barred individual from entering other military installations. As a result, an individual identified by one commander as a potential threat may pose a threat at other installations.

Directive-type memorandum (DTM) 09-12, *Interim Policy Guidance for DoD Physical Access Control*, dated 8 December 2009, defines DoD policy for installation access, including specific databases to query.[49] This policy does not provide for a database to share information between installations. The HAF Security Forces Center uses DBIDS, a Defense Manpower Data Center product, to close this gap.[50]

DBIDS is an identity authentication system that supports installation access control measures using a networked client/server database. The program supports adding, retrieving, updating, and displaying information for individuals seeking access to instal-

lations. While DBIDS is not limited to accommodate common access card (CAC) holders, implementation for non-CAC holders remains limited. DoD-wide adoption of a DBIDS-like system, with an associated database, would greatly increase the effectiveness of the system and allow for information sharing among the Services. DoD adoption may also lead to supplemental funding for the remaining Air Force installations awaiting DBIDS.[51]

When installation commanders make debarment decisions, the identities of barred individuals are maintained only in local databases. If the information is entered into DBIDS, or a DBIDS-like database, it can be shared with other installations for use by installation commanders in making debarment decisions. The database could also serve as a tool to alert registration personnel and installation gate guards that an individual was barred from another installation.[52] However, even if DBIDS is modified to meet Air Force needs, it will not identify individuals barred from other Service installations unless they make similar commitments.

DBIDS installation is currently complete at 32 bases and in progress at two Air Force bases. Fifteen bases are scheduled to receive the system by October 2010.[53] Thirty-seven active duty bases, 12 Air Force Reserve bases, and 77 ANG bases have yet to fully deploy the system.

Recommendations

31.1   Coordinate with DoD and the other Services to share vehicle registration, debarment lists, and other relevant information required to screen personnel, vehicles, and grant access. (OPR: AF/A4/7)

31.2   Update AFI 31-201, *Security Forces Standards and Procedures*, to govern how debarment information is shared. (OPR: AF/A4/7)

31.3   Revise Air Force policy to require installation commanders to enter debarment information into a central database and to review Air Force debarments when making decisions to grant individuals base access. (OPR: AF/A4/7)

31.4   Fully fund and continue to install DBIDS at all Air Force installations to improve communications between installations. (OPR: AF/A4/7)

31.5   Modify the DBIDS database to reflect debarment actions. (OPR: AF/A4/7)

31.6   Support DoD-wide implementation of DBIDS. (OPR: AF/A4/7)

Sharing Health Information

Finding 32

(This refers to DoD report Finding/Recommendation 2.13.)

- The Air Force follows DoD policy requiring civilian health care providers to provide documentation of TRICARE patient encounters to military treatment facilities; however, civilian medical entities may not fully recognize or report to military leaders the range of indicators of the risk for violence to self or others.

Discussion

The absence of current DoD policies addressing information sharing between military and civilian health care providers creates a potential vulnerability because providers, institutions, and mental health professionals have little guidance on how and when to report specific risk indicators to the military. There is also no requirement to convey medical information to military treatment facilities (MTF) when Service members procure civilian medical care without MTF referral at their own expense. Sharing such protected health information is discretionary for civilian providers. Laws must be changed if DoD and the Services wish to request information from civilian providers beyond what is already allowed by the Privacy Act of 1974 and the Health Insurance Portability and Accountability Act (HIPAA) of 1996.

Four DoD-managed care support contractors (MCSC) obtain information for MTFs from TRICARE network providers who treat military members referred to them.[54] In addition, referring MTF providers should review the results of all off-base referrals to ensure continuity of patient care and communication with the patient's commander as appropriate. TRICARE network providers are held accountable by the MCSC to fulfill requirements for timely, complete consultation reports.[55] If enforced, these two accountability measures should preclude the need for additional policies, programs, and procedures related to TRICARE network provider consults and referrals of military members on active duty.[56]

Sharing information about potential vulnerabilities within legal constraints will require coordination between the TRICARE Management Activity, DoD, and the Services. HIPAA considerations, potential due process issues, and managed care support contract issues may preclude implementing a broader requirement for sharing additional details beyond what is currently permitted by law.[57]

The DoD report noted that Service policies do not reflect the most current DoD-level guidance with regard to sharing protected health information found in DTM 09-006, *Revising Command Notification Requirements to Dispel Stigma in Providing Mental Health Care to Military Personnel.*[58] The DTM focuses on directing providers when and how to report specific military patient information to commanders while appropriately preserving confidentiality. A clear articulation of the need to know—based in operational requirements such as force protection, installation security, or mission-related safety—would support arguments for changes in law, policy, and procedure.

Recommendation

32.1   Coordinate with DoD to establish standardized contract procedures and practices for TRICARE providers to recognize and report, within legal limits, potential indicators of violent behavior for active duty, ANG, and Air Force Reserve members who receive treatment through TRICARE providers. (OPR: SAF/MR)

Finding 33

(This refers to DoD report Finding/Recommendation 2.13.)

- There are no specific DoD or Air Force policies, programs, procedures, or practices that provide commanders, supervisors, and military health care providers visibility on risk indicators for ANG and Air Force Reserve members who seek care from civilian medical institutions when not on active duty orders.

- Air Force and DoD policies do not require civilian health care providers to provide documentation of patient encounters for ANG and Air Force Reserve personnel who seek care while in civilian status, or notify ANG or Reserve leaders when they identify a member who may exhibit indicators of violence.

Discussion

Receiving warning from civilian health care professionals who deem Air Force personnel a potential risk to themselves or others is especially pertinent for ANG and Air Force Reserve members who obtain civilian medical treatment while not on orders. HIPAA-covered entities, including civilian providers, can provide protected health information (PHI) to commanders for fitness for duty and mission-related purposes.[59] Some providers require military members to sign HIPAA-compliant authorizations before forwarding the information to military authorities. However, the Air Force Legal Opera-

> There has to be a way to comply with HIPAA and still ensure commanders/first sergeants get the information they need to ensure the health, morale, welfare and safety of all...
>
> —Survey comment, wing commander

tions Agency, Military Justice Division, would need to evaluate whether military members could lawfully be ordered to provide this information to the MTF, including when the military member seeks and pays for care if not referred by the MTF. If the care affects the member's readiness to perform duties, an order to report such care would have a strong influence on military service and would thus likely be enforceable.

Recommendations

33.1 Coordinate with DoD to develop policies, programs, and procedures for military medical personnel, commanders, and supervisors to receive and review indicators of potentially violent behavior for ANG and Air Force Reserve members who seek care from civilian medical institutions when not on active duty orders. (OPR: SAF/MR)

33.2 Coordinate with DoD to develop policies and procedures for civilian health care providers to alert military leaders when they believe active duty, ANG, and Air Force Reserve members whom they treat pose a threat to themselves or others. (OPR: SAF/MR)

Finding 34

(This refers to DoD report Finding/Recommendation 2.12.)

- Air Force policies correctly refer to, and follow, OSD/Health Affairs policies regarding handling of PHI.

- Air Force policies with respect to mental health do not reference the interim guidance found in DTM 09-006, *Revising Command Notification Requirements to Dispel Stigma in Providing Mental Health Care to Military Personnel*, issued in July 2009.

Discussion

AFIs are consistent with DoD policies regarding safeguarding PHI.[60] However, DTM 09-006, *Revising Command Notification Requirements to Dispel Stigma in Providing Mental Health Care to Military Personnel*, provides interim guidance for sharing PHI.[61] While the DTM is not primarily concerned with PHI, a term normally discussed in the context of the HIPAA of 1996, it does provide guidance on thresholds for notifying commanders of Service members' mental health treatment. The memorandum directs when and how providers report specific military patient conditions or circumstances to unit leaders and how to balance confidentiality with providing mental health information.

Chapter 2 ✦ Sharing Information

The Air Force must revise AFI 44-109, *Mental Health, Confidentiality and Military Law*, paragraph 6, to reference DTM 09-006 or the forthcoming DoDI. AFI 41-210, *Patient Administration Functions*, may also require revision with release of this DoDI since it will require health care providers to report previously protected mental health information. For example, paragraph 2.5.6.2 states: "Access, however, must be balanced with the recognized sensitivity of medical records, which often contain information of a very private nature. Therefore,

before a commander or designee gains access to an individual's protected health information, he or she must establish a need for those records IAW DoDR 6025.18-R, *DoD Health Information Privacy Regulations*, paragraph C7.11 and receive the concurrence of the SJA."[62] Changing this paragraph to align Air Force policy with the DTM and the forthcoming DoDI removes potentially conflicting guidance for providers and allows commanders to access more complete information about potential indicators of violent behaviors. Once these two AFI updates occur, training programs for providers, commanders, and supervisors must be updated to reflect the new reporting guidance.

Recommendations

34.1 Revise AFI 44-109, *Mental Health, Confidentiality and Military Law*, paragraph 6, to reference DTM 09-006, *Revising Command Notification Requirements to Dispel Stigma in Providing Mental Health Care to Military Personnel*, or follow-on DoDI guidance currently in coordination. (OPR: AF/SG)

34.2 Revise AFI 41-210, *Patient Administration Functions,* paragraph 2.5.6.2. to add exceptions for commanders establishing need for and obtaining concurrence with the SJA before obtaining patient information on a military member. (OPR: AF/SG)

34.3 AF/SG incorporate reporting guidance IAW AFI 44-109, *Mental Health, Confidentiality and Military Law*, and AFI 41-210, *Patient Administration Functions,* into all levels of health care provider training, beginning with medical school at the Uniformed Services University of the Health Sciences through the chief of medical staff. (OPR: AF/SG)

Finding 35

- AFRC and ANG commanders have limited ability to identify indicators of potentially violent behavior due to limited close personal observation and interaction with AFRC and ANG members.

Discussion

The ANG has permission to hire 35 psychologists for high-risk (two or more suicides since 2005 or high levels of deployments) wings.[63] The 2012 program objective memorandum is expected to support filling the remaining 54 openings and the conversion of all 89 positions to the general schedule.[64] The directors of psychological health (DPH) at each wing will provide the continuity necessary to identify behavioral indicators that is currently lacking due to the limited close personal contact that ANG commanders have with their personnel. They will manage the CAIB and will be able to report on the pulse of the wing. The DPHs will also be able to complete the increased DoD-directed suicide reporting.[65]

The DPH[66] will work directly for the 89 ANG wing commanders and coordinate the following programs:

- suicide prevention
- CAIB
- Wingman programs
- Air Force resiliency programs
- automated neurocognitive assessment metric testing
- pre-/post-deployment assessments
- mental health referral management
- suicide event reporting.[67]

The AFRC program is designed around seven regional advocates instead of unit-level psychologists.[68] The Reserve is also manning their positions with uniformed psychologists instead of contractors. Combining the Reserve and ANG assets is a consideration; however, it would be difficult and is not currently viewed as being feasible.[69] Yellow Ribbon Reintegration Program (YRRP) funds have been leveraged to hire three four-person regional teams that cover 50 states and four territories. The responsibilities of the DPH program, as outlined by the 2007 DoD Task Force referenced above, is much broader than the YRRP mandate. More effective and sustainable solutions require standardizing training and oversight, removing barriers between

Service components, and allowing for tailored implementation approaches. Refer to appendix B for YRRP information.

Recommendation

(Relevant best practices are identified in appendix B.)

35.1 Continue deploying and expand the ANG DPH and AFRC regional psychological health advocates programs. (OPR: AFRC, NGB)

Sharing Information on Cyberspace Activities

Finding 36

(This refers to DoD report Finding/Recommendation 2.14.)

- Draft DoDI 5420.xxx, *Counterintelligence Activities in Cyberspace*, contains guidance on immediately providing threat information obtained from DoD counterintelligence (CI) activity in cyberspace to affected commands, components, installations, or activities.

Discussion

Revisions to Air Force policy required upon publication of DoDI 5420.xxx, *Counterintelligence Activities in Cyberspace*, must adhere to strict statutory limitations on CI collection and follow DoD procedures for coordinating with other intelligence organizations.

Recommendation

36.1 Publish derivative Air Force guidance upon release of DoDI 5420.xxx, *Counterintelligence Activities in Cyberspace*, to include when the coordinated offices involved in defense cyber activities should alert leaders to potential threats in their command. (OPR: SAF/IG)

Notes

1. Opening Statement, DoD Independent Review Congressional Hearing Conference, House Armed Services Committee, 20 January 2010, 5. http://armedservices.house.gov/pdfs/FC012010/Joint_Testimony 012010.pdf.

2. Air Force Instruction (AFI) 90-501, *Community Action Information Board (CAIB) and Integrated Delivery System (IDS)*, 31 August 2006, 2. Air Force Follow-on Review (FOR) team leads reviewed policies governing the CAIB program during two conferences held at Andrews AFB and during the Compre-

hensive Airman Fitness Summit hosted by Air Mobility Command (AMC). Headquarters Air Force, major command (MAJCOM), and direct reporting unit (DRU) Air Force FOR representatives agreed that the current CAIB structure did not meet the comprehensive requirements for protecting the force against potential internal and external threats. Air Force FOR team leads prefer a forum separate from the CAIB to facilitate discussions among unit leaders to improve awareness of circumstances affecting their personnel and available support options. However, an executive session of the CAIB may be a suitable compromise; the intended purpose of the executive session would involve assisting installation and unit commanders in discussing issues of concern that affect their personnel as well as examining potential indicators of violence. AFI 90-501, *Community Action Information Board (CAIB) and Integrated Delivery System (IDS)*, could be revised to discuss the executive session purpose, meeting frequency, and linkage of issues raised in the executive session for broader CAIB awareness and action.

3. AFI 40-301, *Family Advocacy*, 30 November 2009, 24, par. 4.4.2. The High Risk for Violence Response Team (HRVRT) focuses internally on members of the base community. Trained members of the HRVRT activate at the discretion of the family advocacy officer (FAO), based on the advice of the members (the FAO; the Family Advocacy Program [FAP] clinician who works with the family; members' unit commander; mental health provider; domestic abuse victim advocate; and appropriate representatives from organizations that have legal, investigative, or protective responsibilities). Addressing safety issues and risk factors, the HRVRT develops a coordinated plan for immediate implementation to manage risk to the individual presenting a potential threat, intended victims, and community at large.

4. AFI 10-245, *Antiterrorism*, 30 March 2009, 19, par. 2.11. The Threat Working Group (TWG) reviews, coordinates, and disseminates threat warnings, reports, and summaries. Members include the antiterrorism officer; commanders or designated representatives; appropriate representatives from tenant units and the intelligence community; direct-hire contractor; and members of local, state, federal, or host-nation law enforcement agencies. Depending upon the threat information, subject-matter experts meet to provide information needed to develop predictive intelligence and recommend courses of action to counter threats and reduce risk.

5. The proposal to establish a separate forum for addressing this issue was discussed among HAF, MAJCOM, and DRU representatives at two Air Force FOR conferences (March and April 2010) and the Comprehensive Airman Fitness Summit hosted by AMC and Air Combat Command (ACC) in March 2010. Conference attendees agreed that such a forum is vital to improving information sharing among commanders, civilian directors, support agencies (e.g., chaplain, mental health, medical, family advocacy, equal opportunity, inspector general, sexual assault response coordinator, etc.), as well as investigative and law enforcement entities. Air Force FOR Conference, 30–31 April 2010, Andrews AFB, MD; and Addressing Fort Hood Independent Review Report and Air Force Findings Comprehensive Airmen Fitness Summit, Scott AFB, IL, 16–17 March 2010.

6. ACC proposed its force protection intelligence fusion cell (FPIFC) concept as a recommendation to fill this gap. The FPIFC provides a mechanism whereby intelligence, Air Force Office of Special Investigations (AFOSI), and security forces representatives meet to identify and address DoD threats and hazards and collaborate to conduct intelligence preparation of the operating environment. The goal of FPIFC is to leverage and support timely identification of indicators and warnings of emerging localized threats. The FPIFC and its products are the primary information sources that directly support the installation commander, TWG, defense force commander, emergency management working group, and other organizations in making immediate planning decisions regarding force protection. Air Force Tactics, Techniques, and Procedures (AFTTP) 3-10.X, *Force Protection Information Fusion Cell Operations*, 1–2 (draft). Air Force Space Command (AFSPC) noted that the same Airmen were often appearing in forums such as status of discipline, cross-functional oversight committee, and central registry board, among others. AFSPC voiced concern about missed opportunities to integrate information and help Airmen before their

Chapter 2 ◆ Sharing Information

actions elevated to the level of having these post-incident response forums address them. Based on the desire to intervene before an Airman commits a harmful act, an AFSPC wing commander created a coordinating venue entitled "status of care" (SOC) that brings together each month the wing commander, vice-commander, group commanders, command chief, staff judge advocate, and senior enlisted advisers to review at-risk Airmen. Group commanders submit names, situations, and supervisors to the vice wing commander, who integrates and redacts identifying information before group members review the list. As each individual situation is briefed, the SOC discusses potential strategies and options to assist the member and unit. The forum is designed to assist the commander with avenues and tools that may not have been considered; it is not a substitute for supervisory and commander responsibilities. "Air Force FOR Best Practice Submission, Status of Care Concept," 1, 22 March 2010.

7. Air Force FOR team leads at the HAF, MAJCOM, and DRU levels recommend the following as initial objectives for the Status of Health and Airmen Resiliency Exchange (SHARE):

    a. Implement a secure, comprehensive mechanism for the timely exchange of information;

    b. Make an early identification of behaviors suggestive of potential violence and aberrant activity, to include potential criminal or terrorist activity;

    c. Promote awareness of internal threat indicators and priority intelligence requirements; and

    d. Provide commanders with a comprehensive picture of Airmen/community members with a coordinated plan of action to get AF members well.

The wing commander would chair the SHARE discussion with the proposed rules of engagement. The group would meet monthly, quarterly at a minimum, and ad hoc if necessary. Squadron/unit commanders submit their at-risk individuals to group commanders, who in turn forward to the SHARE administrator, who contacts trusted representatives from the base functional community. Attendees share additional supporting information at the SHARE. Group commanders present the individual with current context to SHARE attendees who, in turn provide amplifying information if available. The group discusses support options, and the commander is responsible for individuals and is accountable for follow-on actions.

8. Specifically, 15,134 top secret (TS)/special compartmental information (SCI), 73,353 secret, 5,000 Periodic TS/SCI reinvestigations, 10,000 Phased TS/SCI periodic reinvestigations, 7,927 Access National Agency Check and Inquiries (ANACI), 15,718 NACI, 1,746 NAC, and 20,477 other checks were conducted during 2009. Defense Security Service, Statistical Data, 6 March 2010.

9. AFI 31-501, *Personnel Security Program Management*, 27 January 2005, 8, http://www.af.mil/shared/media/epubs/AFI31-501.pdf; DoD 5200.1R, *Information Security Program*, 14 January 1997, 8, http://www.dtic.mil/whs/directives/corres/pdf/520001r.pdf; and "HSPD-12: *Policy for a Common Identification Standard for Federal Employees and Contractors*," 27 August 2004, http://www.dhs.gov/xabout/laws/gc_1217616624097.shtm.

10. Defense Personnel Security Research Center, "PERSEREC," http://www.dhra.mil/perserec/pastachievements.html#project21.

11. AFI 31-501, *Personnel Security Program Management*, 8; and William K. Henderson, *Security Clearance Manual* (Pacific Grove, CA: Last Post Publishing, 7 April 2010).

12. DoD Directive (DoDD) 5530.3, *International Agreements*, 11 June 1987, certified current as of 21 November 2003, 21–27; Department of Homeland Security (DHS), "US-VISIT What to Expect When Visiting the United States," 11 April 2010, http://www.dhs.gov/files/programs/editorial _0525.shtm; and AFI 16-201, *Air Force Foreign Disclosure and Technology Transfer Program*, 1 December 2004, incorporating change 1, 11 August 2009.

13. Col Bruce Lovely, AETC/A1, result of query on Air Force Military Personnel System, 3 March 2010.

14. DoD Inspector General, Report D-2008-104, DoD Implementation of Homeland Security Presidential Directive-12, 23 June 2008, 4, http://www.dodig.mil/Audit/reports/fy08/08-104.pdf.

15. Lt Gen Thomas P. Bostick, Deputy Chief of Staff G-1, US Army, Testimony before the Military Personnel Subcommittee of the House Armed Services Committee, 111th Cong., 2nd sess.,17 March 2010, 5; and DoD, Military Accessions Vital to National Interest (MAVNI) Recruitment Pilot, 29 March 2010, http://www.defenselink.mil/news/mavni-fact-sheet.pdf.

16. DoDD 5220.6, *Defense Industrial Personnel Security Clearance Review Program*, 20 April 1999, 16–18, http://www.dtic.mil/whs/ directives/corres/pdf/522006p.pdf.

17. Defense Personnel Security Research Center, Automated Continuing Evaluation System (ACES) (Washington, DC: 7 April 2010), http://www.dhra.mil/perserec/currentinitiatives.html#ACES; Joint Security and Suitability Reform Team, Security and Suitability Process Reform (Washington, DC: 17 December 2008).

18. AFI 36-2907, *Unfavorable Information File (UIF) Program*, 17 June 2005, 6. Officer UIFs may last longer than two years and may transfer with the member to new assignment.

19. Automated Military Justice Analysis and Management System (AMJAMS) provides a Web-based, "cradle-to-grave" real-time, statistical history of military justice. AFI 51-201, *Administration of Military Justice*, 21 December 2007, interim change 1, 3 February 2010, 215; "Information Technology," fact sheet, http://hqja.jag.af.mil/factsheet.pdf.

20. AFI 51-201, *Administration of Military Justice*, 21 December 2007, interim change 1, 3 February 2010, 215; "Information Technology," fact sheet, http://hqja.jag.af.mil/factsheet.pdf.

21. Greg Girard, AF/JAA, to Dr. Anthony C. Cain, e-mail, 9 April 2009, concerns with Finding 2.9.

22. Air Force Manpower Agency, "AF Best Practices Clearinghouse," https://afkm.wpafb.af.mil/community/views/home.aspx?Filter=AF-DP-00-30.

23. Ibid., "Crosstalk."

24. AFI 90-201, *Inspector General Activities*, 19 July 2007.

25. Air Force Manpower Agency, "AF Best Practices Clearinghouse," https://afkm.wpafb.af.mil/community/views/home.aspx?Filter=AF-DP-00-30.

26. AFI 36-2608, *Military Personnel Records System*, 30 August 2006.

27. DoD, Military Personnel Records Information Management Task Force Charter, 10 March 2010, 2.

28. *Protecting the Force*, 19.

29. Col Keith Givens, AFOSI, Andrews AFB, MD, interview with special agent (SA) Jon S. Stivers, Deputy Director/CTO, AFOSI/XI, Andrews AFB, MD, 22 February 2010.

30. Ibid.

31. Office of the Secretary of Defense (OSD), "Interim Recommendations of the Ft. Hood Follow-on Review," memorandum, 12 April 2010, 4.

32. DoD Instruction (DoDI) 5240.6, *Counterintelligence (CI) Awareness, Briefing, and Reporting Programs*, 7 August 2004, 11, http://www.dtic.mil/whs/ directives/corres/pdf/524006p.pdf.

33. DoDD 5240.1-R, *Procedure Governing the Activities of DoD Intelligence Components that Affect United States Persons*, December 1982, http://www.dtic.mil/whs/directives/corres/pdf/524001r.pdf; executive order 12333, US Intelligence Activities, 4 December 1981, http://www.fas.org/irp/offdocs/eo/eo-12333-2008.pdf; and Defense Personnel Security Research Center, Counterintelligence Reporting Essentials (CORE), May 2005, http://www.dhra.mil/perserec/reports/core_brochure.pdf.

34. AFI 71-101, vol. 4, *Counterintelligence*, 1 August 2000, http://www.e-publishing.af.mil/shared/media/epubs/AFI71-101V4.pdf; and AFOSI Manual 71-144, vol. 1, *Counterintelligence and Security Services*, 8 April 2009.

35. Paul Davis and Kim Cragin, *Social Science for Counterterrorism, Putting the Pieces Together* (Arlington, VA: Rand Corporation, 2009), xxxvi, http://www.rand.org/pubs/monographs/2009/RAND_MG849.pdf.

36. Assistant to the Secretary of Defense for Intelligence Oversight, Policy Guidance for Intelligence Support to Force Protection, 18 November 1998, 2.

37. AFI 71-101, vol. 4, *Counterintelligence*.

38. DoDD 5148.11, *Assistant to the Secretary of Defense for Intelligence Oversight*, 21 May 2004, http://atsdio.defense.gov/documents/51481p.pdf.

39. Paul Stockton, Assistant Secretary of Defense Homeland Defense and America's Security Affairs, Coordination Package 03152010, Consolidated Summary of Recommendations, draft 3, 15 March 2010, 1.

40. *Protecting the Force*, 30.

41. Col Keith Givens, AFOSI, Andrews AFB, MD, interview with SA Matthew Simmons, Director, ICON, Andrews AFB, MD, 15 April 2010.

42. OSD, "Interim Recommendations of the Ft. Hood Follow-on Review," memorandum, 12 April 2010, 5–6.

43. www.cttso.gov.

44. AFTTP 3-31.1, *Entry Control*, 29 May 2007, para. 2.4.4.3, 15.

45. Scott Petrowski, office of the Under Secretary of Defense for Intelligence and member of the DoD follow-on review team of the Fort Hood report, stated the PSEAG/DIAC WG study is the "perfect vehicle" for answering recommendation 3.7 to the SECDEF and is requesting updates for later briefings and recommendations. The PSEAG/DIAC WG study will interview subject matter experts throughout the DoD, federal and civilian agencies, and academia. The study will also evaluate operational threat detection/management programs such as the US Secret Service's Exceptional Case Study project and the Transportation Security Administration's Behavior Detection Officer and Screening of Passengers by Observation Techniques Programs. Research projects, to be evaluated by the study, consist of projects within DHS, to include the Future Attribute Screening Technology project which combines multiple physiologic sensor technologies to assist operators in detecting hostility and/or malicious intent, and the Hostile Intent Detection-Automated Prototype project which uses automated intent detection using noninvasive, culturally-neutral behavioral indicators such as facial micro-expressions.

46. DoDI 5200.08, *Security of DoD Installations and Resources*, 10 December 2005, 2, http://www.fas.org/irp/doddir/dod/i5200_08.pdf.

47. Air Force Manual 31-201, vol. 7, *Security Forces Administration and Reports*, 28 August 2009, 10, http://www.e-publishing.af.mil/shared/media/epubs/AFMAN31-201V7.pdf.

48. AFI 31-201, *Security Forces Standards and Procedures*, 30 March 2009, 28–30, http://www.af.mil/shared/media/epubs/AFI31-201.pdf.

49. DTM 09-012, *Interim Policy Guidance for DoD Physical Access Control*, 8 December 2009, 10–11.

50. As the DoD's human resource information source, Defense Manpower Data Center (DMDC) manages databases including identity management systems like DBIDS, Defense Cross-Credentialing Identification System, Defense National Visitors Center, and the Real-time Automated Personnel Identification System card program.

51. The Biometric Task Force is reviewing requirements for an enterprise architecture that gathers and shares data. The DoD Biometric Enterprise Architecture (DBEA) supports the DoD Biometric Enterprise Strategic Plan and will be implemented through guidance in a DoDI to ensure the US government and its allies can share biometric data and operate within a common information structure. The DBEA will establish procedures for inserting and using biometric technologies to support the DoD warfighter and business operations. It will resolve biometric capability gaps, guide biometric system-of-systems development, and align DoD biometric resources. See DoDD 8320.02, *Data Sharing in a Net-Centric Department of Defense*, 23

April 2007, http://www.dtic.mil/whs/directives/corres/pdf/832002p.pdf; and DoD—Biometrics Task Force, "Architecture," http://www.biometrics.dod.mil/CurrentInitiatives/architecture.aspx.

52. DMDC, Defense Biometrics Identification System (DBIDS)/Installation Control Access System (ICAS) Privacy Impact Assessment (PIA).

53. Col Keith Givens, AFOSI, Andrews AFB, MD, interview with Lt Col Scott Ulrich, USAF, deputy commander, Air Force Security Forces Center, 24 February 2010.

54. Some contracts will not pay if the civilian treatment facility fails to provide documentation. The situation is complicated because each contract may be worded differently and processes are not standardized. Standardized wording and contracts would ensure the information is consistently provided to the medical treatment facility (MTF).

55. AFI 41-210, *Patient Administration Functions*, 22 March 2006, 40; Marcia L. Kurtz (legal advisor, Procurement and HIPAA, AFMSA/SG5J), e-mail to Lt Col Kevin P. Seeley, Chief, Enterprise Technology Services, Air Force Medical Support Agency, 22 February 2010; AFI 44-109, *Mental Health, Confidentiality, and Military Law*, 1 March 2000, 1, 6–8; AFI 44-154, *Suicide and Violence Prevention Education and Training*, 3 January 2003, 4. For urgent matters that cannot wait for written communication, disclosure authorization from the patient is not required per DoDI 6025.18-R, *DoD Health Information Privacy Regulations*.

56. National Guard and Reserve members only receive medical care through local MTF and TRI-CARE providers while on active duty orders.

57. Health Insurance Portability and Accountability Act (HIPAA) of 1996, Public Law 104-191, 104th Cong., 2nd sess., 21 August 1996.

58. *Protecting the Force*, 20–21.

59. AFI 41-115, *Authorized Health Care and Health Care Benefits in the Military Health System (MHS)*, 28 December 2001, 6.

60. AFI 44-109, *Mental Health, Confidentiality, and Military Law*, 1 March 2009, 9, http://www.e-publishing.af.mil/shared/media/epubs/ AFI44-109.pdf.

The following policies govern Air Force PHI procedures:

- AFI 41-210, *Patient Administration Functions*, 22 March 2006, 14, http://www.af.mil/shared/media/epubs/AFI41-210.pdf, references DoDI 6025-18R, *Privacy of Individually Identifiable Health Information in DoD Health Care Programs*, 22 March 2006, http://www.dtic.mil/whs/directives/corres/pdf/602518r.pdf.

- AFI 44-109 references DoDI 6490.4, *Requirements for Mental Health Evaluations of Members of the Armed Forces*, 28 August 1997, 6–12, http://www.dtic.mil/whs/directives/corres/pdf/649004p.pdf; and DoDD 6490.1, *Mental Health Evaluations of Members of the Armed Forces*, 24 November 2003, http://www.dtic.mil/whs/directives/corres/pdf/649001p.pdf.

- AFI 44-154, *Suicide and Violence Prevention Education and Training*, 24 November 2003, 5, http://www.af.mil/shared/media/epubs/AFI44-154.pdf; also references DoDI 6490.4, and DoDD 6490.1.

- AFPD 36-60, *Sexual Assault Prevention and Response Program (SAPR)*, 28 March 2008, 2, 5, http://www.e-publishing.af.mil/shared/media/epubs/AFPD36-60.pdf, references DoDD 6495.01, *Sexual Assault Prevention and Response Program*, 7 November 2008, http://www.dtic.mil/whs/directives/corres/pdf/ 649501p.pdf.

61. DTM 09-006, *Revising Command Notification Requirements to Dispel Stigma in Providing Mental Health Care to Military Personnel*, 2 July 2009, 5–6, http://www.dtic.mil/whs/directives/corres/pdf/DTM-09-006.pdf.

62. AFI 41-210, *Patient Administration Functions*, 22.

63. Dale Hamby (Air Force Fort Hood Review) interview by Peter Koeppl (ANG DPH Coordinator), 9 April 2010.

64. Ibid.

65. AFI 44-154, *Suicide and Violence Prevention Education and Training*, 28 August 2006.

66. National Guard Bureau, Presentation to Warrior Resiliency Conference, National Guard Psychological Health (Washington, DC: 3 November 2009); AFI 40-301, *Family Advocacy*, 30 November 2009, 14.

67. AFI 90-501, *Community Action Information Board and Integrated Delivery System*, 31 August 2006; AFI 44-154, *Suicide and Violence Prevention Education and Training*, 3 January 2003; HAF, Memorandum for ALMAJCOM/CC, Automated Neuropsychological Assessment Metric (ANAM), Pre-deployment Automated Neuropsychological Assessment Metric Baseline Testing, 18 November 2009.

68. *An Achievable Vision: Report on the Department of Defense Task Force on Mental Health*, June 2007. See especially Recommendations 5.4 and 5.4.1.16.

69. Hamby, interview.

T

Chapter 3 ◆ Preparing the Force

The Air Force faces a broad array of threats in an uncertain operating environment. To enable appropriate responses, the Air Force must clearly define the term *force protection* and appoint an office of primary responsibility for integrating currently disparate force protection efforts. Only then can we clarify responsibilities, command and control relationships, and reporting procedures.

Emerging technologies will improve timely information sharing. We must also partner with DoD and other government agencies to improve timely threat and incident reporting procedures. For example, participation with the Joint Terrorism Task Force is an important opportunity to strengthen partnerships. Appointing an office of primary responsibility for force protection will be key to forging these partnerships.

Lead Agent for Force Protection

Finding 37

(This refers to DoD report Finding/Recommendation 3.1.)

- Geographic combatant commander (GCC) and military department force protection responsibilities are clear.

- Neither DoD nor Air Force publications include a clear and consistent definition of the term *force protection*.

Discussion

The DoD report implies a degree of misunderstanding regarding the scope of the GCCs' force protection responsibility and that of the military departments, particularly within the continental United States (CONUS).[1] From an Air Force standpoint, GCC responsibilities are clear. United States Northern Command (USNORTHCOM) is assigned tactical control (TACON) for force protection of all US forces in its area of responsibility.[2] As the Air Force component to USNORTHCOM, Headquarters First Air Force (AFNORTH), is assigned force protection responsibilities for the Air Force.[3] These policies and the Unified Command Plan's assignment of force protection responsibilities to USNORTHCOM and AFNORTH are sufficiently clear.

One concern, however, involves the lack of a clear and consistent definition of the term *force protection*. Joint Publication (JP) 1-02, *Department of Defense Dictionary of Military and Associated Terms*, and JP 3-0, *Operations*, define *force protection* as preventive measures taken to mitigate hostile actions against DoD personnel (including family members), resources, facilities, and critical information.[4] Defining *force protection* as actions taken to mitigate *hostile threats* rather than *all threats and hazards* potentially limits the GCC force protection mission assigned by the Unified Command Plan. In contrast, USNORTHCOM Instruction 10-222 (U), *USNORTHCOM Force Protection (FP) Mission and Antiterrorism (AT) Program*, identifies *force protection* as an *all-hazards* mission.[5] Defining *force protection* in this manner enhances the GCCs' ability to protect the force even though it conflicts with definitions in JP 1-02 and JP 3-0.

The current definition of *force protection* also does not consider the full spectrum of threats unit leaders must address for mission assurance. In fact, the same systems and assets required for planning, preparation, and response for terrorist incidents are also used for natural disasters, pandemic diseases, and other non-hostile threats. This is particularly true in CONUS, where national command-level response plans encompass an all-hazards approach.

> The current definition of *force protection* does not consider the full spectrum of threats ...

A revised definition of *force protection* should enable commanders at all levels to protect DoD personnel, facilities, and information from internal as well as external threats. This definition must remain broad enough for commanders to address mission-specific concerns and be appropriately integrated into force protection policies, programs, and procedures.

Current efforts to better define *force protection* are converging toward an all hazards scope: (1) the Office of the Secretary of Defense (OSD) and Joint Chiefs of Staff (JCS) are discussing changing the definition of *force protection* to emphasize all hazards; (2) USNORTHCOM now defines *force protection* as all hazards;[6] and (3) a working group at the Air Force Doctrine Center is updating Air Force Doctrine Document (AFDD) 2-4.1, *Force Protection*, to incorporate an all-hazards approach.[7] Additionally, US Pacific Command has issued a combined Antiterrorism and Defense Critical Infrastructure Program (DCIP) operations order merging the threat-based antiterrorism program with the all-hazards-based DCIP program.[8]

Recommendation

37.1   Engage with the OSD to better define the term *force protection*. (OPR: AF/A3/5)

Finding 38

(This refers to DoD report Finding/Recommendation 3.5.)

- No single agency manages DoD's force-protection-related common reporting system as the counterintelligence and human intelligence (HUMINT) authority.

Discussion

There is no agency that integrates force protection information among DoD agencies. Also, each Service operates criminal and counterintelligence agencies that often compile force protection-related information. Without a DoD-wide integrating agency focused on force protection, unit leaders may not receive required critical information.[9]

Recommendation

38.1   Coordinate with the DoD to identify a single executive agent to manage force protection-related common reporting systems. (OPR: SAF/IG)

Finding 39

(This refers to DoD report Finding/Recommendation 3.1.)

- The Air Force does not have an organizational focal point for integrating force protection policy and guidance.

Discussion

The Air Force has no policy document from which to derive force protection doctrine and policy guidance. Moreover, no Air Force office or agency has responsibility for integrating and synchronizing the efforts of the multiple staff agencies that develop force protection policies. The following organizations at Headquarters Air Force (HAF) address elements of force protection:

- AF/A2 provides policy for force protection intelligence;

- AF/A3/5 is responsible for homeland defense and civil support, continuity of operations (COOP), operations security (OPSEC), antiterrorism, protection of critical infrastructure, and information assurance and security;

- AF/A4/7 offers guidance for air provost and law enforcement operations; integrated defense; chemical, biological, radiological, nuclear, and high-yield explosives (CBRNE); and installation emergency management;

- SAF/AAP issues guidance for personnel security, information security, and industrial security;

- SAF/IG provides policy and guidance for intelligence oversight, counterintelligence, and investigations;

- AF/SE develops policies for occupational safety;

- AF/SG offers policy and guidance for force health protection; and

- Other staff agencies supply specific policy guidance that may be theater dependent.

The Air Force has no integrating policy document to link the myriad functional areas related to force protection and to promote unity of effort in developing and disseminating policy guidance on force protection. Gaps and seams in force protection may develop if various staff agencies responsible for promulgating policy and guidance within their functional areas fail to coordinate closely.

To establish unified force protection policy and better clarify roles and responsibilities, the Force Protection Steering Group should recommend an appropriate HAF office as lead for integrating and synchronizing force protection policy.[10] The force protection lead should chair a HAF Force Protection Summit and oversee the HAF Force Protection Working Group and steering groups. This lead should also revise the charters of these forums to reflect new responsibilities and draft an Air Force policy directive (AFPD) to clarify and establish various roles and responsibilities within the Air Staff on force protec-

tion efforts. In addition, this lead office would coordinate with applicable DoD and Service agencies and address the requirements of multiple Air Force stakeholders.

Recommendations

39.1 Task the Force Protection Steering Group to develop options for appointing a HAF force protection lead. (OPR: AF/A4/7)

39.2 Develop an AFPD to establish and clarify roles and responsibilities within the HAF for the force protection mission. (OPR: AF/A4/7)

Commanders' Tools

Finding 40

(This refers to DoD report Finding/Recommendation 3.2.)

- Force protection programs do not provide multidisciplinary capabilities focused on predicting and preventing insider threats.

Discussion

The Air Force's primary efforts to identify and mitigate internal threats focus on counterintelligence and espionage. Our force faces a variety of internal threats. In most instances, we find early indicators of potential acts of violence associated with internal threats—after the fact.[11] However, even if unit leaders are aware of indicators of potential violence, programs for assessing and reporting those indicators are lacking, increasing the likelihood of gaps in reporting and responding.

As a means of addressing this issue, the Air Force has partnered with the OSD Force Protection Working Group,

In most instances, we find early indicators of potential acts of violence associated with internal threats— after the fact.

which commissioned the Defense Science Board (DSB), to review DoD documents and analytical findings related to workplace violence.[12] The DSB will also evaluate existing threat-assessment programs for success and best practices, including those used by other government agencies, private industry, and academia.[13]

The review will evaluate existing training and education programs to assist DoD personnel in identifying aberrant behavior exhibited by potentially violent actors. Remaining engaged with this effort, the Air Force will gain insight into broader issues related to assessing, protecting against, and countering internal threats.

Recommendations

40.1 Participate in the DSB multidisciplinary group to develop assessment programs for internal threats. (OPR: AF/A4/7)

40.2 Provide commanders with a multidisciplinary capability focused on detecting and neutralizing internal threats, based on recommendations from the DSB independent study. (OPR: AF/A4/7)

Operational Reporting

Finding 41

(This refers to DoD report Finding/Recommendation 3.1.)

- Air Force command and control relationships related to force protection are unclear.

- AFI 10-206, *Operational Reporting*, Attachment 2, "OPREP-3 and Reports Matrix," does not require notifying AFNORTH or USNORTHCOM for certain incidents, despite their force protection implications.

Discussion

Current reporting procedures for CONUS Air Force installations require operational reports (OPREP-3) from the unit of origin to the appropriate MAJCOM and, if required, to the Air Force Service Watch Cell located in the Pentagon.[14] Based on the nature of the event, reports must meet strict timelines to ensure that appropriate organizations are sufficiently informed.

AFI 10-206 addresses required reporting, but inconsistencies in prescribed reporting procedures could lead to incorrect notifications. For example, current procedures under Rule 2M for "deliberate discharge of a firearm resulting in a death" do not demand notification to AFNORTH or USNORTHCOM.[15] However, Rule 3B for "serious crimes/incidents that may involve exercise of domestic or foreign jurisdiction over Air Force personnel or dependents or that may result in extensive news media or congressional interest" requires notification to USNORTHCOM but not AFNORTH.[16] Updating reporting requirements in AFI 10-206, *Operational Reporting*, will improve notification of appropriate entities regarding important incidents that affect Air Force personnel, property, or information.

Further, because AFI 10-206, Attachment 2, does not clearly specify that AFNORTH or USNORTHCOM must be notified when events having implications for force protection occur, reporting may be delayed. Specifically, eight events (death of an active duty Air Force member, death of a civilian, criminal activity, bomb threat, sabotage, change in force protection condition, civil disturbance, and malicious acts) do not require reporting either to AFNORTH or USNORTHCOM; however, any of these occurrences could have serious force protection implications. Adding AFNORTH and USNORTHCOM as minimum essential addresses for force protection-related events will help prevent delays in future reporting and will mitigate subsequent risks.

Recommendations

41.1 Revise AFI 10-206, *Operational Reporting*, to ensure incidents related to force protection within the CONUS are reported according to prescribed timelines to USNORTHCOM, AFNORTH, and appropriate Air Force and DoD agencies. (OPR: AF/A3/5)

41.2 Revise AFI 10-206, *Operational Reporting*, Attachment 2, to ensure AFNORTH and USNORTHCOM are notified for all incident types having force protection implications. (OPR: AF/A3/5)

Finding 42

(This refers to DoD report Finding/Recommendation 3.4.)

• Air Force policies adequately address reporting requirements to share threat information with internal Air Force entities and with external counterparts; however, no DoD-wide standardized reporting procedures exist for sharing threat information.

Discussion

Counterintelligence agents throughout DoD need to share threat information across organizational boundaries. Without standardized processes, agents rely on ad hoc procedures to share information. Lack of standardized processes may create gaps in details and timeliness of information, causing recipients to miss important data and preventing vital information from flowing to operational commanders. AFOSI Manual 71-121, *Processing and Reporting Investigative Matters*, and AFI 10-206, *Operational Reporting*, give clear guidance on following notification procedures as well as elevating threat information.[17]

AFOSI detachments create a suspicious activity report (SAR) when an incident meets criteria outlined in AFOSI Manual 71-121. SARs must fall within one of eight categories:

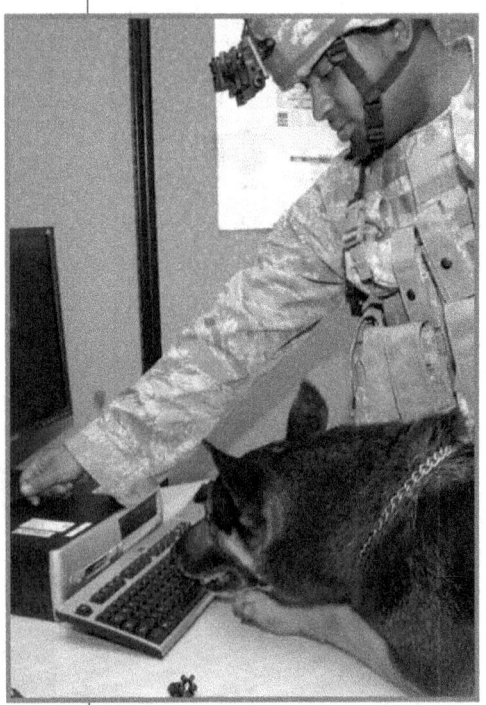

specific threats, surveillance, elicitation, tests of security, repetitive activities, suspicious activities, suspicious incidents, or bomb threats. SARs are reported to the AFOSI Global Watch Center to advise counterpart DoD, local, regional, and federal law enforcement and intelligence agencies as needed. This assists other agencies in identifying and thwarting related suspicious incidents.[18] Though standard practice for AFOSI, these procedures are not standardized among the Services.

The Air Force should participate in DoD efforts to develop specific guidance that improves the timely flow of actionable threat information. DoD plans to establish a principal staff agency for force protection to work with combatant commanders, military departments, defense intelligence agencies, investigative organizations, and counterintelligence organizations to identify sources of required threat information. After defining the threat information and sources, the OPR will establish policies and processes for sharing information with pertinent organizations and agencies. The OSD has set October 2010 as its deadline for developing draft guidance.[19]

Recommendation

42.1   Coordinate with DoD to develop standardized threat-reporting procedures and incorporate any new policies and procedures into existing AFIs as necessary. (OPR: SAF/IG)

Finding 43

(This refers to DoD report Finding/Recommendation 3.6.)

- Current DoD reporting and alerting systems based on phone calls and e-mail can delay the transmission of critical incident reports and limit capacity for simultaneous dissemination, both horizontally and vertically.

Discussion

Legacy communication technology using telephone calls and e-mails may constrain rapid, simultaneous incident reporting. AFI 10-206, *Operational Reporting*, establishes the goal to provide an incident voice report within 15 minutes with a hard copy report following within an hour. A national-level interest event must be reported by telephone to the responsible MAJCOM and combatant command, the Air Force Watch, and the National Military Command Center (NMCC).[20] This reporting process is time-consuming, occurring simultaneously with efforts to coordinate local responses. Current reporting is vertical, to higher levels of command only; other installations and MAJCOMs that may be affected by the incident have to be informed by other means.

Innovative communications, data storing, and sharing options using the Internet could provide Air Force users with near real-time force protection information, trend data, and background sources. Users could potentially see information as it is posted and could access other sites for additional data. Command centers could maintain a constant watch of ongoing events within their communities.

Recommendation

43.1 Participate with the Joint Staff to explore and research technology to improve legacy OPREP-3 reporting systems. (OPR: AF/A3/5)

Finding 44

(This refers to DoD report Finding/Recommendation 3.6.)

- Installation command posts often do not meet the 15-minute requirement to transmit OPREP-3 initial voice reports.

Discussion

According to Air Force Service Watch Cell representatives, OPREP-3 initial voice reporting goals of 15 minutes are often not met.[21] If the voice report is not timely, subsequent notifications are delayed.

Command posts responsible for submitting reports must also communicate information between local responders and installation leaders. Responding to incidents is the first priority and installation commanders typically approve all reporting to include initial voice reports. The initial hard copy reports are frequently delayed as a result.

To improve incident reporting timeliness, command post controllers could be certified to generate initial voice reports on behalf of the installation commander. Controllers should also monitor information and reporting sources outside the installation. All those involved in the reporting process must be well trained, exercised, and inspected to ensure proficiency.

Recommendations

44.1   Ensure those involved in the installation reporting process (e.g., command post representatives, command chain, etc.) are properly trained and proficient in their tasks and have appropriate resources, tools, checklists, and guidance to accomplish them. (OPR: AF/A3/5)

44.2   Evaluate the need for command post controllers to be certified to monitor external information sources, approve, and submit initial voice reports on behalf of the installation commander. (OPR: AF/A3/5)

Finding 45

(This refers to DoD report Finding/Recommendation 3.6.)

- Policies governing operational reporting procedures do not provide specific examples of incident types that are of national-level interest.

Discussion

None of the primary directives governing event notification provide details of the types of incidents meriting national-level response.[22] For example, PINNACLE requirements in AFI 10-206, Section 3.2.1, explain what external factors justify a PINNACLE response (i.e., for national media attention) but do not explain in detail what security breaches merit a PINNACLE designation.[23] Without specific examples, the OPREP-3 PINNACLE reporting might be improperly executed.

Air Force representatives should partner with JCS staff and the other Services to develop and incorporate specific examples of national-interest-level events into policy directives to ensure timely notification of events affecting force protection.

Recommendation

45.1   Coordinate with appropriate DoD, joint, and Service representatives to revise operational reporting policies to include specific examples of incident types that should trigger an OPREP-3 PINNACLE report. (OPR: AF/A3/5)

Finding 46

(This refers to DoD report Finding/Recommendation 3.6.)

- Policies that govern operational reporting procedures do not specify how the National Military Command Center (NMCC) or the GCCs will disseminate incident information.

Discussion

The NMCC or GCCs must disseminate incident information to subordinate units to ensure unity of effort and to synchronize response and recovery actions. Current policies do not provide adequate guidance for this critical phase of the reporting and notification process. Notification from the NMCC and the GCCs to subordinate units could be delayed, especially if an incident involves a coordinated or nearly simultaneous attack against several installations.

AFI-10-206, *Operational Reporting*, clearly defines information flow from the reporting unit to the upper command structure, but it does not provide guidance on horizontal notification of units within the same geographic region. There are no

> There are no standardized procedures for rapidly sharing incident reporting with nearby installations ...

standardized procedures for rapidly sharing incident reporting with nearby installations should an attack occur at multiple DoD installations.

Recommendations

46.1 Coordinate with Joint Staff and USNORTHCOM representatives to revise CJCSM 3150.05C, *Joint Reporting Structure (JRS) Situation Monitoring Manual,* and US Northern Command Instruction 10-211, *Operational Reporting,* to include instructions on how to disseminate incident reports, including rapid horizontal notification. (OPR: AF/A3/5)

46.2 Revise AFI 10-206, *Operational Reporting,* to reflect Joint and GCC policies on disseminating information. (OPR: AF/A3/5)

Intelligence Coordination

Finding 47

(This refers to DoD report Finding/Recommendation 3.3.)

- The Air Force Office of Special Investigations (AFOSI) serves as the focal point for Air Force participation in Joint Terrorism Task Forces (JTTF).

- The current MOU that incorporates AFOSI participation in JTTFs is sufficient.

- Air Force has fully manned its JTTF authorizations in 13 of 103 JTTFs (14 total positions).

Discussion

The DoD report indicated that DoD's commitment to the JTTFs is inadequate. On 7 August 2009, the Federal Bureau of Investigation (FBI) and DoD signed a memorandum of understanding (MOU) formalizing the partnership for AFOSI, Naval Criminal Investigative Service, and Army Military Intelligence participation in JTTFs.[24] This MOU assigns AFOSI as the functional manager for the Air Force role in JTTFs. There are no open issues requiring a change to this relationship or the MOU.[25]

The current MOU between the DoD and FBI, establishing JTTF participation requirements for the counterintelligence agencies within the Services, is sufficient for addressing AFOSI participation. Although DoD does not have an MOU formalizing JTTF participation for all agencies, the current DoD MOU with the FBI meets current Air Force intelligence-sharing requirements.[26] SAF/IGX should coordinate with appropriate DoD agencies to maintain Air Force representation within JTTFs as DoD revises the existing MOU.

To preserve unity of effort and concentrate key resources and expertise at high-priority locations, AFOSI maintains oversight of Air Force participation at high-priority JTTFs nationwide. The Air Force currently has 14 AFOSI civilian criminal investigators assigned at 13 JTTFs and the National Joint Terrorism Task Force (NJTTF).[27] Of these positions, 13 are funded by the Director National Intelligence (DNI) and one is funded by the AFOSI.[28] Expanding AFOSI participation at other JTTFs will require additional manpower and funding; however, AFOSI maintains a prioritized list for assigning additional personnel should resources become available from DNI and the FBI approves Air Force placement at specific locations.

Recommendations

47.1   Participate in DoD revision of MOUs governing participation in JTTFs. (OPR: SAF/IG)

47.2   Coordinate with the FBI and DNI to determine the feasibility of expanding Air Force representation on priority JTTFs. (OPR: SAF/IG)

Finding 48

- There are currently no Air Force personnel assigned to the National Counterterrorism Center (NCTC) or the associated Defense Intelligence Unit (DIU) in Air Force-sponsored billets to support Air Force counterterrorism (CT) analysis.

Discussion

An AFOSI liaison officer (LNO) currently works in the NJTTF, providing valuable law enforcement and counter intelligence collaboration with national investigative agencies.[29] The NCTC is co-located with NJTTF and the Joint Intelligence Task Force-Counterterrorism (JITF-CT) to analyze and assess emerging counterterrorism and counterintelligence threats.[30] The synergy created by these organizations enhances national force protection awareness. NCTC/DIU has offered to host Service intelligence analysts and LNOs.[31]

At present, there are no Air Force-sponsored intelligence analysts working within the DIU. The Air Force should consider the potential benefits of placing an intelligence analyst in the NCTC/DIU to improve CT information sharing and situational awareness of the national counterterrorism picture.[32] Improved collaboration may enhance the Air Force's ability to thwart or mitigate the effects of those intent on causing harm.

Recommendation

48.1   Establish an MOU with NCTC/DIU to establish an Air Force intelligence analyst position and assign an Air Force liaison officer. (OPR: AF/A2)

Finding 49

- The AF does not have real-time signals intelligence (SIGINT) support for counter-intelligence investigations and operations.

Discussion

AFOSI Investigations, Collections, and Operations Nexus (ICON) has a demonstrated need to shape SIGINT support to meet current mission needs and could do so more effectively with an embedded national tactical integration (NTI) element. NTI elements provide time-sensitive, near-real-time SIGINT indications and warning support for CONUS-based air operations centers, numbered Air Forces, and regional cryptology centers. An embedded NTI element in the ICON would enhance AFOSI's indigenous analytic capability against foreign targets and emerging intelligence indicators. Other potential benefits include improving threat information fusion within the force protection community and enhancing situational awareness for unit leaders and regional AFOSI headquarters. The capability would not involve supporting AFOSI's law enforcement mission, except where authorized by DoD Instruction 5240.1-R, *Procedure Governing the Activities of DoD Intelligence Components That Affect United States Persons.*[33]

Recommendation

49.1   Embed a national tactical integration element in the AFOSI Investigations, Collections, and Operations Nexus (ICON) organization to ensure timely signals intelligence (SIGINT) indications and warning support. (OPR: AF/A2)

Joint Basing and Force Protection

Finding 50

- Force Protection exercises and inspections at joint bases may not consistently include all tenant units and joint partners.

Discussion

Force Protection programs are most effective when they are clearly understood and routinely trained, exercised, and inspected. The safety and security of Air Force communities hinge on the vigilance of all personnel who work and live within them. Allowing people to not participate in force protection and emergency management exercises creates potential gaps in awareness of prevention, response, and recovery measures.[34]

AFI 90-201, *Inspector General Activities*, directs compliance inspections to "[e]valuate whether the base exercise program complies with AFI 10-2501 *AF Emergency Management (EM) Program Planning and Operations*. The installation, unit, or activity shall demonstrate the tasks and/or technical operations required to comply with exercise and evaluation program by conducting a *base-wide exercise*."[35] This

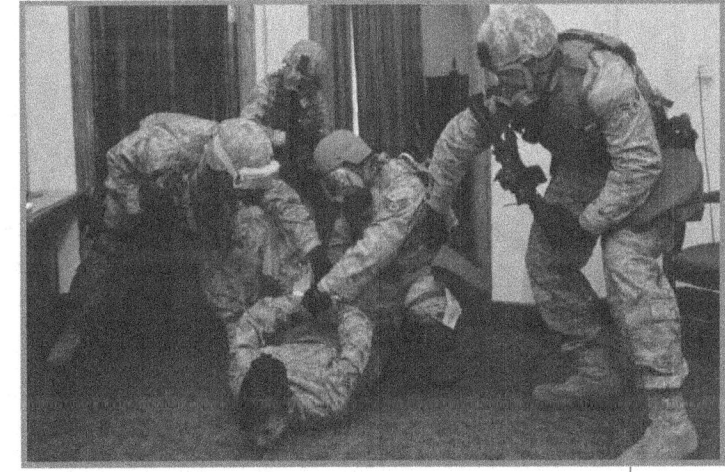

policy directs the evaluation of emergency responders but does not require the general populace to participate in force protection. Exercising emergency responders is important but does not sufficiently stress prevention and mitigation measures.

Emergency management concepts vary between the Services and can slow development and implementation of a common approach to force protection. To this end, the Joint Staff (J3/4) Defense Threat Reduction Agency (DTRA) is addressing joint base inspection standards. DTRA produces Joint Service Integrated Vulnerability Assessment Standards (JSIVA) and benchmarks which the Air Force Vulnerability Assessment Team (AFVAT) uses to create Air Force vulnerability assessment benchmarks.

To overcome gaps between the Services, Joint Base McGuire-Dix-Lakehurst, NJ, established a joint base control center (JBCC). This benchmark structure provides command and control connectivity during crises between the emergency operations cell (EOC) and over 80 tenant units and joint partners. The JBCC maintains direct communication with the host installation EOC and serves as the conduit to distribute information. Doing so allows the EOC to focus on crisis response, while ensuring affected units and personnel receive timely updates.[36]

Recommendations

50.1 Review requirements and coordinate with joint partners and the Defense Threat Reduction Agency for including tenant and joint organizations in base exercises and inspections. (OPR: AF/A4/7)

50.2 Update AFI 90-201, *Inspector General Activities*, to address inspections at joint base locations. (OPR: SAF/IG)

50.3 At joint base locations where the Air Force is lead, the joint base commander must include tenant units in emergency management exercises. (OPR: AF/A4/7)

50.4 At locations where the Air Force is supported by another Service, the senior Air Force commander should ensure Air Force personnel are aware of emergency management procedures and exercise accordingly. (OPR: AF/A4/7)

Notes

1. *Protecting the Force*, 26.
2. Message 071901ZMAY04 (U), chairman, Joint Chiefs of Staff, subject: EXORD [execution order] for Standup of USNORTHCOM CONUS AT-FP [United States Northern Command continental United States antiterrorism/force protection] Responsibility.
3. HQ USAF/CC Message 261834ZMAR09 (U), subject: Designation of 1 AF (AFNORTH) [First Air Force (Air Forces Northern)] as POC [point of contact] for USAF Force Protection Issues. This message also rescinded AF/XO message 012247ZDEC04 (U), subject: Designation of NORTHAF POC for Force Protection (FP) Issues.
4. *Protecting the Force*, 25. See Joint Publication 3-0, *Joint Operations*, 13 February 2008, III-25, http://www.dtic.mil/doctrine/dod_dictionary/data/f/623.html.
5. USNORTHCOM Instruction 10-222, *USNORTHCOM Force Protection (FP) Mission and Antiterrorism (AT) Program*, 17 February 2010, 5, par. 1.2.1.
6. Ibid.
7. The revised document, to be listed as Air Force Doctrine Document (AFDD) 3-10, *Force Protection*, is currently in technical coordination prior to four-letter coordination.
8. USPACOM OPORD [United States Pacific Command operations order] 5050-08, 18 March 2008, FRAGO [fragmentary order] 1, 23 July 2009, 1, par. 1.a.; and 2, par. 1.c.
9. The Counterintelligence Field Activity preceded the Defense Counterintelligence and Human Intelligence Center (DCHC). The latter was created in 2008 to manage the DoD's counterintelligence and HUMINT operations. A suborganization of the Defense Intelligence Agency, it nevertheless has no classic intelligence function and is more closely aligned with the Air Force Office of Special Investigations (AFOSI) than with the AF/A2. Defense News Release, no. 651-08, "DoD Activates Defense Counterintelligence and Human Intelligence Center," 4 August 2008, http://www.defense.gov/releases/release.aspx?releaseid=12106.
10. We explored three possible courses of action in an effort to identify an appropriate Air Force integration office for force protection: (1) designate AF/A3/5 as the office for integrating force protection policy via a matrix organization, (2) designate AF/A4/7 for that function, or (3) establish a special staff to integrate force protection policy (e.g., SAF/FP) with assigned and matrix personnel. Major commands

(MAJCOM) and direct reporting units (DRU) firmly rejected the third option due to concerns about manpower and cost but favored having the Headquarters Air Force (HAF) Force Protection Steering Group analyze the first two options for the HAF FP Summit and approval by the Secretary of the Air Force. The force protection office of primary responsibility (OPR) should develop an Air Force policy directive to define force protection efforts by staff agencies and provide overarching policy to support an Air Force doctrine document on force protection.

11. "Air Force Follow-on Review (FOR) Background Materials," tab 3, Air Force Research Institute (Maxwell AFB, AL: Air University, 2010), 1.

12. The Defense Science Board task force is sponsored by the Under Secretary of Defense for Acquisition, Technology, and Logistics; the Chairman of the Joint Chiefs of Staff; and the Under Secretary of Defense for Policy. "Terms of Reference" (draft), in *Defense Science Board (DSB) Study on Behavioral Indicators of Potential Insider Threats to the Department of Defense and Violence in the Work Place* (Washington, DC: Defense Science Board, 1 May 2010), 2.

13. The DSB will interview DoD and civilian officials (threat-assessment professionals and first responders, as well as those in academe, private business, health affairs, law enforcement, force protection, and intelligence), peer and subordinate groups, witnesses, and others to identify behavioral indicators of potential violence. The DSB plans to assess the adequacy of suitability criteria conducted in periodic checks and those provided to coworkers and supervisors. If the current criteria are inadequate, the DSB will suggest possible alternatives that are more effective, given the large number of people involved and the range of activities requiring suitability determinations.

14. AFI 10-206, *Operational Reporting*, 15 October 2008, 9, par. 1.3.2; 18, par. 3.4.

15. Ibid., 73.

16. Ibid., 74.

17. AFOSI Manual 71-121, *Processing and Reporting Investigative Matters*, chap. 6; and AFI 10-206, *Operational Reporting*, sec. 3.2, 14.

18. Ibid., chap. 6.

19. Alan Gorowitz, team lead, "OSD [Office of the Secretary of Defense] Fort Hood Follow-on Review Information Sharing Team Meeting Notes," 1 April 2008.

20. AFI 10-206, *Operational Reporting*, 15 October 2008, 14, par. 3.2.1.

21. Air Force Service Watch Cell representatives; interview, 3 February 2010.

22. Chairman of the Joint Chiefs of Staff Manual 3150.03C, *Joint Reporting Structure Event and Incident Reports*, 1 February 2009; and United States Northern Command Instruction 10-211, *Operational Reporting*, 16 April 2009.

23. For example, does someone firing a single round at a person on an installation constitute national-level interest? What about exposing an improvised explosive device on an installation? See AFI 10-206, *Operational Reporting*, 15 October 2008.

24. DoD/Federal Bureau of Investigation (FBI) Joint Terrorism Task Force Memorandum of Understanding (JTTF MOU), 7 August 2009, 2, sec. I, par. A.

25. The 12 April 2010 Secretary of Defense *Interim Report for the OSD Follow-on Review Related to Fort Hood* indicates that the Under Secretary of Defense for Policy (USD[P]) will serve as the DoD lead for providing policy guidance and developing DoD-wide goals and objectives for JTFF collaboration. By September 2011, USD(P) will begin drafting and coordinating a consolidated MOU between the FBI and DoD, including the DoD Inspector General's Defense Criminal Investigative Service, to clarify responsibilities and ensure consistency among all agencies. USD(P) will review personnel and data from a resource study provided by the Under Secretary of Defense for Intelligence (USD[I]) to ensure that the commitment of resources to JTTFs meets DoD requirements. Resource and organizational requirements, including requests for additional manpower, will be determined no later than October 2010. A realignment

plan, if required, will be completed by October 2012. SecDef [Secretary of Defense], memorandum, subject: Interim Recommendations of the Fort Hood Follow-on Review, 12 April 2010, 5.

26. SAF/IGX and HQ AFOSI representatives, Mr. Jude Sunderbruch, AFOSI HQ XRC, interview by Preparation Team, HAF OSI HQ, 9 March 2010.

27. The FBI has 103 JTTFs nationwide. Air Force JTTF billets are located in Boston, Colorado Springs, Las Vegas, Los Angeles, Miami, New York City, Omaha, Orlando, Salt Lake, San Antonio, Tampa, Tucson, and the National JTTF in Washington, DC. These locations were selected based on personnel levels, resources, and Air Force interests.

28. SAF/IGX and HQ AFOSI representatives, Mr. Jude Sunderbruch, AFOSI HQ XRC, interview.

29. Federal Bureau of Investigation and the Department of Defense, standard memorandum of understanding, 21 July 2009, par. 4.

30. Executive Order 13354, *National Counterterrorism Center*, 27 August 2004, sec. 3.

31. Dustin Gard-Weiss, "DIA/JITF-CT Mission Management," e-mail memorandum, 4 December 2009.

32. Meeting between Connie Wright, Chief, Force Protection Intelligence Integration and Capabilities Division, Headquarters Air Force; Thory Wolfe, Director, Operations Center; and John Sinisko, Chief/SIO, Information Sharing Division, JITF-CT-DIU, National Counterterrorism Center, 11 February 2010; Executive Order 13356, *Strengthening the Sharing of Terrorism Information to Protect Americans*, 27 August 2004, sec. 2; and Executive Order 13388, *Further Strengthening the Sharing of Terrorism Information to Protect Americans*, 25 October 2005, sec. 2.

33. Air Force Intelligence, Surveillance, and Reconnaissance Agency, "Bullet Background Paper on Air Force National Tactical Integration Support to OSI," 8 April 2010. See also DoD Instruction (DoDI) 5240.1-R, *Procedure Governing the Activities of DoD Intelligence Components That Affect United States Persons*, December 1982, 56.

34. See appendix C. The AFMA survey confirmed that tenant units are not routinely integrated into force protection exercises and inspections.

35. AFI 90-201, *Inspector General Activities*, 17 June 2009, 31, par. 3.3.7.2.3.

36. "Joint Base Control Center Concept Briefing," 87th Air Base Wing, 16 April 2009 [POC, Lt Col David Searle (87th Mission Support Group/CONS)]. Joint bases at Charleston, SC, and McGuire-Dix-Lakehurst, NJ, have also conducted tabletop exercises in concert with joint partners on their installation.

Force development relies on a continuum of learning that provides competency development across members' careers. Integrating prevention and force protection concepts into this continuum represents a necessary step for securing the force against violence and internal threats. As such, providing training and education to all military, civilian, and contractor personnel on potential threats, across a spectrum of violence, can increase Total Force protection. The Air Force must collaborate with DoD on violence education and training policies, programs, and procedures. These programs will better equip Air Force members to identify possible indicators of violence, and as vigilant Wingmen, to mitigate associated risks and take appropriate actions. The majority of these issues and programs are appropriate for the Force Management Development Council (FMDC) to address.

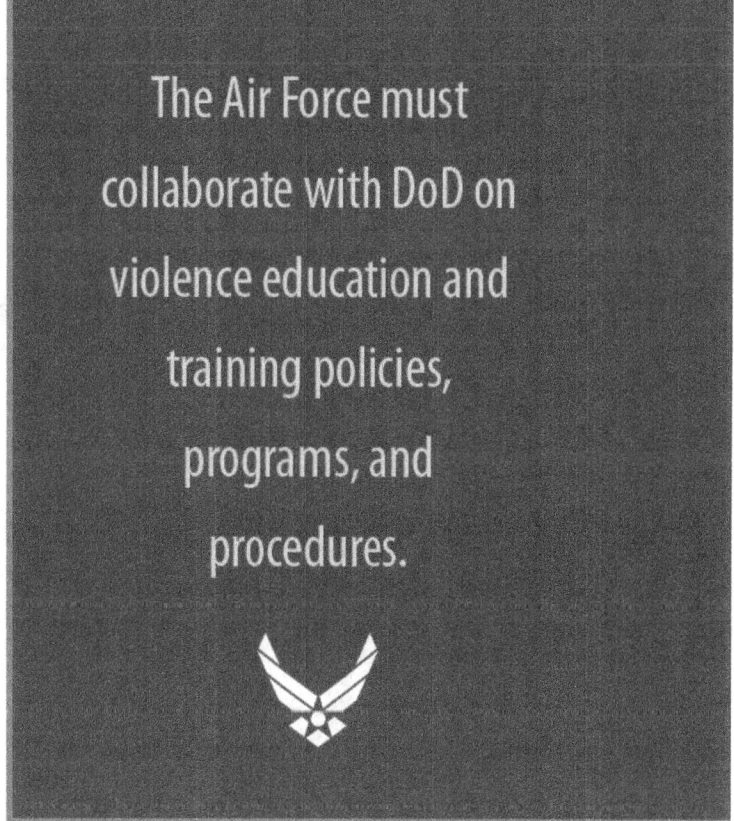

Currently, most Air Force violence prevention training does not adequately prepare personnel to handle the full spectrum of violence. Violence-related training and education should capture all types of threats with specific emphasis on detecting, preventing, or minimizing injury from both internal and external threats. Failing to address all aspects of force protection can severely compromise the safety and well-being of Air Force members and ultimately jeopardize the mission.

Officer Development

Finding 51

(This refers to DoD report Finding/Recommendation 2.12.)

- Air Force training for commanders on protected health information (PHI) is not consistent.

Discussion

Health Insurance Portability and Accountability Act (HIPAA) guidelines prohibit disclosing PHI. In addition to HIPAA, health information is protected by numerous laws including the Privacy Act, Freedom of Information Act, Drug Abuse Offense and Treatment Act, and Comprehensive Alcohol Abuse amendments.[1] However, exceptions are permitted in accordance with DoD 6025.18-R, *DoD Health Information Privacy Regulation*, to allow unit leaders to access PHI when necessary for mission accomplishment.

Commanders and civilian directors frequently cite improved health information sharing and relaxation of HIPAA as most needed to ensure the health and safety of their unit personnel.[2] Sixty-two percent of unit leaders surveyed perceived that HIPAA constrains information sharing on personnel concerns between Air Force leaders and care providers.[3]

HIPAA is a topic of discussion addressed by the Surgeon General during wing, group, and squadron precommand training courses; however, there is no standardized HIPAA curriculum across these courses. To ensure clarity and consistency in commander training, the Air Force Surgeon General should annually review, validate, and disseminate HIPAA training resources presented in these courses.

New Air Force commanders receive the Air Force Judge Advocate General's School (AFJAG) publication, *The Military Commander and the Law*. This publication discusses HIPAA along with permissible disclosures, minimum necessary standards, and commander access to information.[4] In addition, military treatment facility (MTF) leaders are required to meet with all new commanders and first sergeants to provide a TRICARE Commander's Tool Kit including a section outlining HIPAA rules and identifies the privacy officer (PO) for the relevant MTF.[5] MTF POs are experts on PHI issues and are a valuable resource for commanders.[6] Therefore, to solidify commander understanding of PHI issues and to establish working relationships, POs should meet with all new commanders whom they support.

Recommendations

51.1   Annually review, validate, and disseminate HIPAA training resources to wing, group, and squadron commander courses. (OPR: AF/SG)

51.2   Revise AFI 41-210, *Patient Administration Functions*, paragraph 1.4.2.2, HIPAA Privacy Officer Responsibilities, Education, Training, and Communication, to provide commanders initial patient privacy orientation within 90 days of their assignment. (OPR: AF/SG)

Finding 52

- Separate accession programs for line officers and direct commission officers (e.g., medical, chaplain, and legal) may create an unintended gap in leadership, officership, and military professionalism.

Discussion

AFI 36-2013, *Officer Training School (OTS) and Enlisted Commissioning Program (ECPS)*, establishes two separate programs within OTS: Basic Officer Training (BOT) and Commissioned Officer Training (COT). Of the officers trained at OTS, 38 percent are trained via BOT while 62 percent are trained via COT.[7]

To ensure a common foundation for all officers, AFI 36-2014, *Commissioning Education Program*, establishes a standard list of core competencies taught at all commissioning venues, including COT.[8] Although the standards are common and annual reviews aim to ensure equivalency, course length for direct commission officers is significantly shorter than for all other officers. The four-and-a-half week COT course differs from the 12-week BOT course in the depth of instruction available to officers and opportunities for students to demonstrate professional competence as part of the course.[9]

Given these significant differences in initial training, COT and BOT officer candidates do not begin their Air Force careers with a common training experience or similar depth of military professional and Air Force–specific knowledge. This initial training difference may contribute to leadership perceptions of inequity or inadequate preparation of direct commission officers to be military professionals within the Air Force officer corps.

The Air Force should review BOT and COT curricula to ensure the programs provide required leadership, officership, and military professionalism competencies. This review should assess the potential for combining COT and BOT courses, as well as whether certain aspects of direct commission officer training could be more effectively conducted in phases over time or via distance learning. The goal is to ensure that all Air Force officers are afforded the same officership and leadership training upon entering the Air Force.

Recommendation

52.1   Assess the requirements for, and implications of, conducting separate officer training courses within OTS to ensure common military professionalism competencies among competitive categories. (OPR: AF/A1)

Finding 53

- Inconsistent support of Air Force personnel in nontraditional developmental positions (e.g., advanced academic degrees [AAD], foreign professional military education [PME], education with industry [EWI], etc.) may create vulnerabilities in accountability and support.

Discussion

Nearly 1,000 Air Force members attend various nontraditional programs (greater than six months) throughout the world. Participants include active duty Airmen involved in endeavors such as AADs at civilian institutions, foreign PME, EWI, foreign exchange fellowships, and medical education programs.[10] The majority of these Air Force members are assigned to programs under the purview of Air University (AU) (for Air Force Fellows) and the Air Force Institute of Technology's Civilian Institution (AFIT CI) Program.

AFI 36-2639, *Education with Industry Program*; AU Instruction (AUI) 36-2213, *Support of Air University Education Program Personnel Attending Civilian Institutions by Air Force Reserve Officer Training Corps (AFROTC) Detachments*; and AFIT Instruction (AFITI) 36-105, *Civilian Institution Programs*, address management and oversight responsibilities for program participants.

AFIT assigns liaison officers (LO) to serve as campus representative for the AFIT commandant at each civilian school where two or more students are enrolled. LOs maintain contact with assigned students and communicate with them weekly to ensure personal issues affecting their military or academic performance are dealt with appropriately.[11]

Individuals who attend programs in foreign countries fall into two categories: the Military Personnel Exchange Program (MPEP) and foreign PME. AFI 16-107, *Military Personnel Exchange Program*, directly assigns day-to-day management of MPEP-assigned personnel to the Air Force International Airmen Division (SAF/IAPA) and regional air component commands through regional program management offices.[12] The sponsoring host-nation military supervisor and the servicing personnel function at the nearest US installation provide continuous support to MPEP personnel and their families.[13]

AFI 16-107 does not apply to members enrolled in foreign education/PME.[14] Current guidance establishes oversight roles and responsibilities only at the programmatic level but falls short when it comes to day-to-day management of individuals in these programs. This lack of leadership oversight and personnel accountability can isolate PME personnel and may make them susceptible to negative influences.

Recommendation

53.1 Revise AFI 16-109, *International Affairs Specialist (IAS) Program*, to include specific command oversight duties within SAF/IA and AU for members attending academic or PME programs in foreign countries. (OPR: SAF/IA)

Chaplain Development

Finding 54

(This refers to DoD report Finding/Recommendation 4.10.)

- Advanced and refresher Chaplain Corps training does not adequately address mass casualty and workplace violence response.

Discussion

Air Force chaplains now receive mass casualty training at their basic course and more detailed mass casualty training upon arrival at their first duty station.[15] The DoD report identified the Army's Chaplain Basic Officer Leadership Course's (CBOLC) comprehensive training for religious support as a possible best practice for other Services to consider.[16]

Based on this recommendation, the Air Force Chaplain Corps College (AFCCC) incorporated this training into the Basic Chaplain Course (BCC) curriculum effective 10 April 2010.[17] This revised training will comply with new DoD policy guidance.[18]

The Air Force Chaplain Corps Education Oversight Board, which provides curriculum-oriented recommendations, will recommend updates to advanced chaplain and chaplain assistant training programs, building on curriculum revisions incorporated in the BCC. Upon approval by the Chief of Chaplains, the AFCCC will develop relevant instructional materials and programs.[19]

Recommendation

54.1   Revise advanced chaplain and chaplain assistant training and refresher courses to include mass casualty and workplace violence response familiarization training. (OPR: AF/HC)

Finding 55

(This refers to DoD report Finding/Recommendation 4.10.)

- AFI 52-104, *Chaplain Service Readiness*, does not address the need for chaplains to provide spiritual support in response to workplace violence.

Discussion

AFI 52-104 includes procedural checklists and required training for chaplains to provide spiritual support for deployed operations, humanitarian support, and response to natural disasters and national emergencies, but does not address workplace violence.[20] Updating the AFI to include mass casualty response resulting from workplace violence will align policy with the recently revised curriculum at the AFCCC and will improve the corps' ability to respond to all types of traumatic events.[21]

Recommendation

55.1   Revise AFI 52-104 to address training and provide guidance on the requirement for chaplains to provide spiritual support in response to incidents involving workplace violence. (OPR: AF/HC)

Finding 56

(This refers to DoD report Finding/Recommendation 4.10.)

- The Civil Air Patrol (CAP) Chaplain Corps Region Staff College does not include training on mass casualty response.

Discussion

Responding to emergencies is a critical aspect of the CAP Chaplain Corps mission. CAP provides chaplain support, when available, in response to emergencies such as disasters, aircraft accidents, or acts of terrorism involving the CAP, the Air Force, or local communities.[22]

CAP Regulation 50-17, *CAP Senior Member Professional Development Program*, establishes a formal, in-residence training program at the Chaplain Corps Region Staff College.[23] This program covers the main CAP mission areas and includes critical incident stress management and disaster response; however, it does not include training on mass casualty response. The DoD report highlighted the value of having well-trained chaplains who responded during the Fort Hood incident.[24] Without mass casualty training, CAP chaplains may not be as effective in meeting emergency-response mission requirements.

Recommendation

56.1 Air Force Chief of Chaplains and the CAP should review and update Chaplain Corps Region Staff College training to ensure CAP chaplains are prepared to respond to the full range of emergencies, to include mass casualties. (OPR: AF/HC)

Finding 57

(This refers to DoD report Finding/Recommendation 4.10.)

- Contract clergy may not be prepared or permitted to provide spiritual support in the aftermath of mass casualty incidents.

Discussion

AFI 52-105, volume 4, *Chaplain Service Contracts*, provides for contracted clergy to meet religious needs within the Air Force community, and AFI 52-104, *Chaplain Service Readiness*, requires installations to maintain liaisons with civilian clergy in the community to prepare for emergency-response scenarios.[25]

The Air Force contracts with civilian clergy to meet specific faith group requirements (e.g., lead worship services,

Installations may rely on contracted clergy in circumstances when Air Force chaplains and civilian clergy are unavailable ...

hear confessions), but the contract statement of work does not require the full range of military chaplain duties such as general counseling or Airman visitations.[26] Specifically, contract clergy are not required to respond to mass casualty incidents despite requirements specified in AFI 52-104.[27]

Installations may rely on contracted clergy in circumstances when Air Force chaplains and civilian clergy are unavailable to respond adequately to mass casualty incidents. Workplace violence is also not identified as a contingency response scenario in AFI 52-104.[28] Finally, there is no apparent requirement for contract clergy training, to include training concerning workplace violence and mass casualty incidents.

Air Force installations depending on contract clergy for spiritual support require clergy with comprehensive capabilities; lack of workplace violence training for contracted clergy presents a potential gap in pastoral care for Air Force communities in times of crisis.

Recommendation

57.1 Evaluate training requirements and appropriately resource contracted clergy to provide support during mass casualty incidents on military installations. (OPR: AF/HC)

Care Provider Development

Finding 58

(This refers to DoD report Finding/Recommendation 5.2.)

- The Air Force has no policies, programs, or procedures specific to health care provider resiliency.

Discussion

The Air Force has policies and programs addressing generic issues of readiness and resiliency, including the Airman Resiliency Program (ARP) established in 2010.[29] The intent of the ARP is to provide tailored support based on risk of developing post-traumatic stress symptoms, depression, anxiety, suicide, or other adverse conditions.[30] However, certain care provider specialties (e.g., chaplains, trauma center professionals, mental health specialists, mortuary affairs personnel) may require additional resiliency support to cope with stressful or traumatic events.[31] As noted in the DoD report, current readiness and resiliency programs do not provide adequate support to care providers needing to recover from occupational stress.[32]

The Air Force's Warrior Resiliency Program Senior Review Group is reviewing resiliency issues within the Air Force.[33] The group is evaluating readiness issues specific to care providers (e.g., compassion fatigue, secondary trauma) to determine how to integrate these issues into a tiered ARP.[34] Under the ARP, risk for stress is categorized into three tiers based on severity of risk. Ultimately, appropriate tier placement for care providers should adequately address the need for additional policies, programs, or procedures specific to care provider resiliency.

The Army, Navy, and various civilian organizations are likewise addressing the issue of provider resiliency.[35] Awareness of their work should continue to contribute to developing successful Air Force resiliency training, program development, and delivery.

Recommendation

58.1   Incorporate provider-specific resiliency care in the ARP. (OPR: AF/A1)

Finding 59

(This refers to DoD report Finding/Recommendation 5.2.)

- There are no current mechanisms for the Air Force to collaborate with civilian resources on resiliency matters.

Discussion

Because no data or outcome trials exist for resiliency in military settings, the Air Force may benefit from forming partnerships with civilian entities to develop ARPs and procedures. Research groups such as the Defense Centers of Excellence for Psychological Health and Traumatic Brain Injury specializing in post-traumatic stress disorder have gained great synergy by combining military and civilian resources.[36]

Recommendation

59.1   Develop a process to collaborate with civilian entities in addressing resiliency issues. (OPR: AF/SG)

Finding 60

(This refers to DoD report Finding/Recommendation 5.2.)

- Resiliency and self-care education and training have not been integrated into DoD and Air Force military medical education and training materials.

Discussion

The Air Force Surgeon General (AF/SG) has a representative on each of the four Uniformed Services University of the Health Sciences curriculum committees charged with developing and integrating health care provider skills and readiness concepts into applicable training.

As previously discussed, the Warrior Resiliency Program Senior Review Group is actively reviewing resiliency issues within the Air Force and integrating them into existing training and education programs (e.g., suicide awareness) across all education and training venues. Further, the group has begun identifying and addressing the needs of caregiving specialties such as chaplains, mortuary affairs, and medical technicians.[37]

Each of these career fields is addressed within the tiered system of resiliency care. As the ARP develops, providing resiliency and self-care matters early in accession training, as well as throughout specialty training (e.g., primary care manager training) and continuing education (e.g., Aerospace Medicine Primary Course), will help identify and provide coping tools beneficial to these professional caregivers.[38]

Recommendation

60.1 Coordinate with Assistant Secretary of Defense for Health Affairs to incorporate resiliency and readiness self-care skills into initial and follow-on training and education programs for military health care providers. (OPR: SAF/MR)

Force Protection Training and Education

Finding 61

(This refers to DoD report Finding/Recommendation 2.1 and 2.2.)

- Air Force policies and procedures addressing indicators of potential violence are consistent with DoD policy but do not adequately address workplace violence, radicalization, and internal threat education and training.

Discussion

Leadership training on different forms of violence varies in frequency and availability, as does the effectiveness of that training. In our survey of commanders and civilian directors, 98 percent indicated they had received Air Force training to prevent suicide and sexual assault in the past year. Annual training on these two topics is mandatory for the entire Air Force population. Training to prevent other types of violence is not mandatory and is less common.

Our survey revealed variations in prevention training. At least 60 percent received training in the past year on internal security threats, family violence, and domestic terrorism. Less common is training on hostage-taking, physical fights or assault, shooting sprees or mass killings, or homicide. Less than half received training on preventing other abusive behaviors that may be linked to self-harm or workplace violence, such as verbal abuse (43 percent) and bullying (23 percent). Current research on bullying distinguishes this form of aggression from other negative workplace behaviors, particularly in terms of intensity, frequency, and duration of numerous negative acts, which may include harassment but extend beyond it.[39]

We also surveyed unit leaders on whether they had received Air Force–sponsored training in the past year to *respond* to those same forms of violence. The frequency rates for receiving this training were similar to those for prevention training, although training on the response to violence was less common on several items than it was for training on prevention.[40] Instruction on how to respond to violence, however, appears to be more effective than training guidance on prevention: more than 70 percent of Air Force leaders reported that their training provided the skills and tools they needed to respond to various forms of violence, with that figure surpassing 90 percent for suicide and sexual assault response training.[41]

The Air Force introduced DoD workplace violence prevention training in 1999 through AFI 44-154, *Suicide and Violence Prevention Education and Training*, which provides guidance for violence awareness training to include common motivations, scenarios, and risk factors for violence; targets of and precipitants to violence; and post-incident support.[42] AFI 44-154 further supports force development training and education goals by defining annual violence prevention education and training requirements for AU PME courses, commander courses, and community education programs.[43]

In 2008, however, AFI 44-154 requirements for workplace violence awareness training were rescinded to streamline ancillary training.[44] As a result, accession, military and civilian supervisor, commander, and AU PME courses no longer address workplace violence, although related issues are referenced in leadership lessons associated with the Air Force Institutional Competencies List (ICL).[45]

Recommendation

61.1 Reinstitute workplace violence prevention education and training as outlined in AFI 44-154, *Suicide and Violence Prevention Education and Training*, across the career-long continuum of learning. (OPR: AF/SG)

Finding 62

(This refers to DoD report Finding/Recommendation 2.1 and 2.2.)

- Current antiterrorism level 1 (AT-1) training does not include information on identifying and responding to internal threats or radicalization.

Discussion

AFI 10-245, *Antiterrorism (AT)*, implements DoD Directive (DoDD) 2000.12, *DoD Antiterrorism (AT) Program*, and DoD Instruction (DoDI) 2000.16, *DoD Antiterrorism (AT) Standards*.[46] It establishes responsibilities and guidance for the Air Force AT program and integrates security precautions and defensive measures. The primary focus of AFI 10-245 is on external threats such as terrorism and those associated with chemical, biological, radiological, nuclear, and high-yield explosives.[47]

DoDI 2000.16 specifies requirements for AT training and is supplemented by requirements in AFI 10-245 that all military and civilian personnel, as well as local, national, or direct-hire third-country citizens, must complete regardless of grade or position.[48] Given that these policies focus on external threats, AT Level 1 training does not address how to identify or respond to internal threats or radicalization.

The success of current force protection may be impacted by the effectiveness of formal training to detect and respond to potential internal threats. In our survey of commanders and directors, nearly 80 percent of respondents reported consulting Air Force policies and guidance to educate themselves on how to assess indicators of potential violence by a member of their unit. Nearly 70 percent report using Commander's Course guides or information, over 65 percent consult Air Force training materials, and 55 percent refer to Air Force or DoD Web sites to obtain risk assessment information.[49] These findings suggest a revision of AFI 10-245 by the Director of Air Force Security Forces may prove beneficial to addressing internal threat identification and response. Further, table 2.2, "Minimum AT Awareness Training Requirements," should be updated to include "indicators and response to internal threats." These updates should be incorporated into current AT training and education programs.

Recommendation

62.1   Revise AFI 10-245 to integrate response procedures for defending the Total Force against internal threats (e.g., active shooter) into existing training across the continuum of learning. (OPR: AF/A4/7)

Notes

1. AFI 41-210, *Patient Administration Functions*, 22 March 2006, 13, http://www.af.mil/shared/media/epubs/AFI41-210.pdf.

2. Air Force Manpower Agency (AFMA), "Follow On Review: Issues from Ft. Hood Survey," data collection period 22 February–8 March 2010, appendix C.

3. Brig Gen Sharon K. G. Dunbar, USAF, "AF Follow On Review (FOR): Lessons from Fort Hood" (presentation, 9 April 2010), 47.

4. AFJAGS, *The Military Commander and the Law* (Maxwell AFB, AL: AFJAGS Press, 2009), 272–75, http://milcom.jag.af.mil/Military_CC_and_Law_2009.pdf.

5. Maj Pell, HQ USAF/SGMA, "Operation Command Champion (OCC), 2001 Campaign," talking paper, 28 June 2001; Lt Gen Paul K. Carlton, Surgeon General, memorandum, subject: Operation Command Champion (OCC), 2001 Campaign; and Lt Gen Charles B. Green, Surgeon General, to ALMAJCOM/SG, memorandum, subject: Operation Command Champion, 25 October 2009. Operation Command Champion supports DoDI 6000.14, *Patient Bill of Rights and Responsibilities in the Military Health System (MHS)*, 5 September, 2007.

6. AFI 41-210, *Patient Administration Functions*, 8.

7. BOT is a 12-week program open to all civilian applicants including Air Force Reserve, Guard, sister Service members, and active duty Airmen pursuing the opportunity to become an Air Force commissioned officer. COT is a four-and-a-half-week program that provides initial officership training and leadership developmental education to direct commissioned officers serving in the profession-oriented JAG Corps, Chaplain Service, Nurse Corps, Medical Corps, and Dental Corps. AFI 36-2013, *Officer Training School (OTS) and Enlisted Commissioning Programs (ECPS)*, 23 October 2008, 65, 85. Dr. Donald Giglio (Holm Center Commander's Action Group) e-mail to Ms. Ladonna McGrew, 12 April 2010.

8. AFI 36-2014, *Commissioning Education Program*, 22 April 2008, 8–16.

9. Most direct commission officers do not attend in-residence officer developmental education courses (e.g., Squadron Officer College and intermediate developmental education). Therefore, for the majority of non-line, direct commission officers, COT is the only formal officer training and education they receive during their Air Force careers. Capt Je Raley, Holms Center, AETC/CRDL, "Differences between Basic Officer Training (BOT) and Commissioned Officer Training (COT) Curriculum," talking paper, 18 March 2010.

10. AFITI 36-105, *Civilian Instruction Programs*, 28 April 2006, 1–2.

11. Ibid., 15.

12. AFI 16-107, *Military Personnel Exchange Program (MPEP)*, 2 February 2006, 7–8.

13. Ibid., 9–27.

14. Ibid., 1.

15. Maj Michael S. Rash, USAF, Chief, Education Division, USAF Chaplain Corps College, to Col Jerry Pitts, AF/HCX, e-mail, 26 March 2010.

16. *Protecting the Force*, 45.

17. On 10 April 2010, the Army chaplain course Religious Support during Mass Casualty Operations to Wounded and Dying Soldiers was adapted into the AF Chaplain Corps College's BCC. This material will form the foundation for revisions to the advanced chaplain and chaplain assistant training and refresher courses to address mass casualty and workplace violence response. Rash to Pitts, e-mail.

18. Robert Gates, Secretary of Defense, "Interim Recommendations of the Fort Hood Follow-on Review," 12 April 10. The interim guidance directs the Under Secretary of Defense for Personnel and Readiness to publish a policy by July 2010 directing that new chaplains get mass casualty incident training at the earliest point.

19. USAF Chaplain Corps Education Oversight Board Charter, 27 February 2009.

20. AFI 52-104, *Chaplain Service Readiness*, 19 August 2009, 45–49, 71–79.

21. Specifically, attachments 2 and 6 of the AFI must be updated to incorporate mass casualty response.

22. Civil Air Patrol Regulation (CAPR) 265-1, *The Civil Air Patrol Chaplain Corps*, 15 October 2009, 2.

23. CAPR 50-17, *CAP Senior Member Professional Development Program*, 22 September 2009, 25.

24. *Protecting the Force*, 44–46.

25. AFI 52-105, vol. 4, *Chaplain Service Contracts*, 10 April 2008, 4; and AFI 52-104, *Chaplain Service Readiness*, 16.

26. AFI 52-105, vol. 4, *Chaplain Service Contracts*, 4.

27. AFI 52-104, *Chaplain Service Readiness*, 16.

28. Ibid., 72–83.

29. AFI 10-403, *Deployment Planning and Execution*, 13 January 2008, 133–41; AFI 44-153, *Traumatic Stress Response*, 13 March 2006, 4; Col John Forbes, USAF, "Airmen Resiliency Training" (presentation, 22 February 2010); and Lt Gen Bruce Green, USAF, "Tiered, Targeted and Tracked Interventions" (presentation, 22 February 2010).

30. Green, "Tiered, Targeted and Tracked Interventions."

31. Sharon Rae Jenkins and Stephanie Baird, "Secondary Traumatic Stress and Vicarious Trauma: A Validation Study," *Journal of Traumatic Stress* 15, no. 5 (October 2002): 423–32; and Amy R. Hesse, "Secondary Trauma: How Working with Trauma Survivors Affects Therapists," *Clinical Social Work Journal* 30, no. 3 (September 2002): 293–309.

32. *Protecting the Force*, 51–53.

33. Lt Col Charles Motsinger (Deputy Chief Medical Information Officer, Workflow Integration and Business Process Reengineering Division, Air Force Medical Support Agency [AFMSA]/SG6), interview with Lt Col William Isler (Chief, Deployment Mental Health, Air Force Medical Operations Agency, AFMOA/SGHW), 25 February 2010.

34. Ibid. Secondary trauma, also referred to as compassion fatigue, is the effect on therapists from working with traumatized persons. See Jenkins and Baird, "Secondary Traumatic Stress and Vicarious Trauma," 423–32; and Hesse, "Secondary Trauma," 293–309.

35. LTC Edward Brusher, *Transitioning the Provider Resiliency Training (PRT) Program into the Care Provider Support Program (CPSP: Program Expansion and Revision)* (Falls Church, VA: DASG-HSZ, 10 December 2009); LTC Graeme Bicknell and LTC Edward Brusher, DASG-HCZ, "Professional Quality of Life (ProQOL) Scale Score Comparisons," information paper, 23 November 2009; Bicknell and Brusher, DASG-HCZ, "MEDCOM Provider Resiliency Training (PRT) Program," information paper, 1 December 2009; Bicknell and Brusher, DASG-HCZ, "Provider Resiliency Training (PRT) provision across Department of Defense," information paper, 23 November 2009; and Motsinger and Isler, interview.

36. Examples include the "Strong Star" program in San Antonio and the "Home Base" program, a collaboration between the Boston Red Sox and Massachusetts General Hospital, working with the Army-funded Center for Integration of Medicine and Innovative Technology (CIMIT). CIMIT, "Soldier Medicine: Addressing Soldier Care, Disaster Response and National Healthcare Needs," http://www.cimit.org/about-soldiermedicine.html.

37. Col John Forbes, MD, Deputy Director, AFMSA, Crystal City, VA, talking paper, "AF Resiliency Program (AFRP)," 25 March 2010; Forbes, "Airman Resiliency Training" (presentation, 22 February 2010); and Forbes, "Tiered, Targeted and Tracked Interventions" (presentation, 22 February 2010).

38. AF medical training venues include initial and new staff orientation programs conducted at each clinic as new providers and staff arrive, primary care manager training, intermediate executive skills courses, chief of medical staff (SGH) course, monthly professional staff meetings (conducted by the SGH and includes all privileged providers), mandatory monthly training (e.g., Personal Reliability Program training), Graduate Medical Education (medical residency training), Aerospace Medicine Primary Course, and continuing educational programs that involve AF health care providers. E-mail correspondence provided by Col Angela Thompson, USAF, AF/SG8X, 12 April 2010.

39. AFMA Survey, appendix C. See also for example, one evaluation of the research on workplace bullying operationalizes "bullying as occurring when an individual experiences at least two negative acts, weekly or more often, for six or more months in situations where targets find it difficult to defend against and stop abuse." Pamela Lutgen-Sandvick, Sarah J. Tracy, and Jess K. Alberts, "Burned by Bullying in the American Workplace: Prevalence, Perception, Degree and Impact," *Journal of Management Studies* 44, no. 6 (September 2007): 837–62.

40. AFMA Survey, appendix C.

41. Ibid.

42. AFI 44-154, *Suicide and Violence Prevention Education and Training*, 3 January 2003, 1, rescinded AFI 44-154, 1 July 1999, which introduced violence prevention.

43. Force development involves integrating education, training, and experience through integrated competencies—the career-long continuum of learning. See AFI 36-2640, *Executing Total Force Development*, 16 December 2008, 4; and AFI 44-154, *Suicide and Violence Prevention*, 4–5.

44. Maj Gen Thomas Loftus, assistant surgeon general, Office of the Surgeon General, AF/SG3, to ALMAJCOM/SG, memorandum, 8 April 2008.

45. The Institutional Competencies List identifies the basic, intermediate, proficient, skilled, and advanced levels of knowledge and corresponding officer, enlisted, and civilian grades associated with each proficiency level. It serves as the foundational document for the continuum of learning across all training venues.

46. AFI 10-245, *Antiterrorism (AT)*, 30 March 2009, 1; DoDD 2000.12, *DoD Antiterrorism (AT) Program*, 13 December 2007; and DoDI 2000.16, *DoD Antiterrorism (AT) Standards*, 2 October 2006.

47. AFI 10-245, *Antiterrorism (AT)*, 4–10.

48. DoDI 2000.16, *DoD Antiterrorism (AT) Standards*, standard 25, table E3.T2, 28–30; and AFI 10-245, *Antiterrorism (AT)*, table 2, 28.

49. Dunbar, "AF Follow On Review."

Aggressive unit leadership is required to accelerate the Air Force drive to prevent violence while accomplishing assigned missions. The DoD report identified commanders as our "key assets to identify and monitor internal threats."[1] Commanders and supervisors are responsible for enhancing force protection and maintaining situational awareness regarding the health, safety, and effectiveness of their personnel. With this in mind, we've identified initiatives that should improve unit leader abilities to support subordinates and prevent violence.

Sponsorship Programs

Finding 63

- Guidance regarding the Air Force Sponsor Program appears in two AFIs.

- The benefits of the Sponsor Program do not consistently reach all Air Force personnel.

Discussion

Moving to any new location is stressful for individuals and their families. Sources of stress include the ability to sell one's house, find renters, and find a new home; they also include the need for a spouse to secure employment, for children to transition into new schools, and for individuals to adjust to their new work environment. Some of these activities can present financial difficulties and pose uncertainties. Children may face adjustment challenges, leading to behavioral and academic problems. New assignments may take Airmen and their families to unfamiliar or even foreign cultures that may be frustrating to understand. Moves may also disrupt many of the social networks individuals rely on for friendship and support.

The Air Force's Sponsor Program was designed to help lessen the stresses associated with these moves by assisting Air Force personnel and their families as they transition during a permanent change of station. This program is a component of the Air Force Individualized Newcomer Treatment and Orientation (INTRO) Program, governed by AFI 36-2103, *Individualized Newcomer Treatment and Orientation Program*. Additional requirements regarding sponsor training are currently found in AFI 36-3009, *Airman and Family Readiness Centers.*

When notified of a new assignment, Airmen have an opportunity to request a sponsor to help ease the transition to the new location.[2] In 2009, 77.4 percent of Airmen who had

a permanent change in duty assignment requested and were assigned a sponsor; 22.6 percent elected not to have a sponsor.[3] Sponsors are normally assigned to newcomers based on similar demographics (e.g., family, grade, unit) and help them adjust to their new unit and Air Force community by quickly establishing relationships with peers and superiors. These relationships and acceptance in a new environment build resiliency.

Recommendations

63.1 Incorporate Sponsor Program guidance found in AFI 36-3009, *Airman and Family Readiness Centers,* into AFI 36-2103, *Individualized Newcomer Treatment and Orientation Program,* to consolidate Sponsor Program policy. Cross-reference consolidated policy appropriately. (OPR: AF/A1)

63.2 Require sponsors for all first-term Airmen and new officer accessions to support relocation to first duty stations, and update AFI 36-2103 accordingly. (OPR: AF/A1)

Finding 64

- The Air Force does not consistently track sponsor training, sponsor actions, or feedback from sponsored Airmen and their families.

Discussion

Airman and Family Readiness Center (A&FRC) staffs currently provide sponsor training. AFI 36-3009 states, "First-time sponsors and those who have not been trained as a sponsor during the past year must receive sponsorship training."[4] A&FRC coordinates to make sponsor training available. Although the sponsor checklist found at table 1 in AFI 36-2103 provides detailed recommendations for sponsor actions, training and feedback are not standardized.[5] Consequently, commanders do not have adequate insight into the effectiveness of their unit's Sponsor Program.

The OSD/Office of Communications, Military Community, and Family Policy (OSD/MC&FP) initiated a program to develop a Web-based program called electronic sponsorship application and training (e-SAT) to provide standardized sponsorship training to all appointed unit sponsors.[6] A sponsor can use this program to create an online record for the newcomer to include a needs assessment, a customizable welcome letter, and a welcome package.[7] The entire process between sponsor and newcomer can be tracked online, establishing e-SAT as the first system to provide metrics on customer satisfaction with the quality of sponsor support.[8] Surveys generated 30 days after newcomer arrival will afford both the newcomer and the sponsor an opportunity to rate e-SAT and their experience with the sponsorship process.

Recommendations

64.1 Incorporate forthcoming DoD e-SAT into the Air Force Sponsor Program to standardize sponsor participation, training, and customer feedback available to commanders. (OPR: AF/A1)

64.2 Make feedback available to commanders from the forthcoming reports function of e-SAT to assist program effectiveness. (OPR: AF/A1)

Finding 65

- Air Force IG inspection checklists do not require comprehensive assessment of the Sponsor Program.

Discussion

At present, eight of 12 MAJCOMs inspect some aspect of the Sponsor Program even though it is not an Air Force–level inspection item listed in AFI 90-201, *Inspector General Activities*.[9] Requiring sponsorship for first-term Airmen and officer accessions and implementing e-SAT will strengthen the Sponsor Program. We recommend including requirements covering sponsor training, newcomer assignment, and feedback tracking in MAJCOM IG inspection checklists.

Recommendation

65.1 Revise the SAF/IG inspection checklists to include Sponsor Program metrics. (OPR: SAF/IG)

Wingman Initiatives

Finding 66

- The Air Force Wingman Program does not provide unit leaders consistent and standardized content to conduct Wingman Day activities that address specific concerns to include force protection and resiliency.

Discussion

In 2004 the Chief of Staff of the Air Force (CSAF) established the Wingman Program to encourage Airmen to look out for their teammates' emotional, physical, social, and professional well-being. Wingman Day also serves as a vehicle for Airmen to get to know one another better and devise coping strategies for difficult times. Today our Chief of Staff uses this tool to engage by personally providing Airmen information, resources, and strategies to help them be more effective.

Commanders have the latitude to tailor Wingman Day activities to address their units' particular challenges, rather than being required to implement a standardized program designed by Air Force headquarters. However, guidance should be provided at all levels (e.g., PME, commanders' courses) to ensure successful Wingman Day planning and to

help embed the Wingman concept into Air Force culture more thoroughly.[10] For example, unit leaders indicate they could benefit from access to MAJCOM statistics related to suicide, violent crimes, and other concerns.

Interactive training scenarios should emphasize realistic leadership situations to enhance communication skills. Adding awareness training on indicators of violence and radicalization to Wingman Day training templates will help Airmen identify at-risk individuals. A range of off-the-shelf training templates would also allow unit leaders to select standardized content to address the needs of their personnel.

A "Knowing Your Airmen" guide, modeled after the one developed by the Air Force Special Operations Command (AFSOC), would prompt leaders to ask about life stressors and circumstances.[11] This would facilitate leader involvement and help resolve potentially volatile situations. The guide would also provide leaders with tools such as real-world scenarios, case studies, counseling approaches, and information about available resources (e.g., health and wellness programs, financial services, sexual assault response coordinators).

AFI 90-501, *Community Action Information Board (CAIB) and Integrated Delivery System (IDS)*, provides the authority and criteria for establishing a cross-functional team to address individual, family, and community concerns. AFI 90-501 is currently being revised to incorporate the Wingman Day program. Examples of successful and unsuccessful practices should be shared with the CAIB/IDS and with leaders who organize Wingman Day so that future events benefit from lessons learned.[12]

Recommendations

66.1 Communicate the importance and value of the Wingman concept and development of Wingman Day through focused messages from senior Air Force leaders to all AF members (e.g., recommended strategic messages, themes, activities, and training templates that address a wide range of behaviors related to violence risk). (OPR: AF/A1)

66.2 Provide unit leaders statistics and background information that MAJCOMs can tailor for installation-level Wingman Days. (OPR: AF/A1)

66.3 Include strategies for executing Wingman Day events in appropriate PME, commanders' courses, and other training venues. (OPR: AF/A1)

66.4 Publish a "Knowing Your Airmen" guide for leaders' use on Wingman Day. (OPR: AF/A1)

Feedback Discussions

Finding 67

- The current Air Force Performance Feedback Program incorporates guidance for personal interviews and written feedback; however, commanders and supervisors do not have consistent methods for meeting program objectives.

Discussion

The current Air Force Performance Feedback Program, as described in AFI 36-2406, *Officer and Enlisted Evaluation System*, facilitates interaction between commanders and Airmen with respect to performance of assigned duties. The underlying philosophy of the process relies on establishing goals and setting standards to provide individual members with a confidential, qualitative framework within which to measure progress and performance.

Although effective when implemented correctly, the Performance Feedback Program is often not fully utilized as a leadership tool. It is beneficial not only to professional success but also to the early identification of stressors. Surveyed leaders also indicated that high operations tempo and mission requirements restrict the time they can devote to conducting feedback, thus degrading program effectiveness.[13]

An Air Force Guidance Memorandum (AFGM) to AFI 36-2406 is in development to support increased automation and accountability in the Performance Feedback Program. The AFGM recommends automating the feedback process. A system such as Virtual MPF could provide automatic notification to the rater that feedback is due, with follow-up notifications if it is not performed on time. Increased visibility at various steps in the process can provide greater accountability for the feedback process as a whole. We recommend modifying the current program to accommodate input from the ratee prior to scheduled feedback sessions.

Recommendation

67.1   Revise AFI 36-2406, *Officer and Enlisted Evaluation System*, via an AFGM, to incorporate greater accountability and automation into the feedback process. (OPR: AF/A1)

Finding 68

- The formal feedback processes can be improved to facilitate greater interaction between rater and ratee during initial and follow-on feedback sessions.

Discussion

AFI 36-2406 prescribes the military feedback process, which is designed to facilitate "private, formal communication" for supervisors to discuss pertinent issues (e.g., work performance, professionalism, professional goals) with their subordinates at regular intervals.

Feedback tools should also be used to increase interaction between Air Force members at all levels. As an example, the Marine Corps' *Honor, Courage, and Commitment* assessment includes the following:

- The critical role of the ratee supporting unit and higher command missions.

- Individual unit readiness index, including assessment of ratee's deployment and medical requirements.

- Supervisor-conducted performance feedback.

- Ratee's assessment of their performance and opportunities to discuss their personal and professional goals.

Recommendation

68.1 Form an integrated process team to evaluate and refine officer, enlisted, and civilian feedback tools and processes. (OPR: AF/A1)

Health-Related Feedback

Finding 69

- Air Force policy does not specify that Physical Evaluation Board liaison officers (PEBLO) update commanders and first sergeants on Medical Evaluation Board (MEB) and Physical Evaluation Board (PEB) results affecting Airmen in their units.

Discussion

AFI 36-3212, *Physical Evaluation for Retention, Retirement, and Separation*, consolidates guidance for the complex, lengthy, and often stressful MEB and PEB processes.[14] Although the instruction contains a section on "control of member during PEB processing," it lacks guidance on how and when PEBLOs should notify impacted Airmen and their commanders and first sergeants (e.g., in person, by e-mail, by phone call, in writing via mail or distribution—during the duty day, not on a Friday). The 61-page PEBLO Guide also lacks guidance on the importance of communicating information to Airmen as well as their unit leaders.[15] A gap exists in both policy and practice: at present, Airmen may be notified of MEB results—potentially life-changing events—without commander, first sergeant, or supervisor awareness.

Coping with the potential loss of a military career can challenge an Airman's resiliency and may lead to behavior that puts the Airman or others at risk. At the conclusion of an

MEB or a PEB, PEBLOs should notify commanders and first sergeants as soon as reasonably possible so they can ensure adequate support for affected Airmen. Likewise, Airmen should have time to arrange for a supervisor, first sergeant, or commander to participate in the medical board discussion to provide Wingman and unit support as needed. PEBLOs are enablers of this unit-leadership support. Revised guidance should thus ensure that adverse information is not passed to an Airman at the end of the duty day or end of a work week, as squadron support may be less available compared to the time when notifications occur during normal duty hours within a regular work week. Timing should also afford Airmen the opportunity to immediately ask the PEBLO important follow-up questions.

> Coping with the potential loss of a military career can challenge an Airman's resiliency and may lead to behavior that puts the Airman or others at risk.

PEBLOs must therefore be well trained and must coordinate information among the primary medical care provider, local MEB, Airman and his/her commander and first sergeant, public health flight, PEB, and force support squadron. Modifying AFI 36-3212 will clarify important pre- and post-notification procedures for health care providers, unit leadership, and Airmen.

Recommendations

69.1 Modify AFI 36-3212, *Physical Evaluation for Retention, Retirement, and Separation*, to include PEBLO duties to relay MEB/PEB processes and timely updates to affected Airmen and their commanders and first sergeants. (OPR: AF/SG)

69.2 Revise the *Disability Counseling Guide for Physical Evaluation Board Liaison Officers (PEBLO)* to incorporate material from the updated AFIs. (OPR: AF/SG)

Health Care Leadership

Finding 70

(This refers to DoD report Finding/Recommendation 5.3.)

- Sustaining high-quality health care requires balancing operational demands, compensation, and quality of life for the number of Air Force health care professionals available.

Discussion

Compassion and caregiver fatigue attracted significant attention in the DoD report.[16] Today's elevated operations tempo often magnifies stress associated with these phenomena.[17] Similar stressors are also experienced by medical professionals in garrison, who often maintain the same level of patient care. Fully implementing the Family Health Initiative/Medical Home concept and addressing some of the critical shortfalls that exist in many Air Force Medical Service (AFMS) career fields may mitigate some of these issues.[18]

Recommendation

70.1   Review AFMS force management, and consider changes to compensation, quality-of-life factors, operations tempo, and deployment issues to sustain high-quality health care. (OPR: AF/SG)

Finding 71

(This refers to DoD report Finding/Recommendation 5.3.)

- Air Force health care providers are afforded the same post-deployment programs and opportunity for post-deployment recovery time as combat and combat support personnel.

Discussion

The DoD report highlighted as potentially detrimental to caregiver readiness the Army policy of requiring caregivers assigned to Brigade Combat Teams to remain in their assigned teams for a minimum of 90 days after return from deployment. Air Force health care providers are currently afforded the same post-deployment programs and opportunities for recovery as all other Airmen, operational or support.

Recommendation

71.1   None.

Finding 72

(This refers to DoD report Finding/Recommendation 5.3.)

- The DoD and Air Force do not address issues of stigma and confidentiality for members who seek treatment for stress or other mental health concerns.

Discussion

The Office of the Under Secretary of Defense for Personnel and Readiness (OUSD[P&R]) has announced plans to convert DTM 09-006, *Revising Command Notification Requirements to Dispel Stigma in Providing Mental Health Care to Military Personnel*, into a DoD instruction (DoDI) addressing stigma concerns among Service members who seek mental health treatment.[19] The new instruction will clarify information communicated to commanders when a member seeks mental health care.[20] AFI 44-109, *Mental Health, Confidentiality and Military Law*, addresses issues referenced in the DTM at the Air Force level.[21]

DTM 09-006 and AFI 44-109 do not address treatment sought by health care providers. Clarifying and communicating proper uses of mental health treatment information should reduce perceived stigmas associated with treatment. This could encourage Airmen, including mental health care providers, to seek mental health care, when needed, by reducing their concerns over possible personal and career impacts.

Clarifying and consolidating policy related to all aspects of mental health care, including treatment, can reduce overall concerns (and associated stigmas) by reducing inconsistencies in how commanders interpret and apply policy. The Air Force is in the process of centralizing policy with respect to mental health issues through a comprehensive mental health AFI, which will incorporate guidance on mental health issues currently found throughout multiple AFIs, policy letters, and memoranda. It will also implement Air Force Policy Directive (AFPD) 44-1, *Medical Operations*, and establish guidance for Air Force mental health services.[22]

Publishing a comprehensive mental health AFI, including guidance on reducing stigmas for health care providers who seek treatment, will benefit the Air Force health care community.

Recommendations

72.1   Coordinate with OUSD(P&R) to integrate existing policies and provide appropriate guidance to sustain high-quality care, as well as publish an anti-stigma DoDI based on DTM 09-006. (OPR: AF/SG)

72.2   Address health-care-specific stigma concerns as part of the ongoing biennial review process for AFI 44-109, *Mental Health, Confidentiality and Military Law*. (OPR: AF/SG)

72.3   Consolidate Air Force mental health guidance into a 40-series AFI. (OPR: AF/SG)

Finding 73

(This refers to DoD report Finding/Recommendation 5.4.)

   • Air Force policy does not consistently allow senior (O-6) physicians to remain clinically active and regularly available to serve as clinical peers and mentors to junior caregivers.

Discussion

Senior clinicians typically serve in command and administrative roles, removing them from regular patient care.[23] This often leaves junior clinicians without the benefit of mentoring from more seasoned clinicians.[24] In 2008, the AFMS launched a pilot initiative—the Senior Clinician Billet Program—that returns O-6 physicians to full-time practice, enabling them to serve as mentors during clinical practice.[25]

AFMS officers are encouraged to sustain clinical activity across the duration of their careers.[26] Officers are expected to step into career-enhancing leadership positions (e.g., command, departmental chair, chief of the medical staff), as annotated in the Medical Corps Officer Career Path.[27] Placing senior physicians in clinical mentoring roles maintains high-quality health care and preserves the breadth of experience and expertise within the AFMS.

Recommendation

73.1   Augment chiefs of medical staff by continuing the current Senior Clinician Billet Program pilot project, and evaluate the program within six months of implementing the 2010 O-6 assignment plan. (OPR: AF/SG)

Total Force Leadership

Finding 74

- Air Force leaders lack knowledge about how best to manage Total Force personnel who might pose a threat to themselves or others.

Discussion

Air Force operations increasingly require unit leaders to serve with Total Force personnel: active duty, reserves, National Guard, DoD civilians, contractors, dependents, as well as personnel from other Services. Our survey of commanders and civilian directors asked whether they were aware of their authority to address various types of personnel who may pose credible threats to themselves or others. Results indicate gaps in understanding that may impair leaders' ability to ensure a safe working environment. Closing this gap should present a stronger, more resilient Total Force.

All active duty commanders surveyed indicated they are aware of their authorities for active duty personnel, while only 79 percent report awareness of their authorities with DoD civilians. Further, and surprisingly, active duty commanders are more familiar with their authorities with regard to dependents (74 percent) than they are with reserve personnel (65 percent). In fact, these commanders indicated the same knowledge in addressing reserve personnel as they did other Service personnel (also 65 percent). Active duty commanders reported being least familiar with their authorities with respect to DoD contractors (60 percent) and ANG members (58 percent).

Civilian directors also conveyed levels of disparity in their awareness of Total Force personnel. Although 93 percent are aware of their authorities for potentially dangerous DoD civilians, 83 percent reported the same awareness for active duty personnel and 75 percent for contractors. Only 45 percent indicated familiarity with authorities to address dependents or Reservists, compared to 42 percent for other Service personnel. Similar to active duty commanders, civilian directors are least familiar with their authority for Air National Guard members (34 percent). Responses from ANG and AFRC commanders reflected patterns similar to active duty and civilian leaders.[28]

Uncertainty regarding authorities may lead to hesitant, ineffective, or diminished responses. Unit leaders appeared most likely to understand, document, and refer or report personnel within their affiliation.[29] Gaps in understanding may be rooted in training; only 40 percent believe their commander training sufficiently addressed sharing information on civilian employees, dependents, and contractors.[30] Knowledge gaps on authorities, procedures, and information sharing for Total Force personnel may lead to inaction or slow response even when leaders are concerned about individuals. When asked why they might be hesitant to report personnel concerns to official agencies or individuals, "unclear guidance" and "unclear lane of authority" were among the most common reasons indicated by roughly one-third of respondents.

As the Air Force continues to integrate Total Force operations and operate in joint environments, training and education must provide leaders with greater awareness of how to address all members of the force.

Recommendations

74.1   Revise applicable professional military education and professional continuing education programs to include learning outcomes focused on authorities, procedures, and programs that support Total Force teaming and leadership. (OPR: AF/A1)

74.2   Revise reference materials for officer, enlisted, and civilian members to clarify authorities, procedures, and programs that support Total Force teaming and leadership. (OPR: AF/A1)

Notes

1. *Protecting the Force*, 3.

2. The Checklist for Sponsor Guidance says the sponsor's role is to provide information and assistance and to help the newcomer's move be as smooth as possible. AFI 36-2103, *Individualized Newcomer Treatment and Orientation Program*, 3 June 1994, 9.

3. Department of the Air Force, "Air Force Sponsorship Program," *Airman's Roll Call*, 23 July 2008. Of the 105,317 Airmen who changed duty locations in 2009, 97,173 were eligible for sponsorship. More Airmen request sponsors when assigned outside the continental United States due to a lack of understanding of lawful requirements, currency, culture, traffic, utilities, and so forth.

4. AFI 36-3009, *Airman and Family Readiness Centers*, 18 January 2008, 15.

5. AFI 36-2103, *Individualized Newcomer Treatment and Orientation Program*, 3–4.

6. According to the A&FRC policy chief, e-SAT will officially be announced in May 2010 at the Joint Services Agency Relocation Training Conference. DoD, "e-Sponsorship Application & Training," https://apps.mhf.dod.mil/esat.

7. Gretchen Shannon, Chief, Airman and Family Readiness Policy, AF/A1S, to Lt Col Janice Langer, Associate Director, Medical Corps, AF/SG, e-mail, 22 March 2010.

8. A forthcoming report feature will allow commanders to generate feedback reports based on the newcomer's rating of his/her experience with his/her sponsor or a sponsor's experience with the training. Pam Cunningham, program manager, Relocation Program, OSD/Military Community and Family Policy, to Thomas A. Kelly, Deputy Chief, Personnel Readiness Division, AF/A1PR, e-mail, 26 March 2010. See also Lorraine M. Neuser, Deputy Chief, Airman and Family Readiness Policy, AF/A1DF, to Thomas A. Kelly, e-mail, 24 March 2010.

9. AFI 90-201, *Inspector General Activities*, 17 June 2009.

10. Examples of effective Wingman programs include a Wingman Familiarization Tool developed organically within a unit through the use of focus groups. The tool involves programs centered around

positive choices with regard to relationships, alcohol and drugs, financial matters, and negative emotions; and a Wingman Tool Kit comprised of games that pose questions related to suicide prevention, financial and family readiness, physical fitness, chaplaincy, and other programs involving Airmen taking care of Airmen. Maj Gen Kurt Cichowski, vice-commander, Air Force Special Operations Command, to Lt Gen Richard Newton, Deputy Chief of Staff, Manpower and Personnel, AF/A1, e-mail, 10 April 2010; and Theresa D. Gardiner, "Wingman Tool Kit" (best-practice document, 7 December 2005).

11. Cichowski, e-mail.

12. Air Force Public Affairs Strategy and Assessment Division (SAF/PAX), "Identification as Airman, Wingman, Warrior," *Communication Research Bulletin* 31 (7 February 2008). See also Husna Mirza (AF/A1S), "2008 Wingman Day Feedback" (information paper, February 2009.)

Academic studies cite means to facilitate psychological commitment from individuals and influence long-term behavior, including making short public statements in a small-group forum (e.g., oath of office, change of command, promotion, marriage ceremonies) and publically signing a contract. Robert B. Cialdini, *Influence: Science and Practice*, 4th ed. (Needham Heights, MA: Allyn & Bacon, 2001), 52–97. Incentives such as quarterly, annual, or "best Wingman" awards have proven their value in enhancing Airmen's positive impression of the Wingman program. Mirza, "2008 Wingman Day Feedback."

13. AFMA Survey, appendix C.

14. AFI 36-3212, *Physical Evaluation for Retention, Retirement, and Separation*, 2 February 2006, Incorporating Through Change 2, 27 November 2009. The USAF Physical Disability Division's PEBLO Guide includes 12 references, five of which are lengthy Air Force instructions.

15. AFI 48-123, *Medical Examinations and Standards*, 24 September 2009; AFI 10-203, *Duty Limiting Conditions*, 25 October 2007; AFI 41-210, *Patient Administrative Functions*, 22 March 2006; AFI 36-3212, *Physical Evaluation for Retention, Retirement, and Separation*.

16. *Protecting the Force*, 52–53.

17. Charles R. Figley, *Treating Compassion Fatigue* (New York: Routledge, 2002).

18. Lt Col Timothy J. Kosmatka (AFMOA), "FHI Implementation: The Road to a Medical Home" (presentation, 19 January 2010); and Capt Joe Lupa (AFPC/DPAPA), "Medical Corps: Career Field Data" (presentation, 31 January 2006).

19. The DTM was disseminated to MAJCOM mental health consultants in July 2009 and will remain in effect until its conversion into a DoDI. Lt Col Catherine A. Bobenrieth, Chief, Mental Health Branch, Psychiatry Consultant to Air Force Surgeon General, to author, e-mail, 7 April 2010.

20. Concerns about stigmas often center on a Service member's worry that shared details about mental health treatment will result in unfavorable command perception, negative career impact, and the potential for being ostracized. DTM 09-006, *Revising Command Notification Requirements to Dispel Stigma in Providing Mental Health Care to Military Personnel*, 2 July 2009.

21. The AFI is currently undergoing biennial review, and a discrepancy relating to confidential substance evaluations will be addressed as part of the process. AFI 44-109, *Mental Health, Confidentiality and Military Law*, 1 March 2000; and Lt Col Catherine A. Bobenrieth, interview, 7 April 2010.

22. The proposed 44-series AFI—developed over the past year with inputs and reviews from all MAJCOM mental health consultants, a Tiger Team of mental health professionals, and the AFMOA Mental Health Division staff—is expected to be forwarded for coordination by May 2010. Bobenrieth, e-mail.

23. Col Arnyce Pock (Chief, Medical Force Management, AF/SG1), interview, 9 April 2010.

24. Col Arnyce Pock (presentation, Clinical Systems Program Assessment Review Conference, 5 December 2008); and Pock (presentation, Medical Corps Developmental Team Meeting, 16 September 2008).

25. Pock (presentation, 5 December 2008); and Pock (presentation, Medical Corps Pre-Game Plan Conference, December 2008).

26. AF/SG1M and AFPC/DPS, "Career Counseling Tool," 29 January 2010; and Lt Col Janice Langer (AF/SG1M), "Talking Paper on Medical Corps (MC) Career Progression," information paper, 9 February 2010.

27. AF/SG1M and AFPC/DPS, "Medical Corps Office Career Path Guide," chart, 22 January 2010; and AF/SG1M and AFPC/DPS, "Office Career Time with Projections," chart, 22 January 2010.

28. AFMA Survey, appendix C.

29. Ibid., 9.

30. Ibid.

Many Air Force emergency preparedness and response policies, programs, and practices are well designed and well implemented. However, we found room for improving installation emergency management programs, notifications system, and on-scene command procedures. Although Air Force policies address "high-risk situations," including active shooter response, our approach to traumatic stress response is not fully integrated into the emergency-response program.

Currently, no Air Force–level working group exists to synchronize emergency management functions, and there is no appointed office of primary responsibility for mass-notification systems. Also, there is no Air Force–level office with primary responsibility to oversee and codify the exercise evaluation team (EET) program. This lack of senior management and oversight leads to redundancy and gaps in programs where the seams and responsibilities have not been resolved. It also leads to a proliferation of nonstandard systems in lieu of a best-practices approach.

We also recognize the important role of a common operational picture (COP) to respond effectively to an emergency. Although the DoD has not established standards, requirements, and capabilities for a COP, we recommend that the Air Force continue to define its needs through its Emergency Response Operations Community of Interest. These policies and associated programs will require updates as DoD policy requirements emerge.

Responsibility for Emergency Response

Finding 75

(This refers to DoD report Finding/Recommendation 4.6.)

- No Air Force-level working group exists to synchronize emergency management functions.

Discussion

Air Force instructions require MAJCOMs and installations to establish working groups to foster discussions and synchronize efforts of emergency-response organizations.[1] AFI 10-2501, *Air Force Emergency Management (EM) Program Planning and Operations*, requires all tasked agencies to coordinate on the Comprehensive Emergency Management Plan (CEMP) 10-2.[2] Installations are also required to convene an emergency management working group (EMWG) semiannually to synchronize plans and programs.[3]

Although there is no specific requirement for an Air Force–level EMWG, AF/A4/7 recently identified the need for a HAF working group to synchronize policy efforts to support the Installation EM program.[4] AF/A4/7 held an initial working group meeting in April 2010.

Recommendation

75.1   Establish and chair a HAF-level working group to synchronize Air Force Emergency Management policy and programs. (OPR: AF/A4/7)

Finding 76

(This refers to DoD report Finding/Recommendation 4.4.)

- The Air Force has no appointed OPR for mass notification systems.

Discussion

Timely, accurate notification of an impending threat and appropriate response can reduce the risk of mass casualties. Installations may not have the most effective means for notifying personnel in the event of emergencies because there is no HAF OPR for mass notification systems (MNS). In the event of an incident on or near an Air Force base, the installation command post (CP) is responsible for mass notification.[5] Draft AFI 10-221, *Installation Command and Control*, defines the duties of CP controllers as initiating "base control procedures via sirens, klaxon, telephone and network alerting systems, Giant Voice or Installation Notification and Warning System (INWS), and other mass notification systems."[6]

Most Air Force installations employ an MNS; however, the absence of Air Force–wide standards results in varied capabilities across installations. Net-Centric Alert Systems, which include such measures as pop-up alerts on computers and text messages to mobile phones can be used to activate Giant Voice notification systems. In March 2008, AF/A3O identified the need for MNS requirements, and the "Air Force–Wide Network Centric Emergency Notification Management System" is in draft.[7] Air Mobility Command developed a performance work statement for an integrated system that was delivered to SAF/ CIO A6 in February 2010.

Some installations remain limited to Giant Voice capability while others do not even have access to Giant Voice capabilities.[8] Several MAJCOMs have incorporated state-of-the-art systems into their emergency-response plans. Available advanced systems include integrated capabilities, Giant Voice in populated areas, pop-up messages on network computers, e-mail messages, text messages, and television and radio messages, as well as notification on land-mobile radios and on land or mobile telephones. Total Force commanders and civilian directors reported on the quality of alert procedures, rating e-mail alerts, telephone recall, and Giant Voice as primarily "good" more than "very good." Figure 1 highlights variations in ratings within and outside the continental United States (CONUS).[9]

Air Force policies, programs, and procedures should be updated to reflect current technologies such as text messaging and e-mail to alert personnel who may or may not be physically located on the installation.

Alert Procedures: CONUS vs OCONUS

The following Installation alert procedures for ongoing threats are:

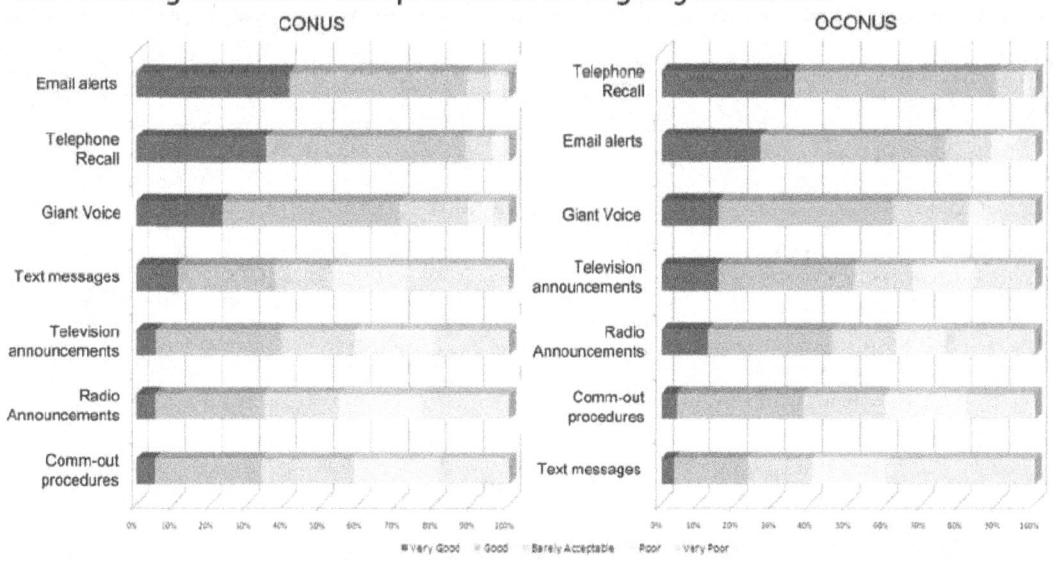

Figure 1. Comparisons of alert procedures

Recommendations

(Relevant best practices are identified in appendix B.)

76.1   Appoint the Director of Operations (AF/A3/5) as the OPR for the MNS. (OPR: AF/A3/5)

76.2   Evaluate mass notification technologies and recommend viable, tailored solutions for installation use. (OPR: AF/A3/5)

Exercise Evaluation Team

Finding 77

- There is no Air Force–level office with primary responsibility to oversee the EET program.

Discussion

Exercise evaluations are critical commanders' tools for assessing installation emergency management capabilities and practices. Inspector general (IG) checklists, installation-level EETs, Joint Staff Integrated Vulnerability Assessments, and Air Force Vulnerability Assessment Teams are used to evaluate the effectiveness of the Air Force Incident Management System (AFIMS).[10]

Although AFIs require exercises for emergency response, the EET program should have Air Force–level oversight to ensure that program and mission requirements are properly updated, exercised, and evaluated. The Air Force Inspector General (SAF/IG) is currently leading a working group of key stakeholders to identify the appropriate Air Force–level OPR for EET and to better define the Air Force EET program.

Recommendation

77.1   Determine the appropriate HAF-level OPR for EET policies, programs, and procedures. (OPR: SAF/IG)

Finding 78

- Tenant units are often not included in installation emergency management exercises.

Chapter 6 ✦ Responding and Recovering

Discussion

AFI 10-2501, *Air Force Emergency Management (EM) Program Planning and Operations*, provides guidance on the installation emergency management program and requires installations to include tenant units in base exercises. Our survey of unit commanders and civilian leaders confirmed that tenant units are much less involved in installation emergency-response exercises than required.[11] Approximately 20 percent of field operating agencies (FOA) and direct reporting units (DRU) report they were "not sure" if their organization practiced emergency response in the past year.

Air Force and MAJCOM IGs should assess tenant participation in emergency management exercises. Air Force host installation and tenant unit leaders should actively seek routine engagement related to emergency management issues.[12]

Recommendation

78.1   Include tenant units in installation emergency management exercises. (OPR: SAF/IG)

Finding 79

(This refers to DoD report Finding/Recommendation 4.5.)

● Air Force policy includes an operational approach to raise and lower the force protection condition (FPCON) level as needed.

Discussion

The DoD report emphasized that local command and control procedures for responding to FPCON changes should allow commanders flexibility to lower FPCON when appropriate to accelerate recovery efforts. AFI 10-245, *Antiterrorism (AT)*, provides installation commanders the authority to raise and lower the installation FPCON as necessary.[13] Commanders may not, however, lower the FPCON below that established by the combatant commander. The instruction requires installations to provide specific details regarding local implementation of each condition.[14] FPCON implementation measures are required in the installation's antiterrorism plan.[15]

To ensure that installations can receive support from off-base responders during an incident, AFI 31-101, *Integrated Defense*, gives specific guidance requiring local plans to include "instructions to allow expedited emergency entry for off-base Fire, Medical, or Law Enforcement personnel as identified in mutual aid agreements."[16]

Recommendation

79.1   Ensure that installation exercises include situations requiring changes in the FPCON. (OPR: SAF/IG)

Emergency Management Systems

Finding 80

(This refers to DoD report Finding/Recommendation 4.1.)

- DoD guidance identifying milestones for accomplishing full operational capability of the DoD installation emergency management program will require reassessment of the Air Force emergency management program.

Discussion

In March 2004, the Department of Homeland Security published the National Incident Management System (NIMS) in response to Homeland Security Presidential Directive 5.[17] In that directive, the President mandated a single, comprehensive system for national incident management.[18] NIMS outlines core doctrine to enable a "balance between flexibility and standardization" in preparation for, response to, and recovery from incidents.[19] National preparedness and response activities have grown from this core con-

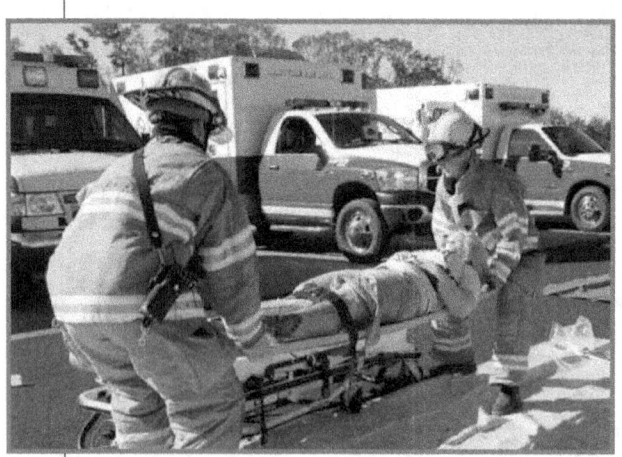

cept. The National Response Framework (NRF) is the operational guidance of NIMS and discusses roles, responsibilities, authorities, and the overall approach to incident management.[20]

The DoD instituted the installation emergency management program to align Services' preparedness, response, and recovery actions within national-response guidance. DoDI 6055.17, *DoD Installation Emergency Management (IEM) Program*, establishes guidance related to the installation emergency management program but does not identify program requirements for initial operating capability (IOC) and full operating capability (FOC). Air Force guidance for implementing the installation emergency management program and aligning with national-response policies—specifically, the implementation of AFIMS—

identified milestones for IOC and FOC.[21] All installations reached Air Force Installation Management System (AFIMS) FOC in February 2010.[22] When DoD guidance is updated to include milestones, Air Force installation programs should be assessed to determine the feasibility of reaching FOC by the DoD deadline of 13 January 2014.

Recommendation

80.1   Revise the Air Force emergency management program to comply with the DoD's forthcoming installation emergency management program policy. (OPR: AF/A4/7)

Finding 81

(This refers to DoD report Finding/Recommendation 4.4.)

- Mass Notification System procurement and sustainment currently depend on the availability of installation discretionary funds or reprogrammed funds from other programs.

Discussion

Although MNS is a costly system, its funding is currently an installation responsibility. One installation estimated the cost to upgrade the current MNS at $4.5 million to provide full coverage.[23] AFRC estimates the initial cost for its MNS to have been $1.2 million in 2007, with a sustainment cost of $600,000 each year.[24] A formal acquisition program would help standardize MNS capabilities and provide centralized funding for procurement and sustainment.

Recommendation

81.1   Establish a formal acquisition program for MNS capabilities, including procurement and sustainment support. (OPR: AF/A3/5)

Emergency Communications

Finding 82

(This refers to DoD report Finding/Recommendation 4.2.)

- Not all 9-1-1 calls initiated on base are directed to on-base dispatch personnel.

Discussion

Military installations have inherent difficulties related to 9-1-1 emergency phone service. CONUS Air Force bases use 9-1-1 as a universal emergency-response number.[25] However, these calls may be routed to an off-base public safety answering point (PSAP) or to an on-base dispatch center, depending on the mode of communication used by the caller.[26] If an Air Force installation is not identified as that region's PSAP, the commercial provider will route that installation's 9-1-1 calls to an off-base dispatch center. Therefore, even though commercial calls initiated from offices on base generally go through an on-base local exchange and 9-1-1 calls are routed to on-base emergency-response personnel, private phone lines in base housing and dormitories more likely

route through off-base local exchanges, and 9-1-1 calls route to off-base PSAPs. Differences in base telephone routing can delay response and degrade information sharing between on- and off-base responders.

The Air Force has not issued guidance addressing effective 9-1-1 call routing or PSAPs. There are 38 Air Force installations identified as PSAPs, each with varying technological capabilities.[27] Requirements for PSAP capabilities and training vary by state. In addition, cell phones and Voice over Internet Protocol (VoIP) are not routed through local telephone exchanges; these technologies will be addressed in Next Generation 9-1-1.[28]

Recommendation

82.1   Develop policy to ensure effective emergency call routing. (OPR: AF/A4/7)

Finding 83

(This refers to DoD report Finding/Recommendation 4.2.)

- Air Force policy for implementing enhanced 9-1-1 (E9-1-1) gives installation commanders discretion to determine implementation timelines.

Chapter 6 ◆ Responding and Recovering

Discussion

DoD has not published guidance requiring E9-1-1 implementation, although various Air Force policies discuss implementation of the E9-1-1 technology system. AFI 33-111, *Telephone Systems Management*, states that installations "should" migrate to an E9-1-1 system.[29] The August 2009 emergency communications center's (ECC) concept of operations lists E9-1-1 enabling technologies as capabilities needed to support successful execution. The Air Force's on-base telephone exchanges in the CONUS can provide caller information, including location.[30] However, only 33 percent of CONUS installations have the necessary software and computer terminals at the call-reception point to use the service.[31] In addition, for emergency calls directed off base, caller information will not display at the reception point if the local community does not support E9-1-1.

No single Air Force office is responsible for E9-1-1 policy. There are many entities involved in providing E9-1-1 support at various levels:

- The Defense Information System Agency (DISA) is responsible for fielding telephone systems that can support E9-1-1 capability.

- The DoD Emergency Management Working Group is tasked with developing DoD E9-1-1 policy.[32]

- AF/A4/7 is responsible for emergency-response programs, including fire emergency services and security forces.

- The Air Force Network Integration Center/Enterprise Capabilities-Voice Networks Branch manages telephone switches, including E9-1-1 interoperability.

Recommendations

83.1   Designate a single Air Force office responsible for developing Air Force E9-1-1 policy. (OPR: SAF/CIO A6)

83.2   Update Air Force policy to comply with DoD E9-1-1 policy guidance. (OPR: SAF/CIO A6)

Finding 84

(This refers to DoD report Finding/Recommendation 4.2.)

- On-base emergency dispatch centers do not combine all responder capabilities.

Discussion

Many local communities have a combined dispatch center to answer and dispatch responders to fire, police, and medical calls. Civilian communities have found that

consolidating these services yields more efficient use of manpower and resources.[33]

In September 2009 AF/A4/7 issued guidance requiring systematic replacement of Air Force installation dispatch centers with a consolidated dispatch center.[34] This single, integrated ECC will meet E9-1-1 standards and improve response capabilities. However, upgrading base response centers (fire and security forces) requires replacing existing hardware. Costs for installing new consoles range up to $500,000 per location, excluding costs associated with combining dispatch functions.[35]

Recommendation

84.1   Ensure the ECC enabling concept approved in August 2009 is fully developed and funded. (OPR: AF/A4/7)

Finding 85

(This refers to DoD report Finding/Recommendation 4.2.)

- On-base dispatch capability cannot generally provide emergency medical dispatch (EMD) information, including pre-arrival instructions.

Discussion

Air Force installations as a general rule do not have an EMD program. Security forces and fire emergency services receive most 9-1-1 calls. Few installations have advanced ambulance and life-support services. As a result, medical calls are routed to local community 9-1-1 service for ambulance dispatch.

Some civilian communities have implemented EMD programs, which include trained and certified emergency medical dispatchers who provide pre-arrival instructions to 9-1-1 callers using protocols established by the local emergency medical director.[36]

Without an EMD program, personnel on base who answer 9-1-1 calls cannot provide pre-arrival medical-care instructions to callers. This deficiency increases response times to provide basic emergency medical care. The Air Force civil engineer and medical communities are collaborating to develop a basic life support response so on-base fire personnel can respond immediately to medical calls and provide basic assistance until advanced care arrives.

Recommendation

85.1   Evaluate the feasibility of providing an EMD program on Air Force installations. (OPR: AF/SG, AF/A4/7)

Common Operational Picture

Finding 86

(This refers to DoD report Finding/Recommendation 4.5.)

- Although DoD standards, requirements, and capabilities for a COP have not yet been established, the Air Force has established an Emergency Response Operations Community of Interest (ERO COI) to define Air Force needs.

Discussion

The Air Force established the ERO COI to develop standards and provide the groundwork for Air Force implementation comprised of leaders from security forces, fire and emergency services, medical emergency management, and command posts. ERO COI participants exchanged information on missions, goals, and processes related to emergency-response operations. Through the work of the ERO COI, the Air Force established standards to field a COP consistent with the intent of national response guidance and mission considerations.[37]

DoDI 6055.17, *Installation Emergency Management Program*, states that an emergency operations center (EOC) "uses a common operating picture and information management system in order to execute and support actions listed in the IEM Plan and facilitate coordination of incident information."[38] DoDI 6055.17 further defines a COP as "a continuously updated overview of an incident compiled throughout an incident's life cycle from data shared between integrated systems for communication, information management, and intelligence information sharing."[39]

In November 2009, the ERO COI analyzed potential COP solutions. The analysis of alternatives identified 42 required capabilities and two mandatory compliance capabilities to meet requirements from the field.[40] Two systems were found to meet more than 90 percent of Air Force needs.[41] The HAF force protection steering group is scheduled to make a selection for fielding in June 2010.

Recommendation

86.1 Field a COP as a mid- to long-term solution to support emergency-response capabilities. (OPR: AF/A4/7)

Finding 87

(This refers to DoD report Finding/Recommendation 4.5.)

- Until a standard COP is fielded, Air Force installations can continue to use the virtual operations center (VOC) interim tool to provide COP information.

Discussion

Air Force installations must adapt interim solutions until a long-term COP is fielded. Several available Web-based systems provide tactical-level information sharing during emergency response. The VOC system uses SharePoint design templates that can be customized to meet an installation's needs.

Recommendation

87.1 Installations review current COP capabilities and ensure that an interim solution is in place and is practiced as part of the installation emergency management program. (OPR: AF/A4/7)

Finding 88

(This refers to DoD report Finding/Recommendation 4.5.)

- DoD guidance for a COP does not identify minimum system requirements.

Discussion

In March 2010, the DoD's EMWG determined that DoD guidance did not sufficiently define required COP capabilities. The EMWG decided that identifying capabilities would be more cost-effective and mission-enabling than implementing a common DoD-wide solution. Related efforts by the Air Force and Navy will inform discussions on developing required capabilities.[42]

Recommendation

88.1   Coordinate with DoD to develop minimum system requirements for a COP. (OPR: AF/A4/7)

High-Risk Response

Finding 89

(This refers to DoD report Finding/Recommendation 4.3.)

- Air Force policies address "high-risk situations," including active shooter response.

Discussion

Although DoD policy does not currently provide guidance on the active shooter threat, AFI 31-201, *Security Forces Standards and Procedures*, requires security forces to establish policies and procedures for planning, training, and equipping installations to respond to high-risk situations, including active shooter scenarios.[43] AFI 31-201 applies to Air Force military and civilian police responders and directs installations to establish necessary memorandums of agreement (MOA) with local civilian agencies to build an effective response capability.[44]

The Air Force has promulgated specific guidance for preparing, training, and equipping to meet the active shooter threat. Draft Air Force Manual (AFMAN) 31-201, vol. 4, *High Risk Response*, includes preliminary tactics, techniques, and procedures (TTP) under the heading "Active Shooter."[45] In anticipation of the manual's publication, the Air Force's Security Forces Deputy Director released "Interim Guidance for Active Shooter Scenarios" on 21 January 2010.[46] This guidance provides specific TTPs for security forces to prepare for, and respond to, an active shooter incident.

The 21 January 2010 interim guidance directs the installation defense force commander (DFC) or the installation antiterrorism officer (ATO) to assist the installation commander in developing a training briefing suitable for commander's calls or similar forums to educate installation personnel on actions to take during an active shooter situation. The interim guidance includes a requirement for combined exercises with civilian counterpart agencies with which MOAs or mutual-aid agreements have been established. The interim guidance also directs the Air Force to educate all Air Force–affiliated populations on appropriate actions to take when encountering an active shooter.[47]

Several installations have made notable efforts in this area. For instance, Shaw AFB, South Carolina, developed a senior leader seminar focused on responding to an active

shooter event.[48] This forum includes such topics as special considerations for military installations, command and control in a dynamic environment, and active shooter response by security forces. In addition, the workshop includes a tabletop exercise and a basewide active shooter-training presentation for military and civilians.[49] This presentation includes a "shooting incident threat aid" (Figure 2) that can be posted or kept in a convenient location.[50] To provide consistent information and training, the Air Force Security Forces Center (AFSFC) is developing a baseline briefing for MAJCOM review and dissemination that will include best practices seen in the field.

As the interservice lead designated for civilian police training, the Army is publishing a multiservice regulation with common minimum training standards.[51]

Recommendation

(Relevant best practices are identified in appendix B.)

89.1   Continue developing security forces and police-response procedures to high-risk situations through the use of TTPs. (OPR: AF/A4/7)

Finding 90

(This refers to DoD report Finding/Recommendation 4.3.)

- Training and awareness for active shooter response is not formalized.

Discussion

Unit leaders indicate that personnel need to be trained on active shooter response actions.[52] Twenty-five percent of commanders surveyed reported receiving training on how

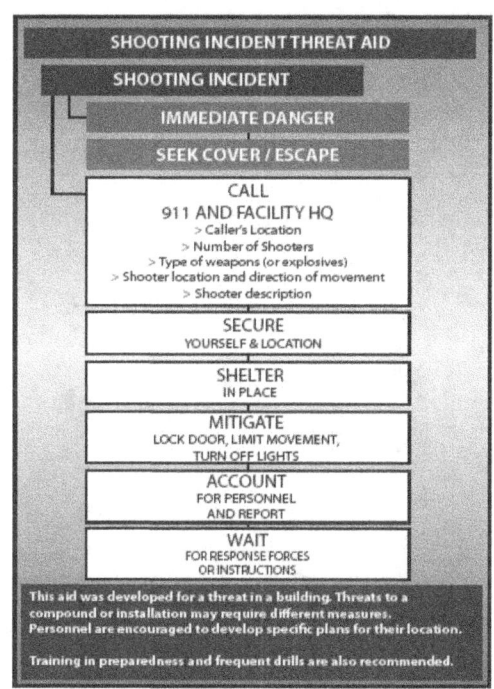

SHOOTING INCIDENT THREAT AID

SHOOTING INCIDENT

IMMEDIATE DANGER

SEEK COVER / ESCAPE

CALL
911 AND FACILITY HQ
> Caller's Location
> Number of Shooters
> Type of weapons (or explosives)
> Shooter location and direction of movement
> Shooter description

SECURE
YOURSELF & LOCATION

SHELTER
IN PLACE

MITIGATE
LOCK DOOR, LIMIT MOVEMENT,
TURN OFF LIGHTS

ACCOUNT
FOR PERSONNEL
AND REPORT

WAIT
FOR RESPONSE FORCES
OR INSTRUCTIONS

This aid was developed for a threat in a building. Threats to a compound or installation may require different measures. Personnel are encouraged to develop specific plans for their location.

Training in preparedness and frequent drills are also recommended.

- Call 911
  - Relay info - S-A-L-U-T-E Report or Your location, # of shooters, type of weapons, shooter location and description
  - 911 call from a base phone goes directly to LE Desk
  - 911 call from a cell phone goes to Sumter Dispatch--costs time
  - 911 may be overwhelmed
- Can also call 803-895-3669/3668 (LE Desk)
- Let dispatcher know you're on SAFB
- Responding SF will yell "Security Forces"
- Stay Calm
- If unable to escape, secure immediate area
- Lock the door
- Block the door using whatever is available-desks, file cabinets, other furniture...
- If the shooter enters your room and leaves, lock/barricade the door behind them
- If safe allow others to seek refuge with you
- After securing the room, people should be positioned out of sight and behind items that might offer additional protection-walls, desks, file cabinets, etc.
- Treat the injured
- Remember basic first aid/SABC
- For bleeding apply pressure and elevate
- Be creative in identifying items to use for this purpose-clothing, paper towels, etc.

Figure 2. Shooting incident threat aid

to respond to shooting sprees and mass killings; three quarters of those reported that the training provided the skills needed to respond effectively. Additionally, as Figure 3 indicates, fewer than one-half of the surveyed unit leaders believe their personnel are informed about actions to take during an active shooter event.[53]

AFI 10-245, *Antiterrorism*, does not specifically address active shooter events.[54] It does, however, mandate annual AT-1 training for all military personnel, civilians, and family members over age 14 who accompany Service members overseas on official orders, as does DoDI 2000.16, *DoD Antiterrorism (AT) Standards*.[55] AT-1 is also offered to all contractors and is mandatory if specified in the contract.

Chairman of the Joint Chiefs of Staff (CJCS) J-34, Office of Combating Terrorism, recently included public reaction to an active shooter event in AT-1 training resources. The Air Force Security Forces Center, responsible for AT-1 updates, will incorporate the new CJCS J-34 training in the updated Air Force AT-1 computer-based training (CBT) course. This will provide a baseline of knowledge, but unit DFCs or ATOs must address installation-specific procedures.[56]

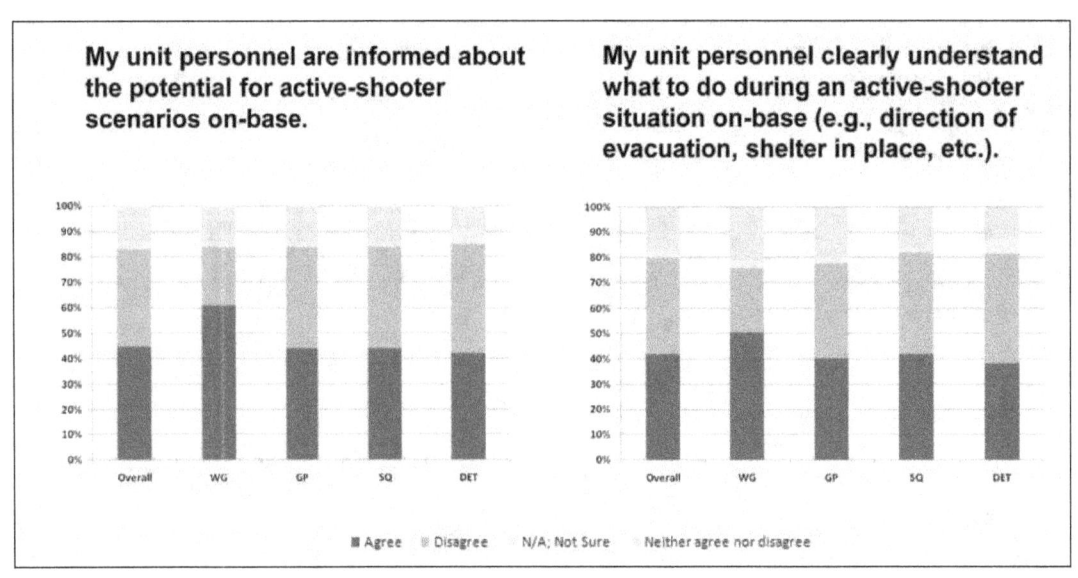

Figure 3. Preparation for active shooter events by organizational level

Recommendations

90.1   Incorporate active shooter response training into Air Force AT-1 training. (OPR: AF/A4/7)

90.2   Incorporate best practices and TTPs for active shooter response into recurring training for military and civilian personnel. (OPR: AF/A4/7)

Finding 91

(This refers to DoD report Finding/Recommendation 4.3.)

- Air Force capabilities for active shooter response must continue to evolve by including lessons learned and best practices from the Fort Hood incident, civilian law enforcement, and such tragedies as the shootings at Columbine and Virginia Polytechnic Institute and State University (Virginia Tech).

Discussion

Several Air Force organizations have implemented procedures based on lessons learned from incidents involving internal threats. After the Columbine shooting in Colorado, the US Air Force Academy (USAFA), in concert with other Service academies, took deliberate steps to improve response capabilities by training cadets and staff on steps to take in the event of an active shooter incident.[57] USAFA identified other improvements through such exercises as ensuring the ability to secure classroom doors to deny shooter access.[58] Air Force agencies are reviewing AFI 10-2501, *Air Force Emergency Management (EM) Program Planning and Operations*, to include references for lockdown procedures.[59]

US Pacific Air Forces conducted extensive training and preparation with DoD dependent schools (DODDS) to ensure they have active, well-trained, and rehearsed plans to respond to an active shooter event.[60] Information gained through these preparation-and-response efforts should benefit all Air Force installations that host local schools.

Developing appropriate TTPs, incorporating best practices, and implementing relevant training will prepare AF members to counter the active shooter threat. Case studies of such internal-threat incidents as Fort Hood should be incorporated into incident-response courses and precommand training at all levels. Doing so will build awareness with regard to leadership accountability and prevention of, preparation for, response to, and recovery from internal threats.

Recommendation

91.1   Incorporate a case study based on the Fort Hood shooting and similar incidents into wing, group, and incident commander training courses. (OPR: AF/A4/7)

Mutual Aid Agreements / Memoranda of Understanding

Finding 92

(This refers to DoD report Finding/Recommendation 4.7.)

- The Air Force does not have clear guidance addressing emergency management mutual aid agreement (MAA) policies, including integrating, tracking, exercising, and inspecting MAAs.

Discussion

Guidance for emergency-response MAAs is contained in several DoDIs and AFIs.[61] Although most Air Force references to MAAs address aid to the local community instead of community aid to installations, several AFIs recognize the need for support from the local community or state and federal agencies.[62] Similar to DoDI 6055.17, *DoD Installation Emergency Management (IEM) Program*, Air Force documents referencing MAAs do not provide overarching guidance for emergency management program-related agreements.[63] Annual review of emergency management agreements is implied, but not specifically stated, as part of the annual review of the CEMP 10-2.

Because MAAs are a critical component of the comprehensive installation emergency management plans, these agreements should be reviewed and exercised annually as part of a review process. AFI 25-201, *Support Agreements Procedures*, discusses mutual benefits under special support conditions in attachment 6; however, no specific information regarding tracking and coordinating responsibilities exists.[64] This section should include functional responsibilities for tracking and exercising. Additionally, appropriate AFIs should be updated following DoD's review of the Fort Hood recommendations.

Recommendation

92.1   Update Air Force policy to address the need to integrate, track, exercise, and inspect MAAs. (OPR: AF/A4/7)

Finding 93

(This refers to DoD report Finding/Recommendation 2.11.)

- Security forces squadrons (SFS) and Air Force Office of Special Investigations (AFOSI) policies do not specify scope and timeliness for MOUs.

Discussion

The DoD report recommended that information-sharing agreements be required with local law enforcement agencies, including standards for scope and timeliness.

Revising AFI 31-101, *Integrated Defense*, to require MOUs with civilian law enforcement agencies will address the gap identified in the DoD report. The updated AFI should specify minimum continuity standards and should provide flexibility for commanders to consider local legal jurisdictions and community relationships for MOUs.[65] SFS and AFOSI commanders should jointly sign MOUs with civilian law enforcement agencies when appropriate. An annual review of MOUs should further facilitate improved levels of information sharing.[66]

Recommendation

(Relevant best practices are identified in appendix B.)

93.1   Modify AFI 31-101, *Integrated Defense*, to require SFSs and AFOSI jointly to establish MOUs with civilian law enforcement agencies to include expectations for scope and timeliness. (OPR: AF/A4/7)

Casualty Assistance

Finding 94

(This refers to DoD report Finding/Recommendation 4.8.)

- Air Force policies governing the Emergency Family Assistance Control Center (EFACC) are not synchronized.

Discussion

AFI 10-2501, *Air Force Emergency Management Program Planning and Operations*, addresses EFACC activation and identifies the EFACC as the focal point for family-assistance services.[67] This instruction is consistent with DoDI 1342.22, *Family Centers*, and AFI 34-1101, *Assistance to Survivors of Persons Killed in Aviation Mishaps and Other Incidents*.[68] AFI 10-2501 and AFI 34-1101 are not synchronized with AFI 36-3009, *Airman and Family Readiness Centers*. Specifically, AFI 10-2501 does not cross-reference AFI 36-3009 when describing the basic execution of an EFACC.[69] AFI 34-1101 and AFI 36-3009 do not have consistent exercise requirements related to the EFACC. Moreover, AFI 36-3009 does not refer to the EFACC toolkit. Updating and cross-referencing these AFIs for consistency and accuracy will solidify the EFACC within the emergency management program.

Recommendation

94.1 Synchronize EFACC-related AFIs to ensure awareness and participation of all pertinent agencies during EFACC execution and sustainment. (OPR: AF/A1)

Finding 95

(This refers to DoD report Finding/Recommendation 4.9.)

- Air Force policy and procedures provide guidance for religious support during mass casualty incidents; however, these policies should be updated to improve response capability.

Discussion

Air Force policy includes chaplain and religious support in the emergency-response framework; however, guidance providing standardized response actions is lacking. The Air Force Chaplain Corps (AF/HC) is integral to cultivating and sustaining the spiritual health and well-being of military personnel, family members, retirees, and civilian employees. Chaplains are expected to perform ministry for their own faith group and provide for the rights and needs of other faith groups in their areas of responsibility, especially

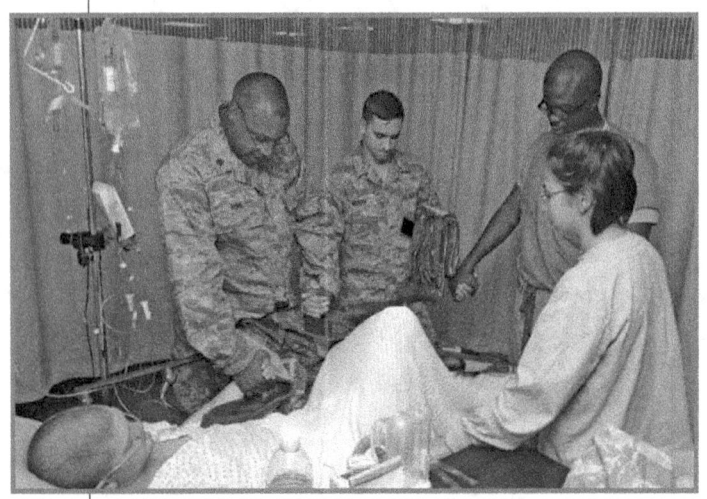

during mass casualty events. The need for spiritual support often intensifies during and following crises.

AFI 10-2501, *Air Force Emergency Management Program Planning and Operations*, addresses religious support and lists chaplain roles and responsibilities.[70] It does not, however, specify a religious-support concept of operations that clearly defines the provision of religious support during and following incidents of workplace violence, response to mass casualties, or recovery actions. Revisions to AFI 10-2501 should ensure response consistency of chaplain support across Air Force installations and inform first-responder training requirements for chaplains.

The guidance in AFI 52-104 includes a sample wing chaplain operation instruction and checklists for major accident response, natural disaster response, national emergencies, and humanitarian support. However, it does not specify chaplain roles and responsibilities following incidents of workplace violence, mass casualty response, and recovery.[71]

Recommendation

95.1 Revise religious support policies to synchronize mass casualty response efforts. (OPR: AF/HC)

Finding 96

(This refers to DoD report Finding/Recommendation 4.11.)

- The Air Force does not have policy or programmed funding to support family attendance at unit memorial services for a deceased military member.

- The Air Force does not have programmed manpower or funding requirements associated with family attendance at unit memorial services for deceased military members.

Chapter 6 ✦ Responding and Recovering

Discussion

The National Defense Authorization Act for Fiscal Year 2010 authorizes round-trip travel and transportation allowances for eligible relatives of members who die while on active duty to attend a memorial service for deceased military family members at a location other than the burial site.[72] In May 2010, DoD published implementation guidance for this legislation, Directive-Type Memorandum (DTM) 10-008 – Travel and Transportation for Survivors of Deceased Members of the Uniformed Services to Attend Memorial Ceremonies.[73]

AFI 34-242, Mortuary Affairs Program, should be updated to reflect the new DoD guidance and address funding family-member travel to attend a unit or installation memorial service.[74] With DoD guidance now established, the Air Force Mortuary Affairs Operations (AFMAO) Center will implement the program, and provide oversight based on the OUSD(P&R) policy memo.[75] AFMAO identified a requirement for one program administrator position and funding requirements for travel reimbursements for civilian family members to attend memorial services.[76]

Recommendations

96.1   Align Air Force policy with DoD guidance to address memorial service attendance. (OPR: AF/A1)

96.2   Fund one civilian position and provide funding to support civilian family requests to attend memorial services. (OPR: AF/A1)

Finding 97

(This refers to DoD report Finding/Recommendation 4.12.)

- Casualty notification and mortuary affairs for private citizens killed on DoD installations or participating in sponsored events are coordinated through MOAs with local government agencies.

Discussion

The DoD report found there was no DoD guidance regarding death of a private citizen on a military installation.[77] This is significant since the death of a private citizen entails two facets: notification and mortuary affairs. The Air Force can prescribe policy regarding notification of next of kin; however, public law must authorize the use of federal funds supporting private-citizen mortuary affairs.

Despite limited DoD guidance, the Air Force provides some guidance in AFI 36-3002, *Casualty Services*, with respect to notifying next of kin. The instruction allows commanders "discretion to notify next of kin of non-DoD civilians if they are killed on an installation or during an orientation flight or a civic leader tour including airlift. If the commander chooses to make notification, the same procedures will be followed as for military members."[78]

Existing AFIs do not require MOUs with local authorities regarding notification. When commanders choose not to notify the next of kin, base support agencies coordinate with off-base civilian organizations to ensure proper notifications are made. Each installation coordinates with local authorities to comply with applicable county and state laws. Air Force policy covering mortuary plans should be updated to include notifications in the MOU.

Unlike casualty notification, mortuary support is an entitlement requiring legislation and funding. Public law does not currently authorize mortuary entitlements for private citizens with no DoD affiliation. The force support squadron develops MOUs with local law enforcement and the coroner's office to ensure appropriate and timely handling and disposition of remains.[79]

Recommendation

97.1 Coordinate with DoD to develop policies and procedures for casualty notification and mortuary support of fatalities involving private citizens on an Air Force installation. (OPR: AF/A1)

Finding 98

(This refers to DoD report Finding/Recommendation 5.1.)

- The Air Force provides a comprehensive, proactive approach to traumatic stress response (TSR), but this concept is not fully integrated into the emergency-response program.

Discussion

AFI 36-3009, *Airman and Family Readiness Centers*, offers guidance on the activation of an EFACC, tasked with integrating services addressing the practical and emotional needs of families of potential DoD casualties and DoD personnel affected by the disaster.[80] Given the EFACC's role in response, it would be logical to include TSR as an organic member of the EFACC; current guidance treats it as a stand-alone team. Guidance covering EFACC and TSR should be updated to clearly identify the relationship between the EFACC and TSR during emergency response.

Published in January 2004, the *Clinical Practice Guideline* (*CPG*) is a joint Department of Veterans Affairs and DoD effort for managing post-traumatic stress.[81] A Veteran Affairs / DoD Working Group is currently revising the *CPG* to address appropriate interventions in the immediate aftermath of traumatic events. The revised *CPG* is expected to be released in summer 2010 and should be incorporated into AFI 44-153, *Traumatic Stress Response*, to replace guidelines listed in section IV.[82]

Recommendation

98.1   Revise Air Force TSR policy to synchronize mental health support services in the aftermath of mass casualty incidents. (OPR: AF/SG)

Finding 99

(This refers to DoD report Finding/Recommendation 5.1.)

- Redundancies among crisis response team (CRT) and TSR team missions cause confusion and inefficiency.

Discussion

The CRT provides mental health support during hostage negotiations and in the aftermath of incidents.[83] CRT and the TSR missions currently overlap. To gain manpower and response efficiencies, mental health support to hostage negotiators should move to the TSR, and its requirement for CRT should be deleted.

Recommendation

99.1   Add hostage-negotiation consultation to TSR team capabilities outlined in AFI 44-153, *Traumatic Stress Response*. (OPR: AF/SG)

Notes

1. AFI 10-2501, *Air Force Emergency Management (EM) Program Planning and Operations*, 6 April 2009, 15, 16. At the Air Force level, five working groups and three organizations are involved in emergency management. At the MAJCOM and installation level, three working groups and three organizations are involved. Working groups at MAJCOMs and installation levels review Air Force Incident Management System (AFIMS) and EM training issues; monitor EM operational plans and exercises; review readiness issues IAW AFPD 10-2, *Readiness*, 30 October 2006, and AFPD 10-4, *Operations Planning: Air*

& Space Expeditionary Force (AEF), 30 April 2009, 1–13; review staff assistance visit, exercise, and inspector general trends; monitor AFIMS and chemical, biological, radiological, nuclear, and high-yield explosives (CBRNE) defense equipment shortfalls; coordinate new AFIMS tactics, techniques, and procedures (TTP) and initiatives; and review CBRNE defense training.

2. AFI 10-2501, *Air Force Emergency Management (EM) Program Planning and Operations*, 6 April 2009, 46–48.

3. Ibid., 15, 16.

4. Lt Col Thomas Taylor, Chief, Incident Management, Air Force Readiness Emergency Services Branch, AF/A7CXR, and Col Elizabeth E. Arledge, A4/7 reserve advisor, AF/A4/7H, 30 March 2010.

5. AFI 10-207, *Command Posts*, 4 April 2008, 28.

6. AFI 10-221, "Installation Command and Control," draft, 11.

7. AF/A3O-AO, "Air Force-Wide Network Centric Emergency Notification Management System," draft, 24 March 2008, 3.

8. There are current Air Force efforts to update and standardize MNS at installations. In a Scope Warrior action item, Air Force Scope Warrior, "Action Item Review" (presentation, 18 November 2009), Air Mobility Command was tasked as the Air Force lead for developing a performance work statement for an integrated mass notification system that includes integrating Giant Voice with a computer desktop notification and other state-of-the-art capabilities. That statement was delivered to SAF/A6 in February 2010. Several MAJCOMs have taken independent steps to standardize MNS capabilities. However, no organization has been named the OPR specifically for MNS. The Air Force FOR team recommends that AF/A3O assume responsibility and update its role accordingly in AFI 10-221 and AFI 10-2501. AF/A3O's continued work in this area, combined with the DoD Emergency Management Working Group's efforts to further define MNS, will remedy this shortfall.

9. Air Force Performance Management (AFMA/MAP), "Follow On Review: Issues from Ft. Hood Survey Results" (presentation, 18 March 2010), 16.

10. See DoDI 6055.17, *DoD Installation Emergency Management Program*, 13 January 2009; and Lt Col Thomas Taylor, Chief, Incident Management, AF/A7CXR, and Col Elizabeth E. Arledge, A4/7 reserve advisor, AF/A4/7H, 30 March 2010.

11. AFMA Survey, appendix C.

12. Source for "FOAs/DRUSs report concerns . . . " AFOTEC, Col Ed Vaughan and commander, 314 AW, "Lessons Learned," briefing, March 2010 AETC Commander's Conference.

13. AFI 10-245, *Antiterrorism (AT)*, 30 March 2009, 25.

14. Ibid., 49.

15. Ibid., 15.

16. AFI 31-101, *Integrated Defense* (FOUO), 7 July 2007, 34.

17. *NIMS and the Incident Command System*, November 2004, http://www.fema.gov/txt/nims/nims_ics_position_paper.txt.

18. Homeland Security Presidential Directive 5, *Management of Domestic Incidents*, http://www.fas.org/irp/offdocs/nspd/hspd-5.html.

19. *NIMS and the Incident Command System*, November 2004, http://www.fema.gov/txt/nims/nims_ics_position_paper.txt.

20. United States Department of Homeland Security, *National Response Framework*, January 2008, 1.

21. Memorandum for ALMAJCOM/CV/FOA/DRU from HQ USAF/A4/7, *Force Incident Management System (AFIMS) Full Operational Capability (FOC) Reporting Instructions*, 22 April 2009.

22. Col Curt A. Van De Walle, Chief, Readiness & Emergency Management Division, AF/A7CX, to AF/A4/7 assistant executive officer, e-mail, 25 February 2010.

23. RFI 7-05-146, "Emergency Management Gaps, Concerns, & Difficulties," Air Force Follow On Review information paper, 11 April 2010.

24. AFRC, "Best Practice #2 (AFRC)" (presentation, 26 March 2010).

25. In October 1999, the *Wireless Communications and Public Safety Act of 1999* (Public Law 106-81) declared 9-1-1 the universal emergency number for telephone service (*Wireless Communications and Public Safety Act of 1999*, Public Law 106-81, 106th Cong., 1st sess., 26 October 1999, secs. 3a3). In 2001 Air Force installations were directed to implement 9-1-1 as the single emergency-response number for all police, fire, and medical emergencies in the continental United States (including Alaska and Hawaii). Overseas, Air Force installations were directed to use 9-1-1 unless it conflicts with host nation emergency-response numbers or intergovernmental agreements (AFI 33-111, *Telephone Systems Management*, 25 March 2005, 20).

26. *DISPATCH Magazine On-Line*, "911 Information," http://www.911dispatch.com/911/index.html .

27. Donald Warner, Air Force Fire Chief, AFCESA/CEXF, to MAJCOM/DRU fire chiefs, e-mail 22 March 2010.

28. National Emergency Number Association, "NG 9-1-1 Project," http://www.nena.org/ng911-project/. Federal Next Generation 9-1-1 policies and procedures are evolving to keep pace with new communication technologies. (The National E9-1-1 Implementation Coordination Office, *A National Plan for Migrating to IP-Enabled 9-1-1 Systems*, September 2009, 2–3.) VoIP is an emerging communication technology challenging conventional E9-1-1 routing mechanisms. VoIP calls are made from traditional phones but move over the Internet rather than traditional phone lines. Consumer and Government Affairs Division, "VoIP and 911 Service," FCC, http://www.fcc.gov/cgb/consumerfacts/voip911.html. With VoIP, individuals can use a phone number from any location as long as there is an Internet connection. This portability, among other characteristics, limits the system's ability to provide location information when a VoIP caller makes an E9-1-1 call. This limitation is being addressed in several ways. More broadly, the FCC continues to update regulations regarding these protocols and the telecommunication industry is working to provide technological solutions. At the local level, users can take several steps users to ensure proper location information is passed to E9-1-1-capable dispatch centers. Information campaigns are cost-effective means for educating installation personnel on how to ensure that their location information is properly displayed on E9-1-1 systems.

29. AFI 33-111, *Telephone Systems Management*, 20.

30. Lt Col Karl Kraan, Deputy Chief, Warfighting Integration and Command & Control Division, SAF/A6WW, phone discussion with Maj Gaycha Robinson and CMSgt Stephen Marotte, Branch Chief, Air Force Network Integration Center/Enterprise Capabilities-Voice Networks, 3 March 2010.

31. RFI 7-01-015, "E911, Mass Notification, Common Operational Picture," Air Force FOR review information paper, 1 March 2010.

32. DoD, "Implementation of Recommendations for the Independent Review Related to Fort Hood," draft, 8 April 2010.

33. Gary Davidson, "Sheriff's Office to Dispatch for Daytona and Holly Hill," *Daily News*, Volusia County Sheriff's Office, 8 July 2004, http://volusia.org/sheriff/press/2004PressReleases/July/040097.htm.

34. Glenn Eckhardt and Lt Col David Scharf, *Emergency Communications Center Enabling Concept*, 19 August 2009, 2.

35. Steven Fuller, AFRC/A7XF, to Donald Warner, Air Force Fire Chief, AFCESA/CEXF, e-mail 19 March 2010.

36. National Academies of Emergency Dispatch, "Standard Practice for Emergency Medical Dispatch," http://www.emergencydispatch.org/articles/standardpractice1.htm.

37. Dating back to 2003, policies leading up to the establishment of a COP include Homeland Security Presidential Directive (HSPD)-5, *Management of Domestic Operations*, 28 February 2003; HSPD-8,

National Preparedness, 17 December 2003; National Response Framework (NRF) (Washington, DC: January 2008); and National Incident Management System (NIMS) (Washington, DC: 18 December 2008), 23. The NRF is the first to introduce a COP in name as part of its key concept of collection, tracking, and reporting incident information. NRF states, "Information must be gathered accurately at the scene and effectively communicated to those who need it. To be successful, clear lines of information flow and a common operating picture are essential." See Department of Homeland Security, *National Response Framework* (Washington, DC: January 2008). HSPD-5 established NIMS as the incident command system to provide a consistent nationwide approach to work effectively and efficiently to prepare for, respond to, and recover from domestic incidents at the federal, state, tribal, and local levels. NIMS guidance defines a COP as "an overview of an incident created by collating and gathering information—such as traffic, weather, actual damage, resource availability—of any type (voice, data, etc.) from agencies/organizations in order to support decision making." See US Department of Homeland Security, *National Incident Management System* (Washington, DC: 18 December 2008), 23.

38. DoDI 6055.17, *DoD Installation Emergency Management (IEM) Program*, 31.

39. Ibid., 39.

40. Of more than 40 systems reviewed, two systems met more than 90 percent of those requirements: Integrated Defense Command and Control (IDC2) and the Incident Information Management System (IIMS) component of Theater Battle Management Core System (TBMCS) Unit Level-Unit Command and Control (UL-UC2). Leveraging existing systems is more cost-effective to the Air Force, and the process of fielding an approved information technology solution can be expedited in what otherwise could be a lengthy approval process. The Analysis of Alternatives found IDC2 incorporated and can meet more than 93 percent of the requirements and appears to be able to meet the needs of the ERO communities. See Michael E. Dickey, *Emergency Response Operations Analysis of Alternatives*, 18 February 2010, 2, 5. Drawbacks, however, still exist. Getting the system fully fielded on the NIPR system is among these problems. Other issues currently being addressed include sustainment and Total Force fielding. Stakeholders represented on the ERO COI meet on a regular basis to provide input to the teams developing IDC2 to resolve open issues. While IDC2 was the clear leader for use at the tactical level, TBMC's UL/UC has a much larger focus on mission-related decision support. However, these two COP tools can integrate and meet all identified requirements.

41. Col Robert K. Mendenhall, Chief, Force Protection and Operations Division, "HAF Force Protection Working Group (FPWG) Meeting Minutes," draft, 26 March 2010.

42. Col Elizabeth E. Arledge, A4/7 reserve advisor, AF/A4/7H, 2 April 2010.

43. AFI 31-201, *Security Forces Standards and Procedures*, 30 March 2009, 31–33.

44. Ibid., 32.

45. AFMAN 31-201, vol. 4, *High-Risk Response*, draft.

46. David R. Beecroft, Deputy Director of Security Forces, DCS/Logistics, Installations and Mission Support, to ALMAJCOM/A7S and ALL SF/CC/SFMs, interim guidance memorandum, 21 January 2010.

47. Ibid., 2.

48. Air Combat Command (ACC), "Best Practice #15 (ACC-Shaw)" (presentation, 26 March 2010).

49. Ibid.

50. Ibid.

51. In response to the DoD recommendation to standardize military law enforcement training and incorporate civilian law enforcement best practices, DoD, through the Joint Security Chiefs Council (JSCC), is reviewing military law enforcement training curriculum to develop and promulgate minimum common training standards for military law enforcement personnel. The JSCC chairman accepted this

tasking, which is included in the DoD Follow On Review Interim Report to the Secretary of Defense (Dickey, interview by Arledge).

52. AFMA Survey, appendix C.

53. Ibid., 5.

54. AFI 10-245, *Antiterrorism (AT)*, 27–28.

55. DoDI 2000.16, *DoD Antiterrorism (AT) Standards*, 2 October 2006, 28.

56. Beecroft, memorandum, 2.

57. Paul M. Ceciliani, United States Air Force Academy (USAFA), "Additional information on USAFA's FOR," information paper, 10 March 2010.

58. Ibid.

59. A7SO, Michael E. Dickey, Chief, Force Protection Branch, Operations, to A7CXR, Lt Col Tom Taylor, Chief, Incident Management, AF/A7CXR, e-mail 21 April 2010.

60. Pacific Air Forces, "Best Practice #10 (PACAF)" (presentation, 30 March 2010).

61. *Protecting the Force*, 42.

62. AFI 10-245, *Antiterrorism (AT)*, 22, 25, 45, 48; AFI 10-2501, *Air Force Emergency Management Program Planning and Operations*, 26 January 2007, 16, 21, 150; and AFI 41-106, *Unit Level Management of Medical Readiness Programs*, 28 July 2009, 9, 20, 33, 46, 136.

63. Ibid.

64. AFI 25-201, *Support Agreements Procedures*, 28 January 2008, 33.

65. AFOSIMAN 71-122, *Criminal Investigations*, 29 May 2008, 1.

66. AFI 25-201, *Support Agreements Procedures*, 28 January 2008, 4–5, http://www.e-publishing.af .mil/shared/media/epubs/AFI25-201.pdf.

67. AFI 10-2501, *Air Force Emergency Management Program Planning and Operations*, 41.

68. DoDI 1342.22, *Family Centers*, 30 December 1992, 3, 6, 7, 11; and AFI 34-1101, *Assistance to Survivors of Persons Killed in Aviation Mishaps and other Incidents*, 1 October 2001, 17.

69. AFI 36-3009, *Airman and Family Readiness Centers*, 18 January 2008, 26–27.

70. AFI 10-2501, *Air Force Emergency Management Program Planning and Operations*, table A4.13, 143, lists the roles and responsibilities of the chaplain as: "1) Determines religious affiliation of victims and assists in comforting the afflicted; 2) Assists with control and assurance of family members of deceased and injured; 3) Ministers to military personnel, their families, and other authorized personnel during contingencies; 4) Serves as OCR for the Mass Care, Housing and Human Services ESF (ESF 6); and 5) Serves as OCR for the Public Health and Medical Services ESF (ESF 8)."

71. AFI 52-104, *Chaplain Service Readiness*, 26 April 2006, 74–79.

72. *National Defense Authorization Act for Fiscal Year 2010*, Public Law 111-84, 111th Cong., 1st sess., 28 October 2009, sec. 631, 170.

73. Office of the Under Secretary of Defense, Personnel and Readiness, Directive-Type Memorandum (DTM) 10-008—Travel and Transportation for Survivors of Deceased Members of the Uniformed Services to Attend Memorial Ceremonies, 11 May 2010.

74. AFI 34-242, *Mortuary Affairs Program*, 2 April 2008, 1–152.

75. Air Force Mortuary Affairs Operations Center, "Travel, Transportation, and Support to Survivors of Fallen Airmen Attending an Installation Memorial Service," draft memorandum, 22 March 2010.

76. The source for the data is based on a five-year average of historical data from Air Force Casualty DCIPs (Defense Casualty Information Processing System) and financial information of travel vouchers filed in relation to burial services. This requirement is based on historical data estimating an average of 190 Air Force active duty deaths per year with an average of 85 percent (or 161) of eligible families expected to use the entitlement. The additional manpower requirement is based on an administrator's duties to re-

ceive, validate, process, and reimburse costs associated with the potential for 966 authorized travelers in accordance with the established Air Force implementation policy.

77. *Protecting the Force*, 47.

78. AFI 36-3002, *Casualty Services*, 22 February 2010, 52–53.

79. AFI 34-242, *Mortuary Affairs Program*, 30 April 2008, 17.

80. AFI 36-3009, *Airman and Family Readiness Centers*, 26–27. The EFACC serves as the staging area where families can obtain disaster relief, contingency information, and services. In addition to Airman and Family Readiness Center personnel, the EFACC may be staffed with representatives from Mental Health, Chapel, Legal, Services, Public Affairs, and the American Red Cross.

81. Department of Veterans Affairs, *VA/DoD Clinical Practice Guideline for the Management of Post Traumatic Stress* (Washington, DC: Department of Veterans Affairs, January 2004).

82. Maj Scott Olech, Chief, Homeland Medical Operations, AFMSA/SGXH, phone conversation with Lt Col Randon Welton, Chief, Modernization Division, AFMC/SGR, 19 February 2010. The VA/DoD Working Group assessed 12 studies that evaluated interventions to prevent post-traumatic stress disorder (PTSD). Additionally, the group reviewed six metaanalyses that addressed PTSD. CPG revisions will outline two treatment options for PTSD: brief cognitive-behavioral therapy (CBT) and psychological first aid (PFA). This update will improve the way clinicians within the DoD and the VA respond to traumatic stress for their patients and therefore obtain more desirable patient outcomes.

83. AFI 41-106, *Unit Level Management of Medical Readiness Programs*, 123.

Air Force (AF) Follow-on Review of Issues Relating to Fort Hood

These Terms of Reference (TOR) address the objectives of the Air Force Follow-on Review of the Secretary of Defense-directed DoD Independent Review of circumstances related to the mass shooting at Fort Hood, Texas on 5 Nov 09. The TOR includes background information, objectives and scope, methodology, duration and limitations and deliverables.

Introduction:

The purpose of the Air Force Follow-on Review (FOR) is to identify and resolve program, policy, and procedural weakness that may create vulnerabilities to the health and safety of Air Force personnel, other supported personnel, and their families. As such, the FOR will thoroughly address all findings and recommendations contained in the January 2010 Report of the DoD Independent Review (DoD IR) relevant to the Air Force. The FOR will identify specific changes required to implement DoD IR recommendations, as well as address other deficiencies identified during the course of the review, with the objective of better protecting Air Force personnel and family members.

Background:

The shooting that occurred on 5 Nov 09, at the Fort Hood, Texas, Soldier Readiness Center resulted in the deaths of 12 Soldiers and one Army civilian, and the hospitalization of 30 victims who sustained gunshot wounds. The President directed a review of intelligence matters related to the Fort Hood shooting, and a military justice investigation is underway. In order to maintain the integrity of these investigations, other reviews underway must not interfere with either of these activities. Nothing herein should be interpreted as expressing any view on the culpability of any individual for the events of 5 Nov 09.

Objectives and Scope:

The FOR will specifically identify gaps and/or deficiencies in Air Force programs, processes, procedures, and training related to the purpose of this FOR, and will recommend improvements. The review will include the following areas:

- Identifying military and civil service personnel, contractors, and civilians who may pose credible threats to themselves and/or others due to internal or external stressors, and consider:
  - Personnel Reliability Programs
  - Personnel assessments to include documentation, reporting, and coordinating pertinent information among appropriate officials

- Medical assessments and/or adverse personnel actions
- Recruitment, background investigations, screening, security clearance, hiring, and placement, with additional focus on recently modified military accession and streamlined civilian hiring authorities
- Transition of personnel deemed not fully qualified or suitable for continued service

- Force protection programs related to potential internal and external threats, from installation to HAF-level, including Air Force reliance on other Services at locations where the Air Force is a supported Service

- Reporting procedures when personnel may be considered a potential threat to themselves and/or others

- Limitations on the ability to communicate, document, and/or share information, to include:
  - Privacy Act and HIPAA issues
  - Transparency and accessibility of information
  - Sufficiency of information sharing between health care providers, helping agencies, commanders, first sergeants, and/or supervisors
  - Effectiveness of documenting and transferring personnel information, particularly during personnel transitions

- Training and education related to identifying, preventing, and/or responding to individuals who may be in distress and/or potentially pose a threat, to include:
  - Life skills and work-life balance
  - Mental health and/or medical concerns/conditions (e.g., PTSD, suicide awareness)
  - Behavioral concerns on and/or off-duty (e.g., unsatisfactory duty performance, isolation, alcohol and/or substance abuse, financial issues, family issues, violent/ aggressive behavior, questionable associations)
  - Risk factors for violence

- Readiness for emergency response to internal and/or external threats and mass casualty situations at AF or Joint Base facilities, to include:
  - Capabilities for responding to alleged perpetrators
  - Initial alert notifications/warning systems, and subsequent communication updates
  - First responder training
  - Memoranda of Agreement with local community and state first responders
  - Personnel accountability
  - Frequency of exercises, use of checklist procedures, and readiness assessments

- Readiness to care for victims and family members in the aftermath of a mass casualty situation, particularly training preparation and periodic assessments, to include:
  - Helping agency and Crisis Incident Stress Management (CISM) team training
  - Memoranda of Agreement with local community and state support agencies
  - Frequency of mass casualty exercises and readiness assessments
- Support of professional care providers (e.g., chaplains, medical, and mortuary professionals)
- Direct personal support, interface, and feedback, to include:
  - Selection and assignment of sponsors and unit wingmen to new unit personnel
  - Training on, and assessment of, sponsor responsibilities
  - Pre-and post-deployment health assessment programs
  - Resiliency and reintegration programs
  - Military and civil service feedback sessions
  - Responsibilities in support of contractor personnel
  - Health questionnaires and assessments over the course of service

Methodology:

- The FOR will entail a Total Force examination of relevant programs, policies, procedures, and best practices ranging from DoD and Air Force levels to MAJCOM, DRU and installation levels.

- FOR participants are authorized to use appropriate interviews, focus groups, data compilation, and other processes they determine sound and necessary to achieve objectives.

- Specific methodology will be established by the AF Lead (AETC/CC).

- MAJCOM/CVs and DRU/CCs will lead their command's effort, working in concert with HAF 2-digit functional experts and the HAF Lead (AF/A1).

- Functional and cross-functional discussions will be required between subject matter experts at the HAF, MAJCOM, DRU and installation levels to identify seams and disconnects among programs, policies, procedures, and training.

- As HAF Lead, the AF/A1 will guide and integrate HAF 2-digit, MAJCOM, and DRU functional and cross-functional efforts and results.

Duration:

The Air Force FOR will begin no later than 15 Feb 10 and conclude by 15 May 10, at which time the AF Lead will submit the results of the FOR to the Secretary of the Air Force and the Chief of Staff.

Deliverables:

The FOR will deliver a concise presentation of areas requiring attention and recommended courses of action to implement DoD IR recommendations and address other gaps and/or deficiencies identified during the course of the review. The FOR will further recommend internal controls to minimize risks, reduce the likelihood of future incidents and mitigate associated circumstances, and will outline best practices (Air Force and otherwise) to improve Air Force policies, programs, procedures, and training. The final product will be in a format that is readily accessible and usable by those who will take follow-on actions.

Support:

Air Force personnel will provide such assistance as required to meet established FOR objectives, scope and timeline, to include access to Air Force records, consistent with law and regulation. To the extent that needed access is impeded by such law or regulation, it will be noted in the report.

Appendix B ♦ Best Practices

The Secretary of the Air Force requested the Air Force Follow-on Review identify best practices, Air Force and otherwise, to improve our policies, programs, procedures, and training. Accordingly, we assessed a number of programs and processes that have proven to be successful, and may be helpful to other installations. Air Force major commands and direct reporting units also conducted a comprehensive review of force protection initiatives for the Air Force Follow-on Review. The list below highlights a limited number of ongoing programs and practices implemented at various Air Force installations or in support of specific commands. Additional noteworthy programs and practices are mentioned throughout the report.

The following best practices range from improving force protection on the prevention, preparation, and response fronts, to improving the resiliency of Airmen and their families. Each example illustrates the results of actively engaged leaders from across the Service to preserve our Air Force community as the safe, secure, supportive environment we expect it to be.

Risk Assessment and Prevention – Collaborative Support

At the 21st Space Wing (21 SW) at Peterson AFB, CO, installation leaders noted that the same names repeatedly surfaced in different personnel forums (e.g., Status of Discipline, Central Registry Board, "Cops and Robbers," Cross Functional Oversight Committee, and Sexual Assault Response Coordinator). Unit leaders realized they may have missed prior opportunities to help troubled Airmen before more serious events occurred. As a result, 21 SW leaders established a "Status of Care" forum in April 2009 to bring appropriate entities (e.g., commanders, medical, legal, chaplains, OSI, etc.) together to review a list of at-risk Airmen. Airmen were discussed by rank and situation, not by name, to protect their privacy. When appropriate, the group discusses potential success strategies for individual situations, assisting squadron and group commanders consider several options for addressing situations. Status of Care is an intervention group rather than a disciplinary forum, although punitive measures may be discussed to assess care. The initiative established by the 21 SW serves as model for the Status of Health and Airmen Resiliency Exchange (SHARE) initiative proposed in Chapter 2 of this report. (POC: 21 SW/DS)

Risk Assessment and Prevention – Deployment Outreach

The Yellow Ribbon Reintegration Program (YRRP) is congressionally mandated in accordance with Section 582 of Public Law 110-181, 28 January 2008, to support National Guard and Reserve members and their families. The YRRP provides information, services, referrals, and outreach opportunities over the course of the deployment cycle. In addition to providing a continuum of support, the YRRP provides a high standard of care for military members and their families. Specifically, the program supports the Air Reserve Components (ARC) with five key events timed during pre-deployment, deployment, and post-deployment. Pre-deployment events prepare military members and their families for deployment by providing training and resources, and offering support services. During deployment, the YRRP provides tailored information and support for families and employers, raising awareness to challenges and stressors associated with deployment. Post-deployment events at the 30- and 60-day points focus on reconnecting military members with their families, employers, and communities, as well as providing information and access to resources to facilitate successful reintegration. These events include a forum for members and their families to address negative behaviors related to combat stress and transition. The third post-deployment event occurs 90 days after return and addresses specific programs focused on the member's adjustment and reintegration, to include a post-deployment health reassessment (PDHRA). While geared to the ARC, the YRRP serves as an important engagement model for building resiliency and a sense of community among deployed Airmen, their families, and even employers. (POC: NGB/A1)

Preparation – Active Shooter Training

After the 2007 Virginia Tech shooting, the US Air Force Academy (USAFA) made active shooter prevention and response a priority. The installation antiterrorism office developed plans and checklists, and then implemented a training program to prepare the installation for an active shooter incident. USAFA updated training to include "key action" words. Once USAFA matched actions to the action words of *cover, communicate, mitigate*, personnel found it easier to know what to do when confronting an active shooter. In exercising these concepts, USAFA reduced estimated casualties by 50 cadets during the first exercise in 2007, to only 4 during a January 2010 active shooter exercise. The innovative planning and training USAFA conducted exemplifies the force protection success that can be achieved by heightening awareness and engaging members within the local Air Force community. (POC: USAFA/ATO)

Preparation – Active Shooter Lessons Learned

USAFA reviewed lessons learned from the February 2008 active shooter incident at Northern Illinois University (NIU) in order to ensure their force protection procedures addressed gaps as well as successes. The NIU action assessment revealed that students ran from the auditorium where the shooter was into other classrooms and auditoriums that could not be locked. Students fled in a similar pattern during the April 2007 Virginia Polytechnic Institute (Virginia Tech) shooting. Students tried to barricade the doors with desks and other items, but the shooter fired shots through the door. Recognizing that survivability may be lower among students who fled into classrooms that could not be locked, USAFA issued work orders to have locks installed on all classroom and auditorium doors. This initiative is due to be completed by June 2010. (POC: USAFA/ATO)

Preparation – Active Shooter Table Top Exercise

Based on the Fort Hood After-Action Report, the 20th Fighter Wing (20 FW) at Shaw Air Force Base, SC tasked its Security Forces to develop a comprehensive active shooter scenario for wing leadership to table top exercise a potential event. The 20 FW Plans and Inspections Office compiled and conducted training on active shooter profile, special considerations for military installations, command and control in a dynamic environment, and active shooter response by security forces members. The scenario was presented in a "rapid slide build" format to simulate how quick an active shooter event can unfold and to ensure leaders understood they would have little time to develop situational awareness during the event. Follow on discussions addressed site safety by Emergency Ordnance Disposal, treatment by medical providers (including Post Traumatic Stress Disorder for survivors and family members of victims), Public Affairs interaction with media, and requirements for interacting with local law enforcement and federal agencies. The table top exercise scenario conducted by the 20 FW is an effective and low-cost means of testing preparedness, response, and recovery to determine gaps in procedures and practice. Consideration of off-base support by local, state, and federal emergency response, medical, law enforcement, and investigative entities and the need for supporting MOUs is equally important. (POC: 20 FW/XP)

Response and Recovery – Mass Emergency Notification

In 2007, AFRC deployed the Installation Warning System (IWS) Alerts Emergency Notification System (ENS), a commercial off-the-shelf system from AtHoc, Inc. AFRC pursued this means of mass notification to address the fact that domicile locations vary greatly among Reserve component forces. AFRC plots members' individual addresses using geospatial information system capabilities. Based on event projections, supportable conclusions can be made with regard to the impact on AFRC forces and where to focus follow-up contact and support efforts. The IWS-ENS capability enhances command, control, and accountability capabilities and is easily adaptable to any real-world or exercise scenario, to include threat events that may occur on as well as off base. (POC: HQ AFRC/A7)

Response and Recovery – Instant Messaging Alerts

The USAFA Command Center implemented an initiative that improved their Installation Notification and Warning System (INWS) while simultaneously adjusting to lower manning from single controller operations. USAFA fielded "Falcon Alert," a local customization of Rave Mobile Safety's "Rave Alert" system. This particular system delivers broadcast emergency alerts via text messaging, e-mail, voice messaging or Really Simple Syndication (RSS) feed. Narrowcast alerts to specific groups or individuals are also possible. User registration requires only 5 minutes; once registered with the system, individuals will receive message updates on emergency matters and other notices via their preferred notification method. A single controller has demonstrated the ability to send text, e-mail, voice messages, and an RSS alert within three minutes after a standard attack notification. USAFA's initiative is illustrative of the mass communication capability that can be gained by leveraging off-the-shelf technology. (POC: USAFA/ATO)

Response and Recovery – Active Shooter Contingency Support

To provide active shooter contingency response for locations with smaller Security Forces units, Air Force Materiel Command (AFMC) implemented a Staff Reaction Force (SRF). The SRF is comprised of six staff personnel who have been trained and appropriately equipped with weapons and communication capability. These individuals keep their equipment readily available and are available to immediately augment any AFMC Security Forces unit in the event of an active shooter situation. (POC: AFMC/IG)

Response and Recovery – Engaging the Community

Representatives from Hickam Air Force Base (AFB) Anti-terrorism, Force Protection, Fire Department, Security Forces, and Safety organizations are members of the local School Safety Committee (SSC). The SSC establishes school-wide phases of Emergency Management (Prevention and Mitigation, Preparedness, Response, and Recovery) efforts. The SSC meets quarterly to review the Hawaiian Department of Education Crisis Management and Safety Guide, and to plan mandatory emergency drills (earthquake, lock down, off-campus evacuation, and shelter-in-place). Base officials attend emergency drills and provide input to after-action reviews conducted by the school. By partnering with the local community school system, Hickam AFB is heightening emergency-response awareness within the local community and at locations frequented by Hickam AFB families. (POC: 15 MSG/CCL)

The practices outlined above are not all inclusive, but reflect efforts to address force protection concerns more effectively. Air Force personnel must remain consistently engaged to identify and address issues, heighten community awareness and participation, and leverage technology to facilitate rapid and accurate communication. Protecting our personnel is not just a concern for unit leaders, but a shared concern within our entire Air Force community. We highlight the noteworthy programs and practices above and others within our report to encourage leaders Air Force-wide to pursue innovation and to share their successes with others. Doing so will better protect and strengthen our communities by more effectively training and preparing to prevent, respond, and recover from the inevitable tragedies in life.

This is a primary source document
provided by the Air Force Manpower Agency.

Preventing and Responding to Violence Survey

The Air Force Manpower Agency conducted a survey to the Air Force Follow-on Review Related to Fort Hood. Responses from unit leaders were used to assess possible deficiencies in information sharing, training and recognition of internal threats, force protection, mass casualty response, and post-incident support. The survey was administered for three weeks to a target population of 4,229 active duty, Guard, Reserve commanders, and civilian directors at the wing, group, squadron, and detachment level. Overall, 2,068 participants completed surveys. Survey sample demographics closely reflect Air Force leadership population demographics.

Where AFMA detected statistically significant differences in survey responses by Air Force affiliation, MAJCOM, organizational levels, or CONUS/OCONUS, the additional results are presented. AFMA conducted further analysis on certain areas where we suspected career field or line/non-line officers' perspectives might also play a role; where significant, these results are presented as well.

The results indicate approximately 25 percent of unit leaders report receiving training in shooting sprees/mass killings of which three quarters report the training provided the necessary skills to respond. Less than half of commanders and civilian directors believe unit personnel are informed about the potential for an active shooter scenario on base and clearly understand what to do during an active shooter situation. Primary and backup slides are included in this appendix.

FOR Survey

- Purpose
  - Identify and assess possible deficiencies in information sharing, training and recognition of internal threats, force protection, mass casualty response and post incident support
- Data Collection Period: 22 February – 8 March
- Distributed to Commanders and Civilian Directors
- Participation Rate – Overall 49% (2,068 Completed Surveys)
  - Active Duty: 55%
  - AF Reserve: 43%
  - Air National Guard: 40%
  - Civilian Directors: 36%
- Agree scales collapsed

Sample Demographics

Survey sample demographics closely reflect population demographics

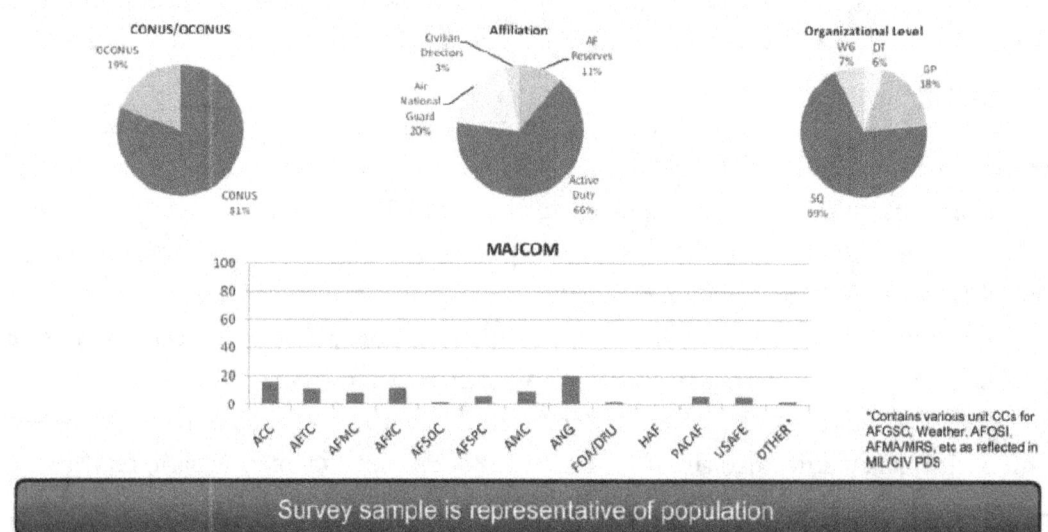

Survey sample is representative of population

Areas of Interest

- Approximately 25% of commanders report receiving training in shooting sprees/mass killings; 75% of those commanders report the training provided skills needed to respond
- Less than half of commanders feel personnel are informed or know what to do during an active-shooter event
- Top 5 reasons commanders are hesitant to report behaviors
  - Not sure there is anything worth reporting
  - Lack of documented proof
  - Unclear guidance
  - Unclear lane of authority
  - Lack of authority
- Most documented behavior is financial problems
- Least documented behaviors are associated with extremist groups
- Information sharing is most constrained by HIPAA

I Would Contact

If I suspected that a member of my unit posed a credible threat to themselves or others, I would contact:

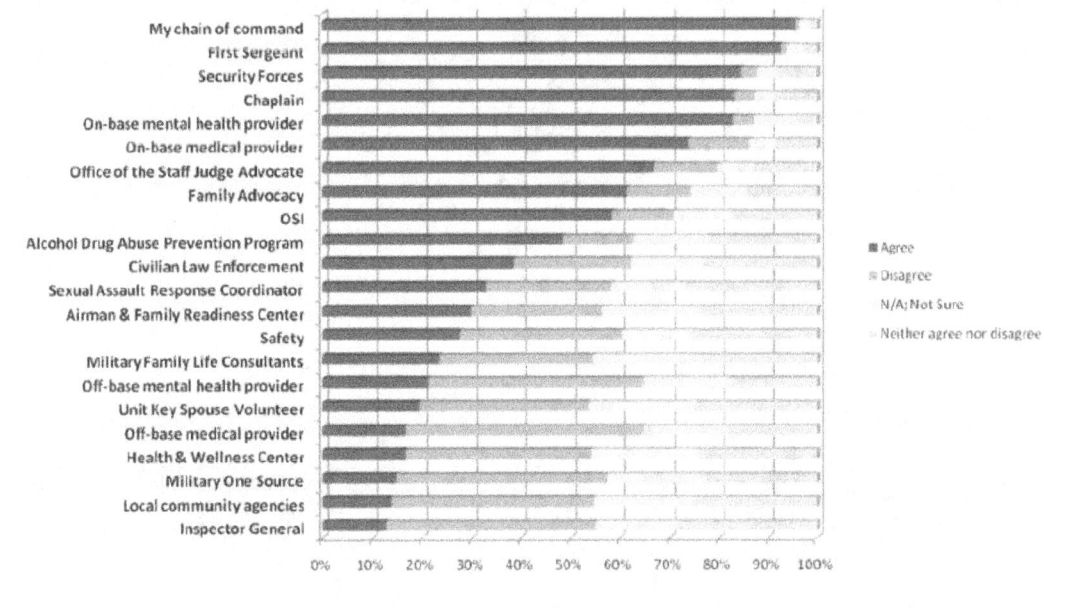

Timely Information

I receive timely information from the following agencies when they determine my personnel may pose credible threats to themselves or others:

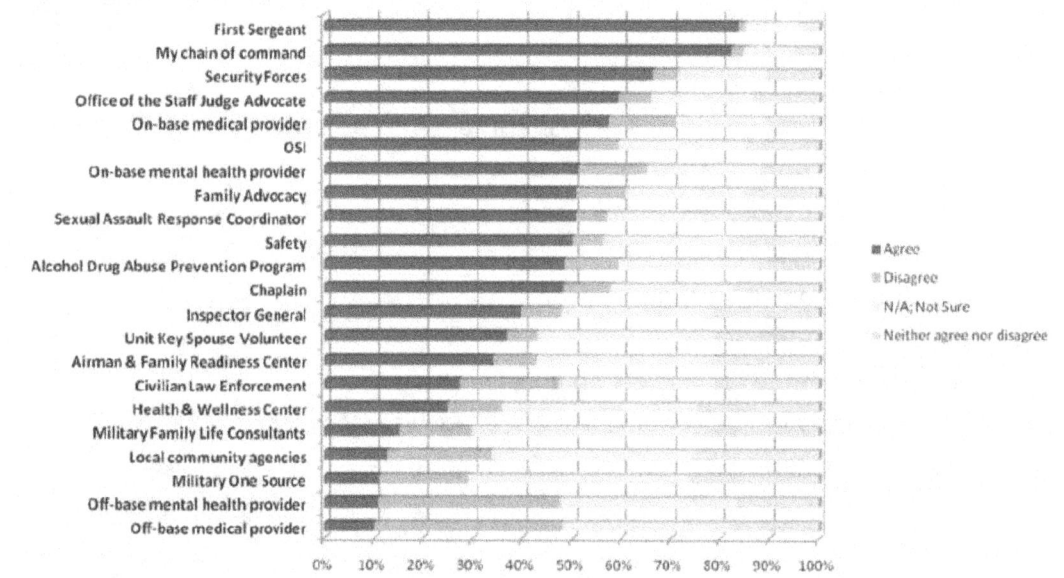

Tools

Other than the agencies previously mentioned, I use the following tools to educate myself on how to assess indicators of a potential for violence by a member of my unit:

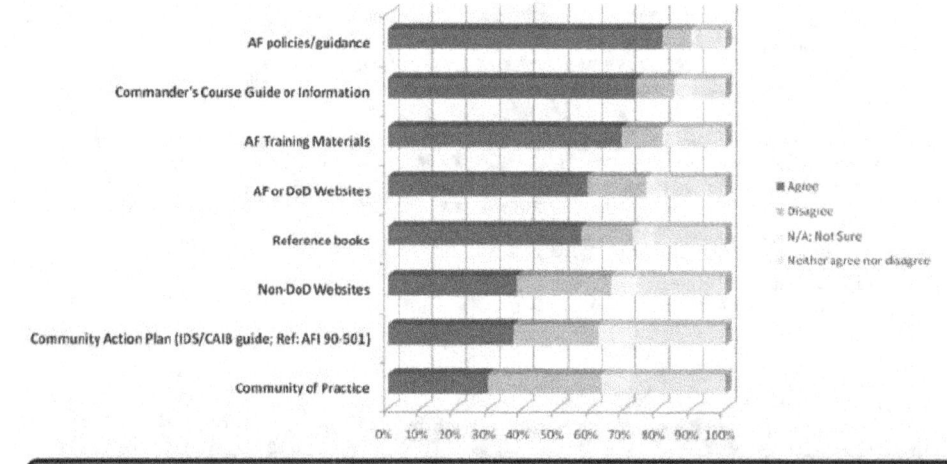

Majority use AF policies/guidance as an educational tool to assess indicators

My Authorities

I am aware of *my authorities* to deal with personnel in the following categories who may pose credible threats to themselves or others:

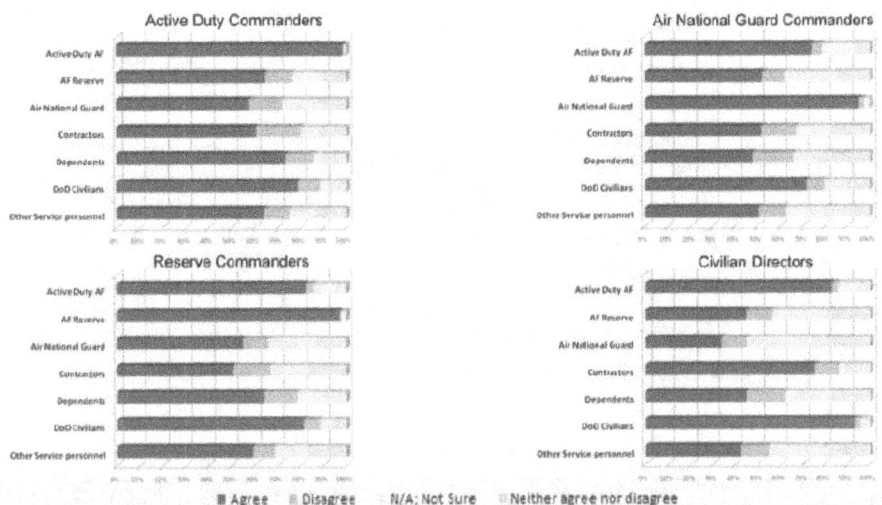

Commanders are most aware of their authorities in their own lanes

Associated Threats

I have the means to verify whether groups and/or networks my personnel are associated with pose a threat to the Air Force community.

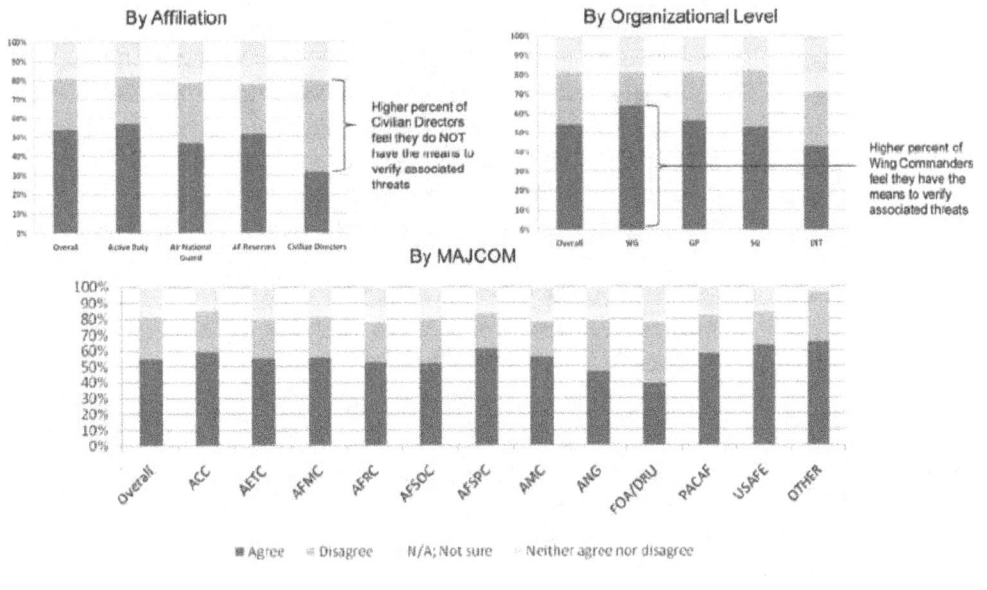

Training to Prevent Violence

In the past year, have you received AF sponsored training to *prevent* the following types of violence?

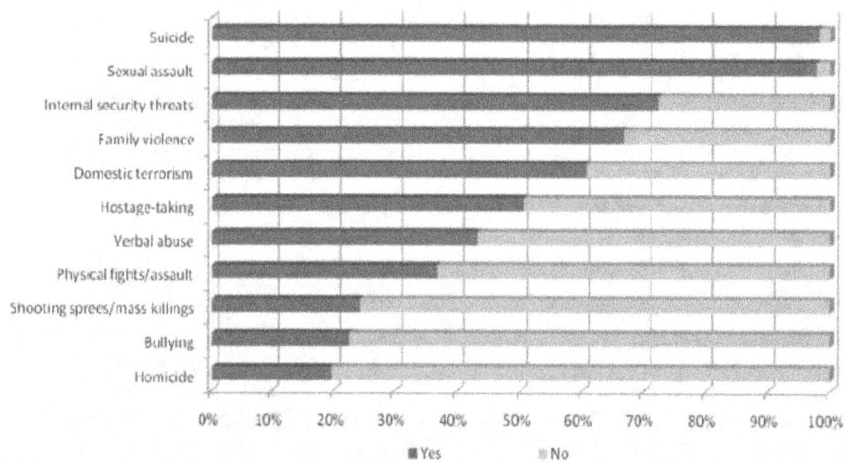

Approximately 1/4 of all AF leaders have received training for prevention of shooting sprees or mass killings

Training to Prevent Violence

The training I received provided the skills/tools I need to *prevent* the following types of violence:

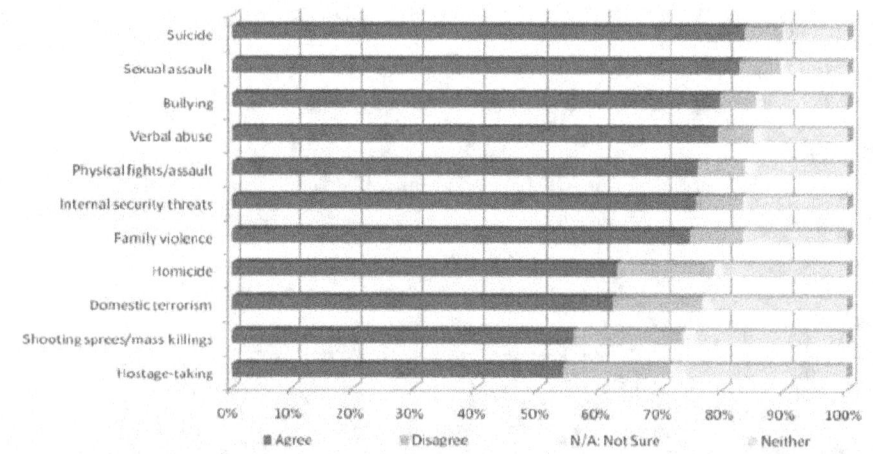

Of those AF leaders who received training in each respective area, just over half agreed training for shooting sprees/mass killings & hostage-taking provided the required skills

Training to Respond to Violence

In the past year, have you received AF sponsored training to *respond* to the following types of violence?

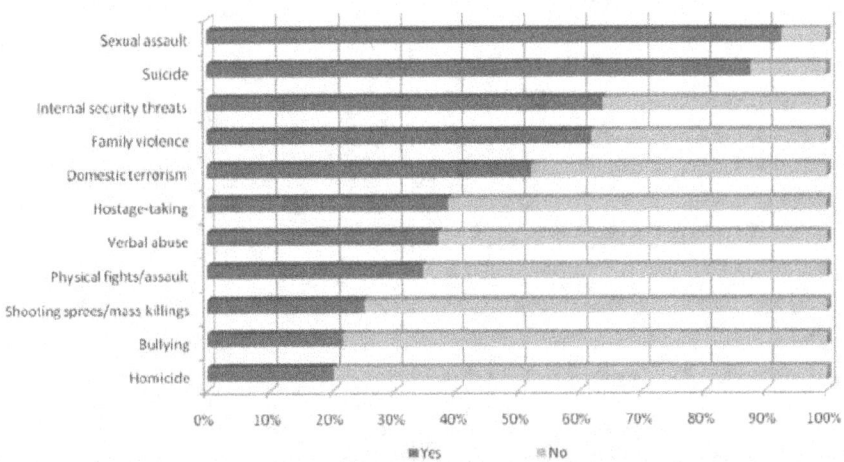

Approximately 1/4 of all AF leaders have received training on how to respond to shooting sprees or mass killings

Training to Respond to Violence

The training I received provided the skills/tools I need to *respond* to the following types of violence:

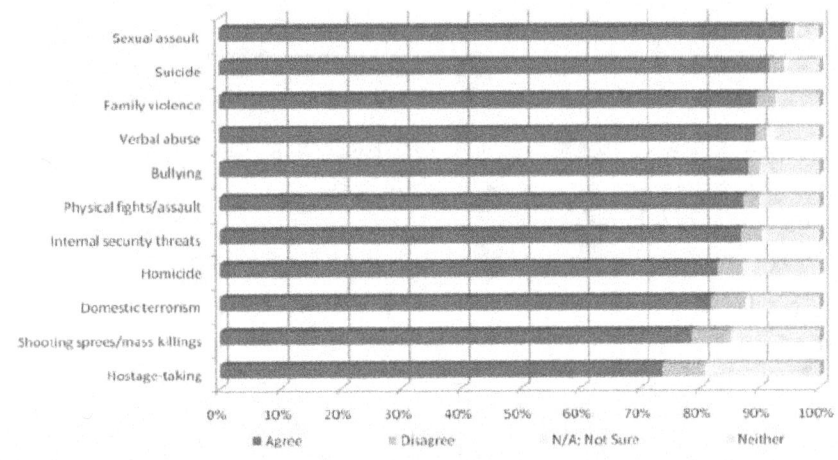

Of the AF leaders who received training in each respective area, 3/4 or more agreed training on how to respond to any type of violence provided the required skills

Emergency Response Practice

My unit practices emergency response actions:

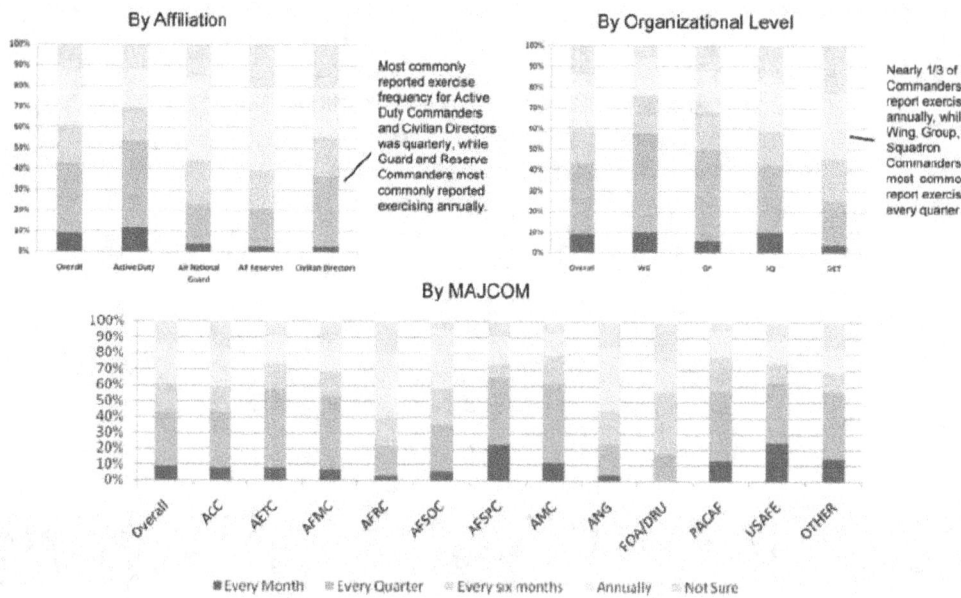

Emergency Response Practice by Career Family

My unit practices emergency response actions:

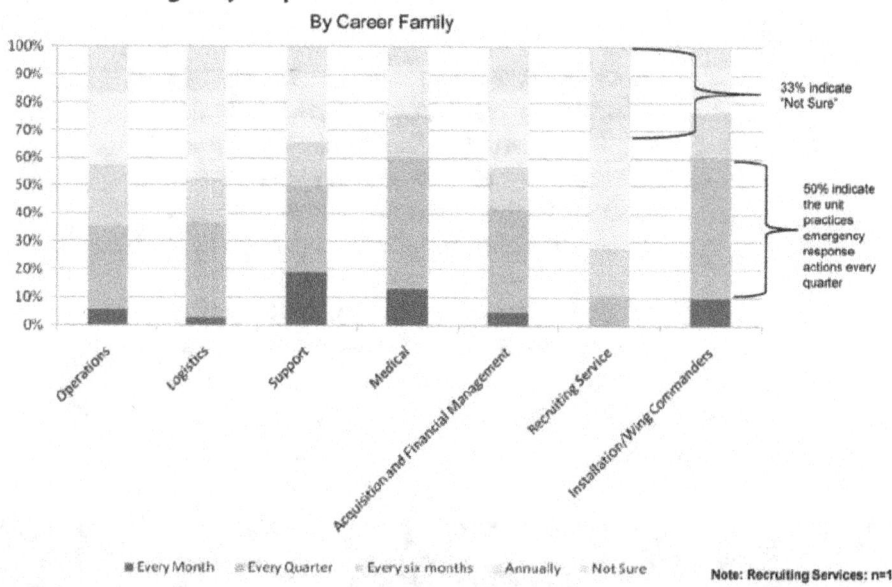

Alert Procedures: CONUS vs OCONUS

The following Installation alert procedures for ongoing threats are:

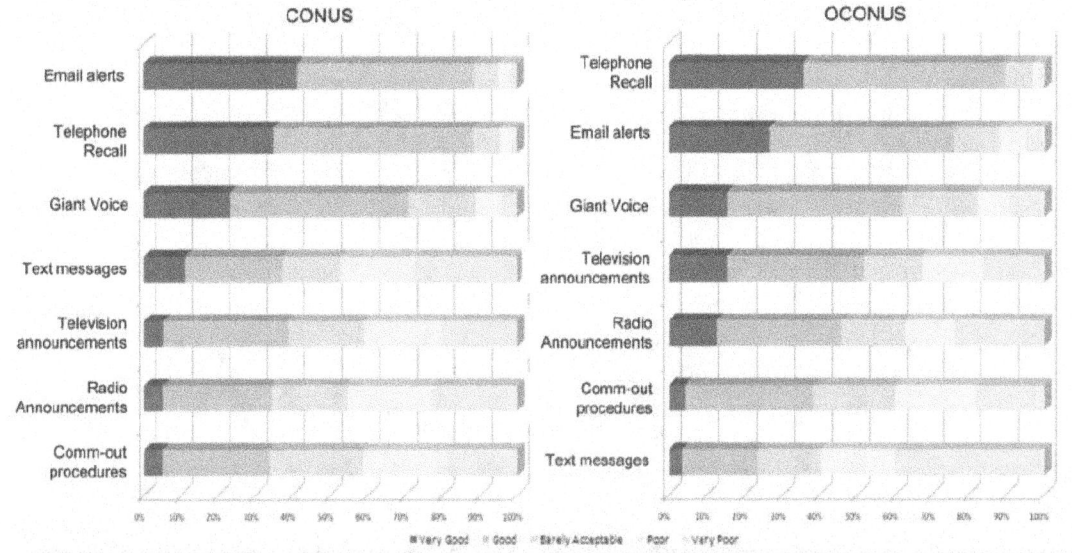

The top three alert procedures among all commanders regardless of affiliation, organizational level, MAJCOM, and CONUS/OCONUS are Email Alerts, Telephone Recall, and Giant Voice

Installation Threat Working Group: Actionable Information

The installation Threat Working Group provides commanders with actionable information.

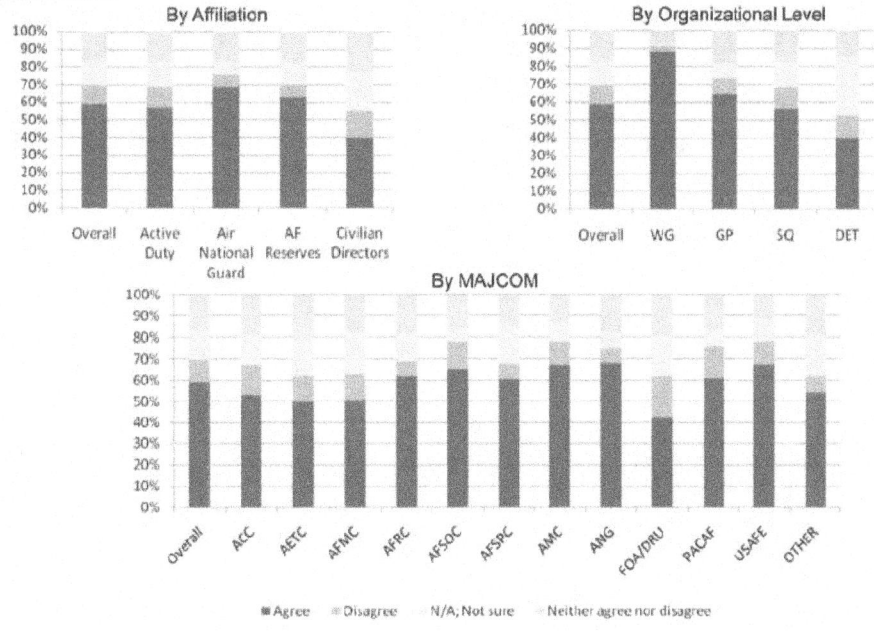

Installation Threat Working Group: Timely Information

The installation Threat Working Group provides commanders with timely information.

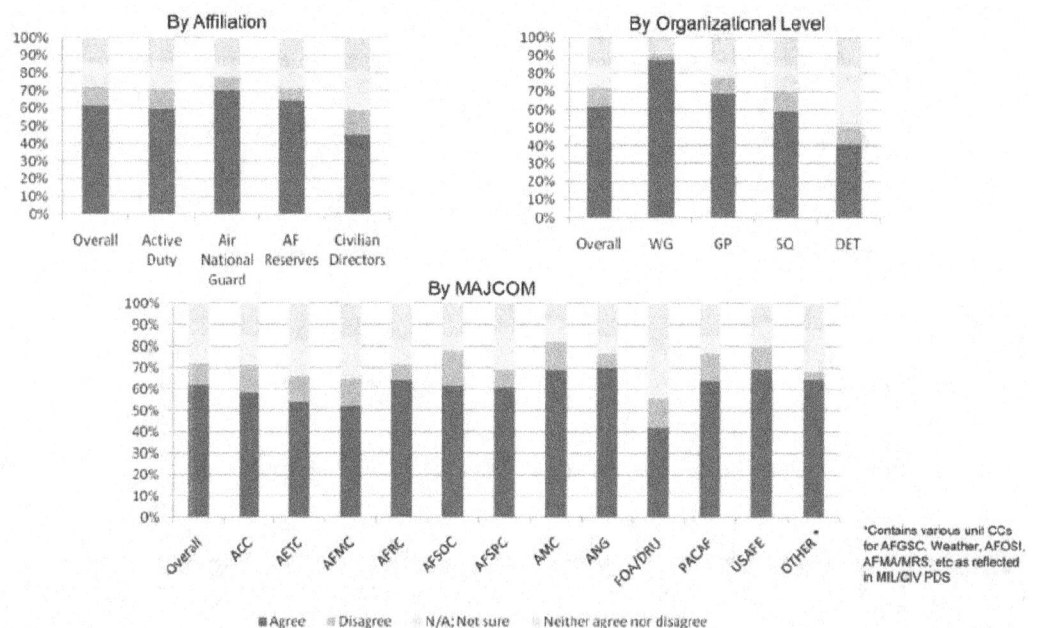

By Affiliation

By Organizational Level

By MAJCOM

*Contains various unit CCs for AFGSC, Weather, AFOSI, AFMA/MRS, etc as reflected in MIL/CIV PDS

■ Agree   ■ Disagree   N/A; Not sure   Neither agree nor disagree

Behaviors Documented by Unit Supervisors

All Commanders n= 2068

Behaviors Documented by Unit Supervisors	Active_Duty	Guard	Reserves	Civilian	Contractors	Family
Financial problems	47	15	11	11	2	5
Abuse of alcohol	44	14	10	12	4	5
Excessive use of alcohol	39	13	8	10	3	4
Mental health problems	35	10	7	9	3	6
Displays of violence	32	10	7	14	6	12
Poor communication skills	32	9	7	15	5	4
Threats of violence	31	11	7	15	6	12
Verbal outbursts	31	11	8	16	5	7
Major physical illnesses	29	10	7	12	3	5
Aggression	28	10	7	13	5	9
Harassing statements	28	11	8	16	6	7
Poor relationships	28	7	5	9	3	8
Divorce/separation	26	7	5	6	2	6
Poor impulse control	22	7	5	9	3	3
Prescription medication abuse	22	6	5	8	2	4
Inability to effectively deal with stress	22	6	5	8	2	3
Excessive stress	20	5	5	7	2	3
Bullying/Belittling behavior	17	7	5	10	3	4
Over the counter medication abuse	16	4	3	6	2	3
Retaliatory behavior	16	7	5	10	3	3
Low self esteem	15	4	3	5	2	3
Antisocial behavior	15	4	3	5	2	2
Social isolation	11	2	2	3	1	1
Display of extremist tattoos, brandings or piercings	10	3	3	3	1	1
Affiliation with groups that pose credible threats	8	3	2	4	2	1
Association with groups known to advocate violence	8	3	2	4	2	1
Association with groups that advocate extremist ideologies	7	3	2	3	2	1

Note: Percents will not sum to 100 because respondents were asked to mark all that apply

Understanding Procedure

All Commanders n= 2068

Understand Appropriate Procedures to Refer/Report Personnel to ...	Not Sure	Active_Duty	Guard	Reserves	Civilian	Contractors	Family
Chaplain	2	73	40	37	39	17	36
First Sergeant	2	73	40	36	29	13	32
My chain of command	1	73	42	38	47	29	35
On-base medical providers	3	73	36	34	34	11	33
Sexual Assault Response Coordinator	2	73	40	37	41	19	33
Security Forces	2	72	40	36	43	24	32
Alcohol Drug Abuse Prevention Program	4	71	32	30	27	7	20
On-base mental health provider	6	71	30	31	29	8	26
Office of the Staff Judge Advocate	3	70	36	33	29	9	20
Family Advocacy	7	69	30	30	26	7	33
Inspector General	5	68	35	34	37	16	20
OSI	7	68	33	33	37	18	26
Airman & Family Readiness Center	10	65	27	30	24	8	32
Safety	6	65	36	32	38	20	20
Health & Wellness Center	13	64	24	27	21	7	21
Unit Key Spouse Volunteer	21	49	20	19	19	8	31
Military Family Life Consultants	27	43	18	19	15	6	22
Military One Source	23	43	24	22	18	7	24
Civilian Law Enforcement	23	41	25	23	31	20	26
Off-base medical providers	27	36	18	16	23	10	21
Local community agencies	32	32	16	15	20	11	19
Off-base mental health provider	30	31	17	14	20	8	17

Document Action by Affiliation

When I refer or report personnel concerns to any of the previously mentioned agencies, I understand how to document the action on the following personnel:

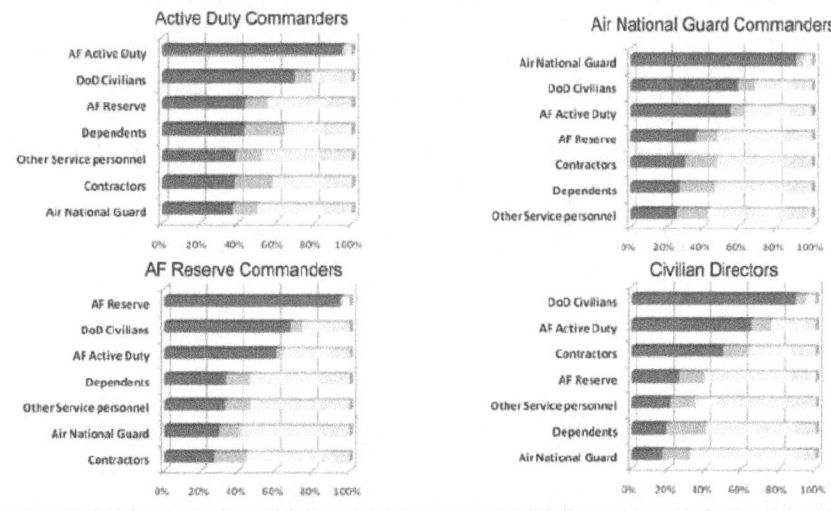

Non ANG commanders least understand how to document ANG actions

Direct Feedback

When I refer or report personnel concerns, I receive direct feedback on actions taken by the appropriate agency.

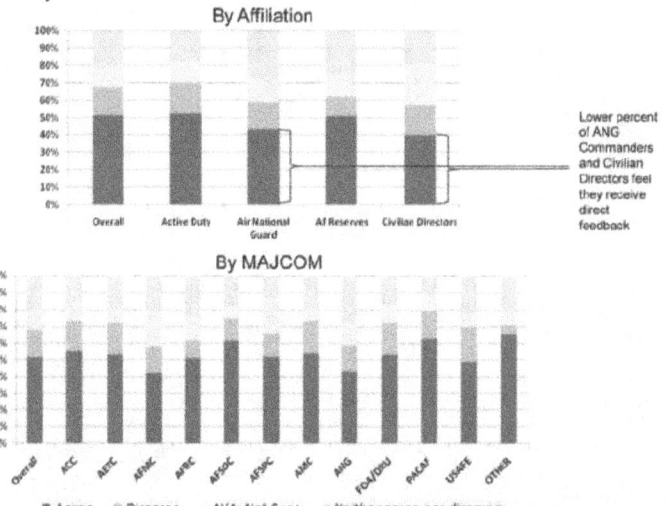

Lower percent of ANG Commanders and Civilian Directors feel they receive direct feedback

There are differences in the feedback received by Affiliation and MAJCOM

Hesitant to Report

Please identify to which of the following agencies you would be hesitant to report personnel:

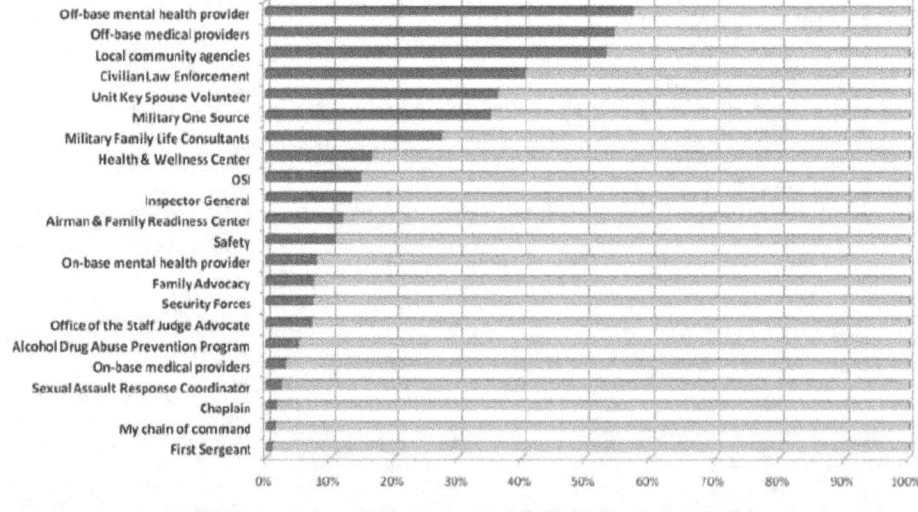

Commanders are more hesitant to report personnel to civilian agencies (except Civilian Law Enforcement); are not as hesitant to report personnel to military agencies

Hesitant to Report

I might be hesitant to report personnel concerns to official agencies/individuals due to the following:

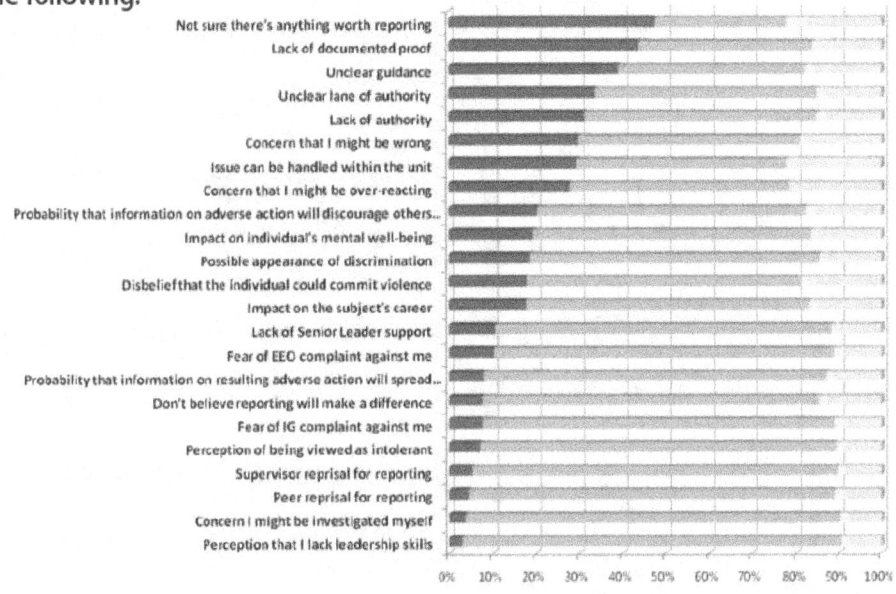

Hesitant to Report

People in my unit might be hesitant to report personnel's possible risk factors for violence to official agencies/individuals due to the following:

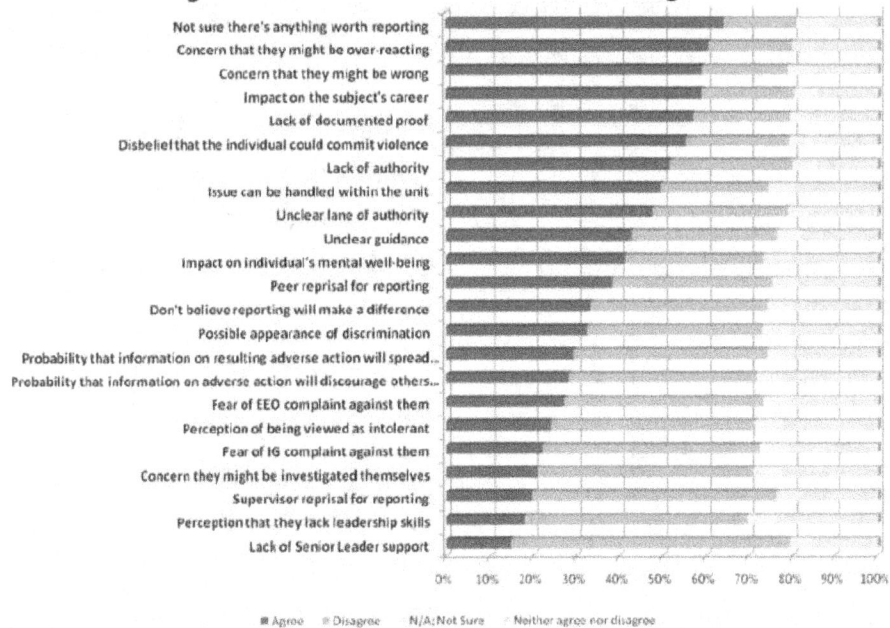

Hesitant to Report

Other commanders might be hesitant to report personnel's possible risk factors for violence to official agencies/individuals due to the following:

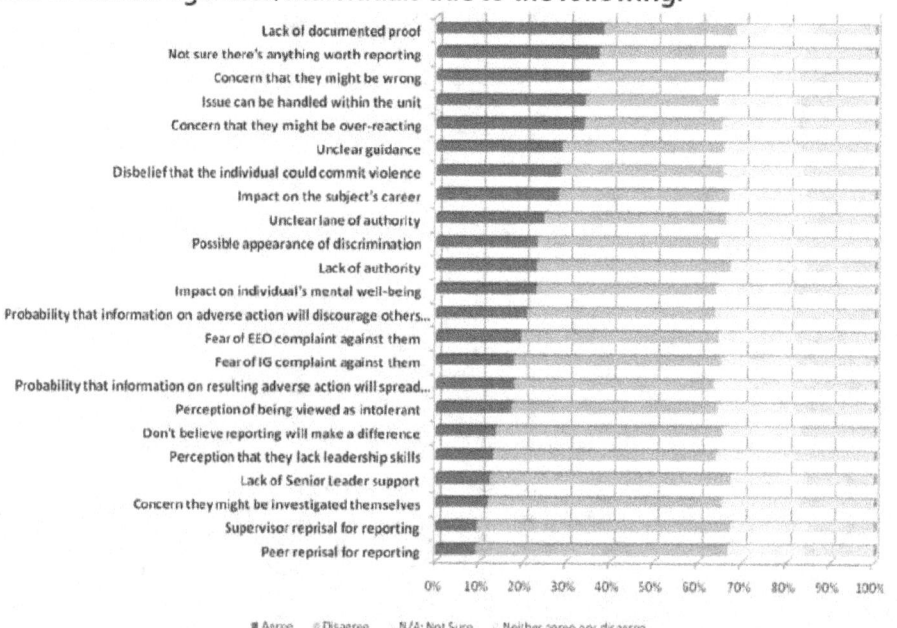

Preparation for Active-Shooter Events by MAJCOM

My unit personnel are informed about the potential for active-shooter scenarios on-base.

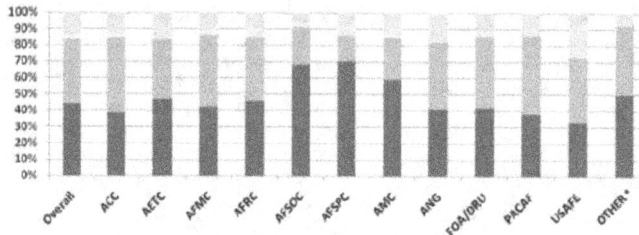

My unit personnel clearly understand what to do during an active-shooter situation on-base (e.g., direction of evacuation, shelter in place, etc.).

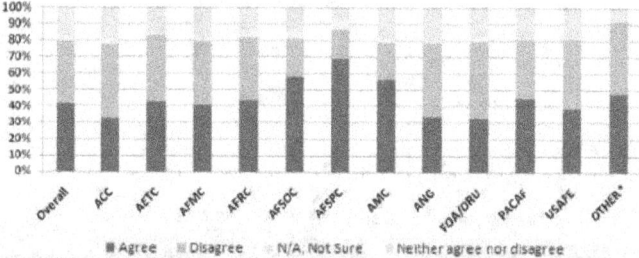

*Contains various unit CCs for AFGSC, Weather, AFOSI, AFMA/MRS, etc as reflected in MIL/CIV PDS

Significant differences in preparation for active-shooter events by MAJCOM

Preparation for Active-Shooter Events by Career Family

My unit personnel are informed about the potential for active-shooter scenarios on-base.

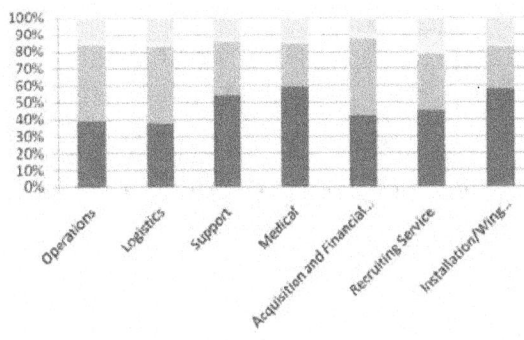

My unit personnel clearly understand what to do during an active-shooter situation on-base (e.g., direction of evacuation, shelter in place, etc.).

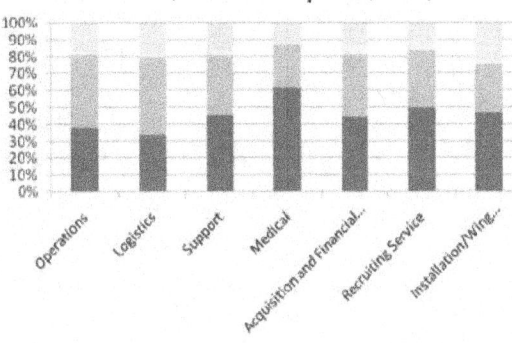

■ Agree   ▨ Disagree   N/A; Not Sure   Neither agree nor disagree

Note: Recruiting Services: n=18

Commander Training

My commander training sufficiently addressed the following:

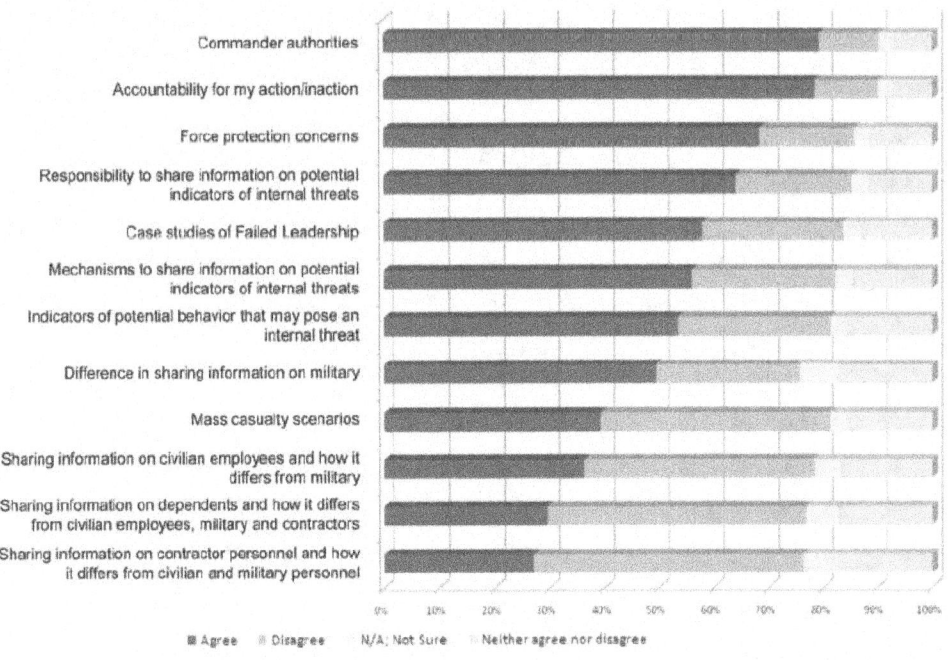

■ Agree   ▨ Disagree   N/A; Not Sure   Neither agree nor disagree

Information Sharing

Information sharing between Air Force leaders and service providers about personnel concerns is constrained by:

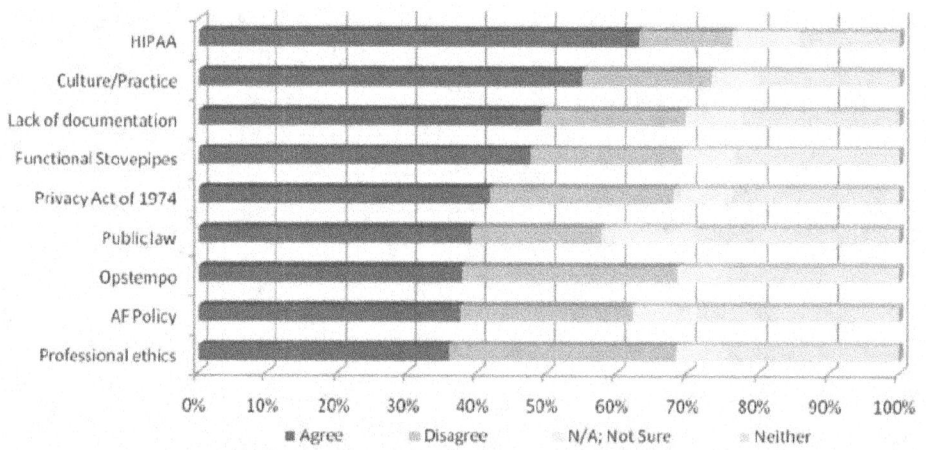

AF leaders most often agree that HIPAA constrains information sharing

Change to Information Sharing

- "What change to information sharing is most needed to ensure the health and safety of your personnel?"
- Background
  - 750 responses
  - 18 areas of concern with at least 10 responses each
  - Top 10 responses accounted for 80% of all responses
  - Analysis focused on identifying areas of concern based on Commander statements
  - Identified responses reflect level of detail provided by Commander statements

Suggested Changes to Information Sharing

- Timely/Complete info on Airman's medical treatment
- Timely/Complete info on Airman's medical treatment (with specific reference to HIPAA)
- Timely/Complete info from agencies (e.g., OSI, Chaplain, etc.)
- Improve guidelines/processes for sharing information
- Improve training for Commander
- Arrange time to interact with Airmen
- Improve training for all Airmen
- Database of relevant information on Airman incidents/behavior
- Fair application of and adherence to standards/discipline
- Timely/Complete info on Airman's medical treatment (with specific reference to civilian health care providers)

Comments on Information Sharing

- "In order to make informed decisions a commander needs all the relevant information in a case, which means more data from care providers to build a whole person picture." Sq CC
- "There has to be a way to comply with [HIPAA] and still ensure commanders/first sergeants get the information they need to ensure the health, morale, welfare and safety of all . . ." Wg CC
- "Unless the Airman self-identifies, there is little I can do until [it is] too late." Gp CC
- "We [don't] share information now. Thus any change would be an improvement." Sq CC
- "Most needed is a MAJOR leadership program of mentorship and cross-talk so leaders can learn from others experience." Sq CC

Top Three Internal Threats

- "What top three internal threats to your installation concern you the most?"
- Background
  - 2,622 responses
  - 53 areas of concern with at least 10 responses each
  - Top 10 responses accounted for 51% of all responses
  - Analysis focused on identifying areas of concern based on Commander statements
  - Identified responses reflect level of detail provided by Commander statements

Top Three Internal Threats

- Disgruntled Airman/civilian employee/contractor
- Alcohol/Drug abuse
- Stress (in general)
- Perimeter defense
- Mass casualty involving firearms
- Emotionally unstable individual
- Terrorist act
- Suicide
- Contractor loyalty
- Family stress (in general)
- Financial stress/poor economy
- Job security

Analysis Notes

- Participation Rate – Overall 49% (2,068 Completed Surveys)
  - Active Duty: 55%
  - AF Reserve: 43%
  - Air National Guard: 40%
  - Civilian Directors: 36%
- Agree scales are collapsed for ease of reporting
  - % Agree = % Strongly Agree + % Agree
  - % Disagree = % Strongly Disagree + % Disagree
- Results are not displayed for demographic groups with less than 10 respondents
- Vertical bar charts display a bar for each demographic group
- Horizontal bar charts display a bar for each question

During My Command

How often do you practice the following?

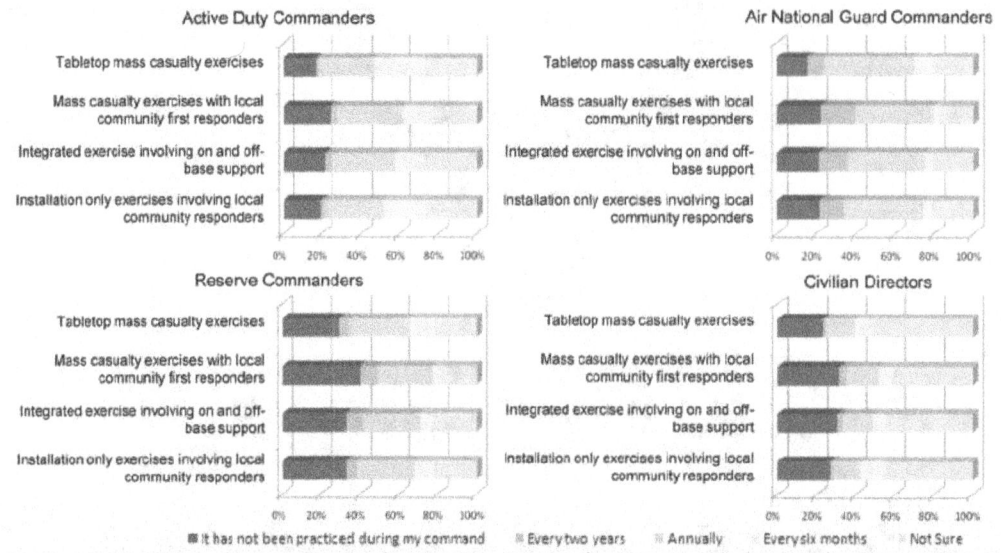

AFRC CCs have highest percents among CCs who chose "It has not been practiced during my command"; Civilian Directors have highest percents among CCs who chose "Not Sure"

Training - Prevent Violence by Career Family

In the past year, have you received AF sponsored training to *prevent* the following types of violence?

In the past year, have you received AF sponsored training to prevent the following types of violence:	Operations	Logistics	Support	Medical	Acquisition and Financial Management	Recruiting Service	Installation/Wing Commanders
	% Yes						
Suicide	99	97	97	100	96	100	99
Sexual assault	98	97	98	99	94	89	99
Internal security threats	73	67	75	75	69	72	72
Family violence	72	56	64	91	61	78	67
Domestic terrorism	59	54	65	70	56	78	63
Hostage-taking	53	45	49	62	52	67	47
Verbal abuse	45	38	41	57	38	33	45
Physical fights/assault	38	33	39	49	27	28	32
Shooting sprees/mass killings	19	19	33	38	20	44	27
Bullying	23	19	22	31	19	22	23
Homicide	17	14	23	37	16	22	19

Green indicates highest % Yes values
Red indicates lowest % Yes values
Note: Recruiting Services: n=18

There are differences in training by career family.
A higher percentage of Medical personnel have been trained to prevent family violence

Training – Prevent Violence by Career Family

The training I received provided the skills/tools I need to *prevent* the following types of violence:

The training I received provided the skills/tools I need to prevent the following types of violence:	Operations	Logistics	Support	Medical	Acquisition and Financial Management	Installation/Wing Commanders
			% Agree			
Suicide	84	82	82	83	85	86
Sexual assault	83	84	79	80	85	86
Bullying	81	74	78	81	82	82
Verbal abuse	80	79	79	75	78	78
Physical fights/assault	74	74	78	76	72	78
Internal security threats	74	76	75	76	80	76
Family violence	74	75	71	73	81	79
Homicide	63	58	64	59	54	76
Domestic terrorism	60	60	63	63	63	70
Shooting sprees/mass killings	52	58	55	57	37	63
Hostage-taking	56	54	54	55	47	55

Green indicates highest % Agree values
Red indicates lowest % Agree values

A lower percentage of Acquisition and Financial Management Personnel felt that training provided the needed skills/tools to prevent shooting sprees/mass killings

Training – Respond Violence by Career Family

In the past year, have you received AF sponsored training to *respond* to the following types of violence?

In the past year, have you received AF sponsored training to respond to the following types of violence:	Operations	Logistics	Support	Medical	Acquisition and Financial Management	Recruiting Service	Installation/Wing Commanders
				% Yes			
Sexual assault	94	92	91	93	94	89	94
Suicide	88	87	85	89	89	89	90
Internal security threats	64	60	64	65	62	67	64
Family violence	66	50	58	62	60	67	69
Domestic terrorism	50	44	58	58	51	61	60
Hostage-taking	40	32	43	45	40	50	36
Verbal abuse	39	34	35	47	31	44	37
Physical fights/assault	34	31	40	43	27	33	33
Shooting sprees/mass killings	19	19	35	37	24	50	30
Bullying	23	17	23	25	18	28	21
Homicide	18	14	27	26	18	28	25

Green indicates highest % Yes values
Red indicates lowest % Yes values
Note: Recruiting Services: n=18

A higher % of Recruiting Service personnel report receiving training for shooting sprees/mass killings (note that Recruiting Service includes only 18 respondents)

Training – Respond Violence by Career Family

The training I received provided the skills/tools I need to *respond* to the following types of violence:

The training I received provided the skills/tools I need to respond to the following types of violence:	Operations	Logistics	Support	Medical	Acquisition and Financial Management	Installation/Wing Commanders
	% Agree					
Sexual assault	95	93	94	94	95	97
Suicide	93	90	92	91	94	93
Family violence	89	86	91	92	92	91
Verbal abuse	90	88	91	89	86	89
Bullying	89	83	90	86	84	95
Physical fights/assault	91	84	89	81	89	85
Internal security threats	86	87	86	89	85	93
Homicide	80	84	85	87	77	79
Domestic terrorism	81	81	83	83	75	86
Shooting sprees/mass killings	77	72	82	81	62	89
Hostage-taking	73	68	74	77	74	84

Green indicates highest % Agree values
Red indicates lowest % Agree values

> A lower percentage of Acquisition and Financial Management Personnel felt that training provided the needed skills/tools to respond to shooting sprees/mass killings

During My Command

How often do you practice the following?

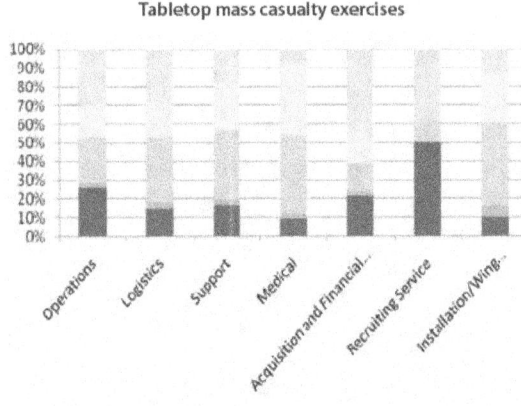

Tabletop mass casualty exercises

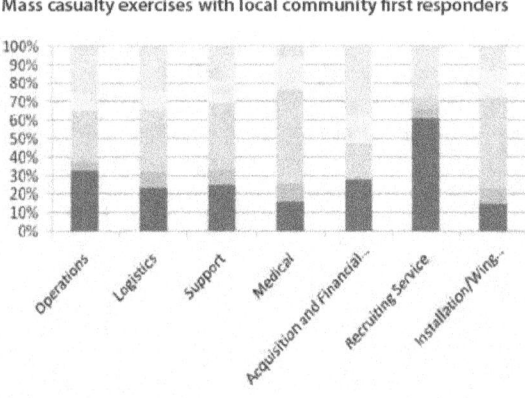

Mass casualty exercises with local community first responders

Note: Recruiting Services: n=18

■ It has not been practiced during my command ■ Every two years ■ Annually ■ Every six months ■ Not Sure

> Operations, Acquisition and Financial Management, and Recruiting Services commanders have the highest % of "Not Sure" and "It has not been practiced during my command"

During My Command

How often do you practice the following?

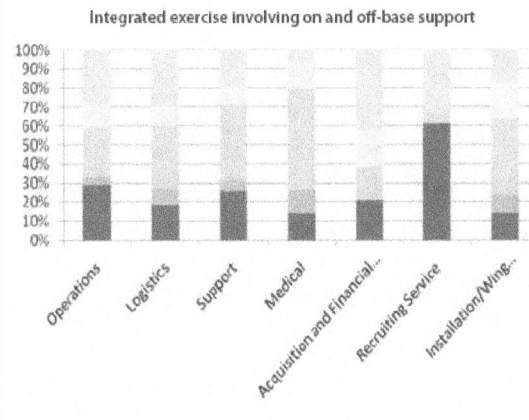

Integrated exercise involving on and off-base support

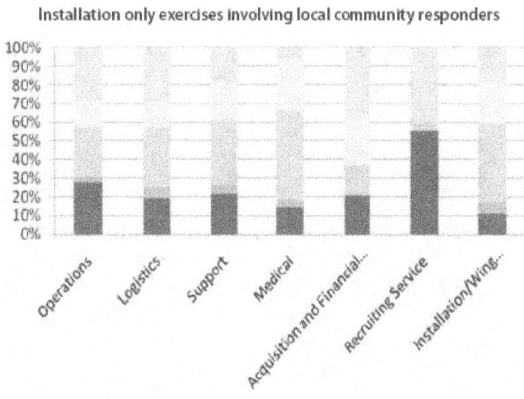

Installation only exercises involving local community responders

Note: Recruiting Services: n=18

▨ It has not been practiced during my command   ▨ Every two years   ▨ Annually   Every six months   Not Sure

Operations, Support, and Recruiting Services CCs have highest % of "It has not been practiced during my command"; Acquisition and Financial Management and Recruiting Services CCs have highest % of "Not Sure"

Behaviors Documented by Unit Supervisors

- Commanders were asked to check all of the behaviors that their supervisors regularly document for AD, Guard, Reserves, Civilians, Contractors, and Family
- Minimal differences in behaviors cited by Active Duty, Guard, Reserve commanders
  - Military commanders indicate the most documented behavior is "Financial problems"
  - Military commanders primarily checked behaviors for personnel under their same affiliation
- Civilian Directors are more likely to cite violent behaviors as the top documented behaviors
- Least documented behaviors reported by all leaders are:
  - "Affiliation with groups that pose credible threats"
  - "Association with groups known to advocate violence"
  - "Association with groups that advocate extremist ideologies"

Behaviors Documented by Unit Supervisors

Active Duty Commanders n= 1362

Behaviors Documented by Unit Supervisors	Active_Duty	Guard	Reserves	Civilian	Contractors	Family
Financial problems	67	3	4	10	3	6
Abuse of alcohol	63	4	5	12	5	7
Excessive use of alcohol	56	4	5	10	4	6
Mental health problems	51	3	4	9	3	8
Displays of violence	46	4	5	14	8	17
Poor communication skills	46	2	3	16	6	6
Verbal outbursts	44	3	4	17	7	9
Threats of violence	43	4	4	15	8	15
Major physical illnesses	42	3	4	12	4	8
Aggression	40	3	4	13	6	12
Harassing statements	40	3	4	16	7	9
Poor relationships	40	2	3	8	4	11
Divorce/separation	37	2	2	6	2	8
Poor impulse control	32	2	2	9	4	4
Prescription medication abuse	32	2	3	7	3	6
Inability to effectively deal with stress	32	2	3	8	2	4
Excessive stress	29	2	2	7	2	4
Bullying/Belittling behavior	24	2	3	10	4	5
Over the counter medication abuse	23	2	2	5	2	5
Retaliatory behavior	22	2	3	9	4	4
Low self esteem	21	1	2	4	2	3
Antisocial behavior	21	1	2	5	2	3
Social isolation	16	1	1	3	1	2
Display of extremist tattoos, brandings or piercings	14	1	2	3	1	1
Affiliation with groups that pose credible threats	11	1	1	4	2	1
Association with groups known to advocate violence	11	1	1	4	2	1
Association with groups that advocate extremist ideologies	10	1	1	3	2	1

Note: Percents will not sum to 100 because respondents were asked to mark all that apply

Behaviors Documented by Unit Supervisors

Air National Guard Commanders n= 405

Behaviors Documented by Unit Supervisors	Active Duty	Guard	Reserves	Civilian	Contractors	Family
Financial problems	5	66	1	6	1	2
Abuse of alcohol	6	58	1	7	1	1
Excessive use of alcohol	5	51	1	6	1	1
Verbal outbursts	3	46	0	7	2	3
Harassing statements	4	44	1	8	1	3
Aggression	4	42	0	8	1	3
Major physical illnesses	4	42	0	5	1	1
Threats of violence	4	41	1	8	2	5
Displays of violence	4	39	1	7	2	3
Mental health problems	2	38	0	4	1	1
Poor communication skills	3	36	1	6	2	1
Divorce/separation	3	29	1	3	1	1
Poor relationships	2	27	0	5	1	2
Poor impulse control	1	27	1	5	1	1
Bullying/Belittling behavior	3	26	1	7	1	2
Retaliatory behavior	3	25	1	6	1	1
Inability to effectively deal with stress	2	21	0	3	1	1
Prescription medication abuse	3	20	1	5	1	1
Excessive stress	2	20	1	3	1	1
Low self esteem	2	13	0	4	1	1
Over the counter medication abuse	1	13	0	3	0	1
Antisocial behavior	1	13	0	2	1	1
Affiliation with groups that pose credible threats	1	12	0	2	1	0
Association with groups known to advocate violence	0	11	0	2	1	0
Display of extremist tattoos, brandings or piercings	1	10	0	2	1	0
Social isolation	1	9	0	1	1	1
Association with groups that advocate extremist ideologies	0	9	0	2	1	0

Note: Percents will not sum to 100 because respondents were asked to mark all that apply

Behaviors Documented by Unit Supervisors

AF Reserve Commanders   n= 228

Behaviors Documented by Unit Supervisors	Active Duty	Guard	Reserve	Civilian	Contractors	Family
Financial problems	8	0	68	18	2	1
Abuse of alcohol	8	0	54	18	2	1
Poor communication skills	6	0	46	18	2	1
Verbal outbursts	6	0	44	19	4	3
Excessive use of alcohol	7	0	43	16	2	1
Harassing statements	6	0	42	16	4	5
Major physical illnesses	5	0	40	15	2	2
Mental health problems	5	0	38	11	2	1
Aggression	5	0	37	14	4	4
Displays of violence	6	0	36	15	4	5
Threats of violence	6	0	34	15	5	6
Divorce/separation	4	0	32	11	1	2
Poor relationships	6	0	31	11	2	2
Poor impulse control	3	0	28	8	2	2
Inability to effectively deal with stress	4	0	27	11	1	1
Retaliatory behavior	4	0	25	10	3	2
Excessive stress	4	0	25	10	1	0
Bullying/Belittling behavior	4	0	24	8	3	2
Prescription medication abuse	3	0	22	9	2	1
Low self esteem	4	0	17	6	2	0
Antisocial behavior	4	0	17	7	2	0
Display of extremist tattoos, brandings or piercings	3	0	14	6	1	0
Over the counter medication abuse	2	0	14	7	2	1
Social isolation	3	0	11	4	1	0
Affiliation with groups that pose credible threats	3	0	10	5	1	0
Association with groups known to advocate violence	3	0	10	5	1	0
Association with groups that advocate extremist ideologies	3	0	10	5	1	0

Note: Percents will not sum to 100 because respondents were asked to mark all that apply

Behaviors Documented by Unit Supervisors

Civilian Directors   n= 73

Behaviors Documented by Unit Supervisors	Active Duty	Guard	Reserve	Civilian	Contractors	Family
Harassing statements	19	0	3	51	11	1
Threats of violence	21	0	3	47	8	3
Displays of violence	18	0	3	45	11	3
Verbal outbursts	15	0	3	45	10	1
Poor communication skills	19	0	0	41	5	1
Abuse of alcohol	22	1	3	38	8	0
Aggression	16	0	3	38	11	1
Financial problems	22	1	3	37	3	3
Major physical illnesses	15	0	1	36	4	1
Retaliatory behavior	16	0	3	34	10	1
Bullying/Belittling behavior	14	0	3	33	11	1
Poor impulse control	14	0	3	26	8	1
Excessive use of alcohol	15	1	3	25	7	1
Prescription medication abuse	11	0	1	25	3	0
Mental health problems	16	1	3	22	3	1
Poor relationships	11	0	0	21	4	1
Inability to effectively deal with stress	11	1	3	21	4	1
Over the counter medication abuse	10	0	1	21	3	0
Antisocial behavior	7	1	1	19	1	0
Low self esteem	11	0	0	18	4	0
Divorce/separation	14	1	1	16	3	1
Excessive stress	10	1	1	16	3	0
Social isolation	10	0	0	10	0	1
Affiliation with groups that pose credible threats	10	0	1	7	3	0
Association with groups known to advocate violence	10	0	1	7	3	0
Association with groups that advocate extremist ideologies	10	0	1	7	3	0
Display of extremist tattoos, brandings or piercings	7	1	1	3	0	0

Note: Percents will not sum to 100 because respondents were asked to mark all that apply

Non-Line Officers

Non-Line officers are held to the same professional standards as Line Officers.

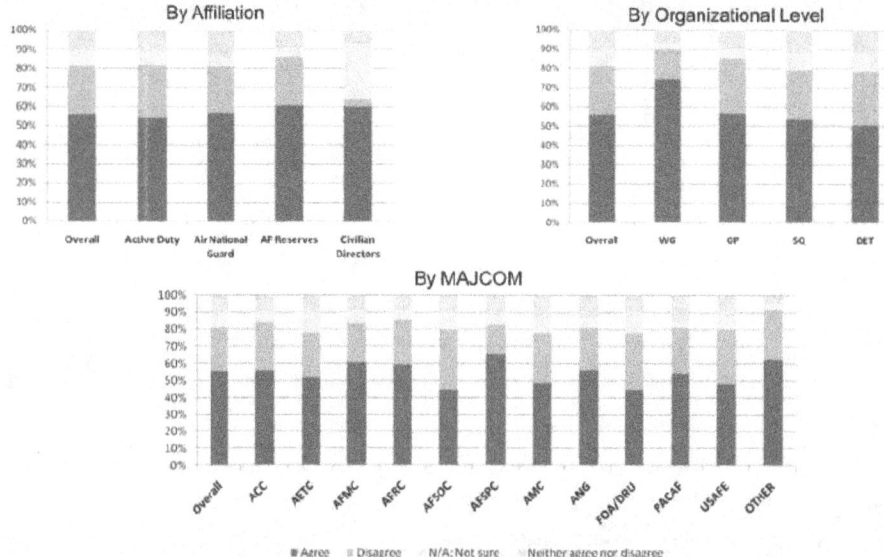

Approximately 56% of commanders feel Non-Line officers are held to the same professional standards as Line Officers

Non-Line Officers

Non-Line officers are held to the same professional standards as Line Officers.

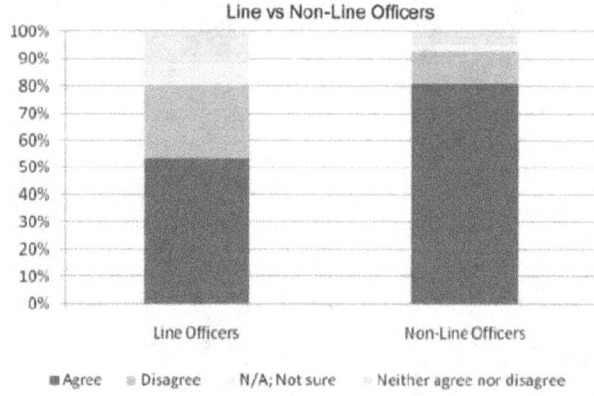

Note: Sample distribution
92% Line Officers
8% Non-Line Officers (only medical)

81% of Non-Line Officers believe they are held to the same professional standards as Line Officers, while 54% of Line Officers agree with this statement

Understanding Procedure

- Commanders were asked to check all of the agencies for which they understood the appropriate procedures for referring or reporting their personnel
- Minimal differences in understanding procedures cited by Active Duty, Guard , Reserve commanders
- Best understood
  - How to refer/report to Chain of Command and Chaplains
  - Appropriate procedures for their own personnel
- Civilian Directors best understood appropriate procedures for active duty personnel as well as civilians
- Least understood procedures by all leaders
  - Local community agencies
  - Off-base mental health provider
- Few leaders report understanding procedures on how to refer contractor personnel

Understanding Procedure

Active Duty Commanders   n= 1362

Understand Appropriate Procedures to Refer/Report Personnel to ...	Not Sure	Active Duty	Guard	Reserves	Civilian	Contractors	Family
Chaplain	1	94	31	35	45	21	48
My chain of command	1	94	33	37	54	35	45
On-base medical providers	2	94	28	33	39	14	45
Alcohol Drug Abuse Prevention Program	2	93	26	30	28	9	26
First Sergeant	2	93	31	34	36	18	42
On-base mental health provider	2	93	26	31	33	10	36
Sexual Assault Response Coordinator	1	93	31	35	46	22	43
Family Advocacy	3	92	26	30	28	9	44
Security Forces	2	92	31	35	48	29	43
Office of the Staff Judge Advocate	2	91	27	31	32	11	27
OSI	4	88	29	33	42	23	34
Airman & Family Readiness Center	6	87	27	30	28	10	42
Inspector General	4	87	28	32	42	19	26
Health & Wellness Center	6	86	26	29	25	8	28
Safety	7	83	27	30	41	23	26
Unit Key Spouse Volunteer	15	68	19	21	24	10	43
Military Family Life Consultants	23	59	18	21	19	7	31
Military One Source	24	55	18	20	20	8	30
Civilian Law Enforcement	25	52	19	21	34	23	33
Off-base medical providers	29	48	13	15	24	12	27
Local community agencies	33	42	13	14	23	13	24
Off-base mental health provider	31	42	12	13	20	10	22

Note Percents will not sum to 100 because respondents were asked to mark all that apply

Understanding Procedure

Air National Guard Commanders   n= 405

Understand Appropriate Procedures to Refer/Report Personnel to ...	Not Sure	Active Duty	Guard	Reserves	Civilian	Contractors	Family
First Sergeant	1	30	92	14	14	5	9
My chain of command	1	30	92	14	25	15	15
Chaplain	1	30	91	13	20	6	11
Sexual Assault Response Coordinator	1	30	88	13	23	10	11
Security Forces	2	30	87	12	23	12	10
Office of the Staff Judge Advocate	3	27	85	10	17	5	4
On-base medical providers	7	28	83	9	16	4	6
Safety	4	26	83	13	23	11	9
Inspector General	6	26	77	12	19	8	8
Alcohol Drug Abuse Prevention Program	10	24	69	8	16	3	6
OSI	14	23	60	10	18	8	7
Family Advocacy	17	20	60	7	12	3	9
On-base mental health provider	20	21	59	6	10	2	4
Military One Source	19	18	55	8	12	5	10
Civilian Law Enforcement	17	19	54	11	20	13	13
Off-base medical providers	24	12	45	4	16	5	8
Off-base mental health provider	26	8	42	3	14	4	6
Airman & Family Readiness Center	27	17	40	6	9	3	7
Local community agencies	26	11	35	6	10	5	8
Unit Key Spouse Volunteer	32	9	33	4	6	2	9
Health & Wellness Center	34	13	27	4	5	2	5
Military Family Life Consultants	35	8	25	4	5	2	5

Note: Percents will not sum to 100 because respondents were asked to mark all that apply

Understanding Procedure

AF Reserve Commanders   n= 228

Understand Appropriate Procedures to Refer/Report Personnel to ...	Not Sure	Active Duty	Guard	Reserves	Civilian	Contractors	Family
My chain of command	2	31	12	95	37	13	19
Chaplain	3	33	12	92	29	8	17
First Sergeant	3	32	11	92	21	5	14
Security Forces	4	33	12	90	34	13	14
Sexual Assault Response Coordinator	2	32	12	90	33	10	16
On-base medical providers	6	33	11	89	25	5	12
Office of the Staff Judge Advocate	5	30	11	88	26	5	9
Inspector General	3	32	11	87	29	7	10
Safety	6	29	10	83	32	10	11
On-base mental health provider	9	32	9	82	23	4	10
OSI	7	32	12	81	28	10	12
Family Advocacy	8	27	10	79	25	4	16
Airman & Family Readiness Center	7	29	10	77	19	5	18
Alcohol Drug Abuse Prevention Program	7	29	9	77	29	4	8
Military One Source	16	21	11	63	20	4	14
Health & Wellness Center	18	27	9	61	15	4	10
Civilian Law Enforcement	17	20	9	60	28	11	14
Off-base medical providers	24	13	6	49	27	7	11
Unit Key Spouse Volunteer	29	13	5	41	12	3	8
Off-base mental health provider	25	12	6	41	25	6	10
Local community agencies	28	13	7	40	20	7	11
Military Family Life Consultants	33	13	6	38	13	3	9

Note: Percents will not sum to 100 because respondents were asked to mark all that apply

Understanding Procedure

Civilian Directors   n= 73

Understand Appropriate Procedures to Refer/Report Personnel to ...	Not Sure	Active Duty	Guard	Reserves	Civilian	Contractors	Family
My chain of command	1	70	16	29	85	42	21
Security Forces	5	64	19	25	82	32	18
On-base medical providers	4	67	11	19	74	16	11
Sexual Assault Response Coordinator	4	66	16	25	74	29	12
Inspector General	8	59	14	23	73	23	10
Safety	11	55	14	23	73	30	10
OSI	5	53	14	21	73	23	14
Alcohol Drug Abuse Prevention Program	10	62	10	16	67	10	10
On-base mental health provider	8	62	10	16	66	14	10
Chaplain	8	62	12	18	64	15	12
Family Advocacy	10	62	10	18	60	14	12
Civilian Law Enforcement	19	33	14	16	55	25	16
Health & Wellness Center	14	51	8	18	52	12	12
Office of the Staff Judge Advocate	16	52	8	14	51	11	8
Off-base medical providers	29	19	4	8	42	15	10
Airman & Family Readiness Center	18	49	10	19	33	10	14
Off-base mental health provider	34	16	3	5	30	11	8
Local community agencies	37	15	1	3	29	10	7
First Sergeant	16	53	14	21	23	8	11
Military One Source	33	27	3	7	14	3	5
Unit Key Spouse Volunteer	37	23	3	7	12	5	7
Military Family Life Consultants	36	26	1	4	11	4	7

Note: Percents will not sum to 100 because respondents were asked to mark all that apply

Preparation for Active-Shooter Events by Affiliation

My unit personnel are informed about the potential for active-shooter scenarios on-base.

My unit personnel clearly understand what to do during an active-shooter situation on-base (e.g., direction of evacuation, shelter in place, etc.).

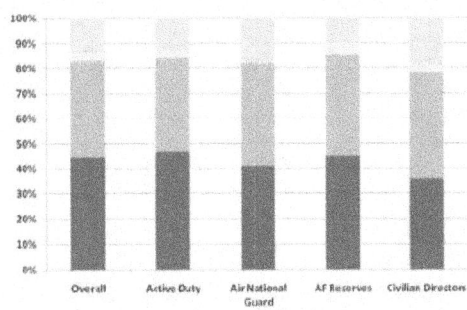
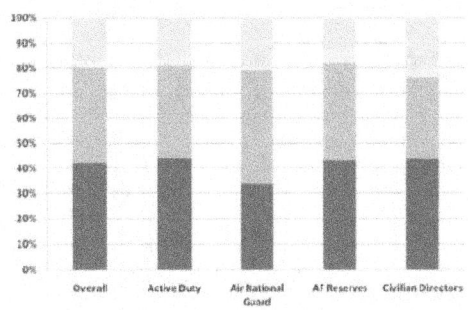

■ Agree   ■ Disagree   N/A; Not Sure   Neither agree nor disagree

Less than half of commanders feel personnel are informed or understand what to do during an active-shooter event

Preparation for Active-Shooter Events by Organizational Level

My unit personnel are informed about the potential for active-shooter scenarios on-base.

My unit personnel clearly understand what to do during an active-shooter situation on-base (e.g., direction of evacuation, shelter in place, etc.).

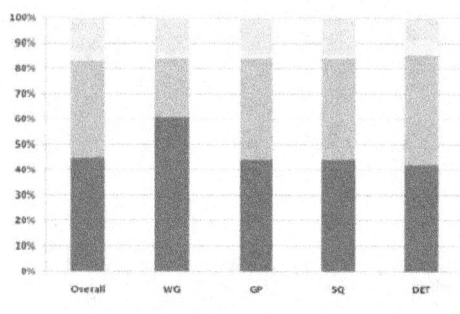 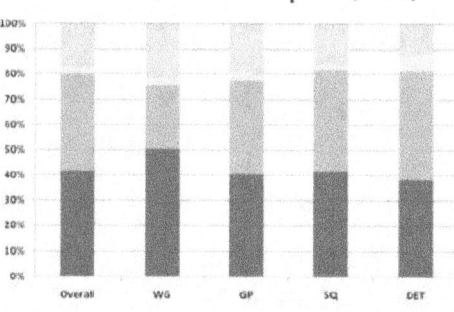

■ Agree ■ Disagree ■ N/A; Not Sure ■ Neither agree nor disagree

Significant differences in perception of preparation by organizational level

Preparation for Active-Shooter Events by CONUS/OCONUS

My unit personnel are informed about the potential for active-shooter scenarios on-base.

My unit personnel clearly understand what to do during an active-shooter situation on-base (e.g., direction of evacuation, shelter in place, etc.).

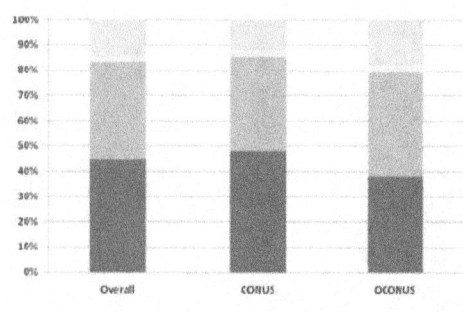 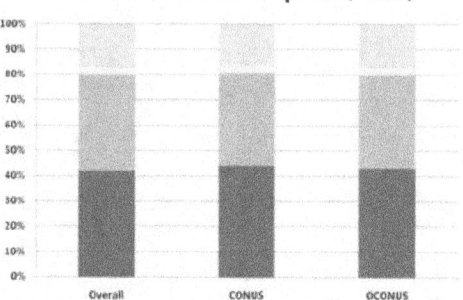

■ Agree ■ Disagree ■ N/A; Not Sure ■ Neither agree nor disagree

Slightly lower percent of OCONUS commanders feel personnel are informed

Commander Training by Career Family

My commander training sufficiently addressed the following:

My commander training sufficiently addressed the following:	Operations	Logistics	Support	Medical	Acquisition and Financial	Recruiting Service	Installation/Wing Commanders
				% Agree			
Commander authorities	77	76	75	83	83	94	84
Accountability for my action/inaction	75	75	75	91	87	94	79
Force protection concerns	62	67	71	76	70	78	76
Responsibility to share information on potential indicators of internal threats	62	63	62	72	70	79	66
Case studies of Failed Leadership	59	53	59	57	65	78	58
Mechanisms to share information on potential indicators of internal threats	63	63	55	69	58	72	67
Indicators of potential behavior that may pose an internal threat	49	51	52	60	61	72	55
Difference in sharing information on military	45	46	52	62	58	44	50
Mass casualty scenarios	28	36	48	69	33	17	52
Sharing information on civilian employees and how it differs from military	26	36	37	46	45	28	41
Sharing information on dependents and how it differs from civilian employees, military and contractors	24	27	29	42	37	22	37
Sharing information on contractor personnel and how it differs from civilian and military personnel	20	25	27	33	38	17	32

Green indicates highest % Agree values
Red indicates lowest % Agree values
Note: Recruiting Services: n=18

Medical Commanders have overall higher % Agree values than other commanders

Commander Training

My commander training sufficiently addressed the following:

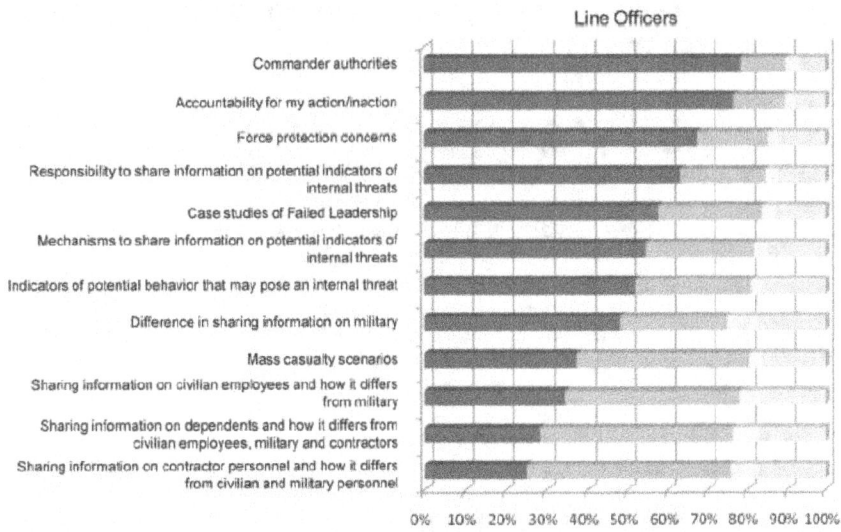

The order of items in the list are relatively the same for both line and non-line officers with the exception of 'mass casualty scenarios' and 'case studies of failed leadership'

Commander Training

My commander training sufficiently addressed the following:

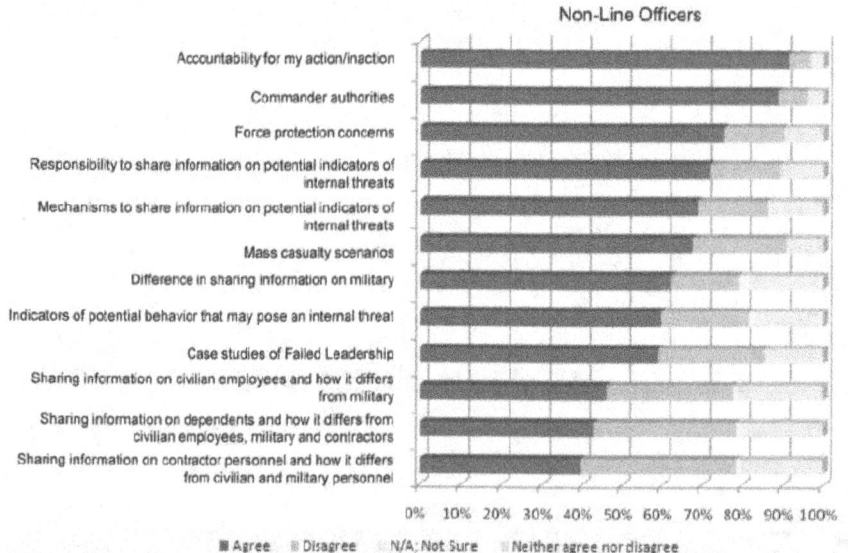

The order of items in the list are relatively the same for both line and non-line officers with the exception of 'mass casualty scenarios' and 'case studies of failed leadership'

Sources of Stress

I have a good understanding of whether the below sources of stress are currently affecting personnel within my unit.

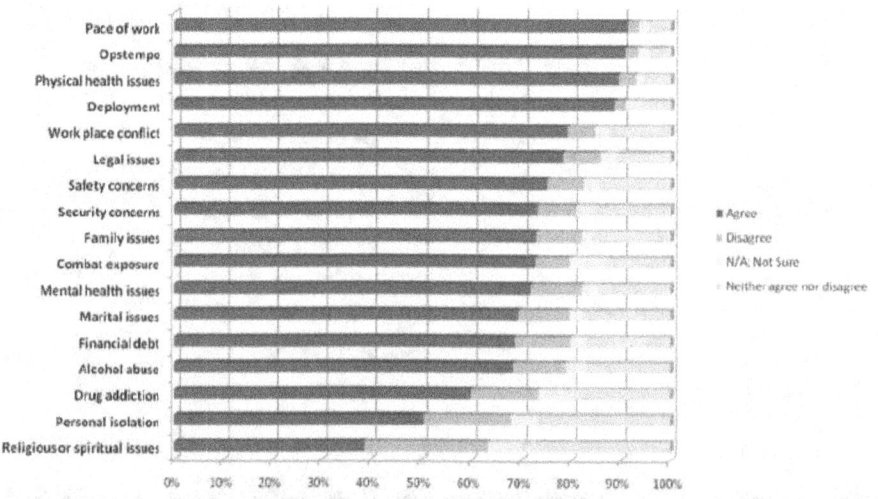

Less than half of commanders feel they have a good understanding of religious/spiritual issues or personal isolation affecting their personnel

Assessment of Programs

Assessment of programs/procedures available to mitigate stressors affecting unit personnel.

All Active Duty, Reserve Commanders and Civilian Directors

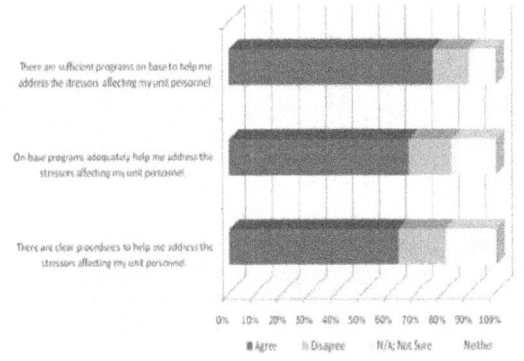

Air National Guard Commanders

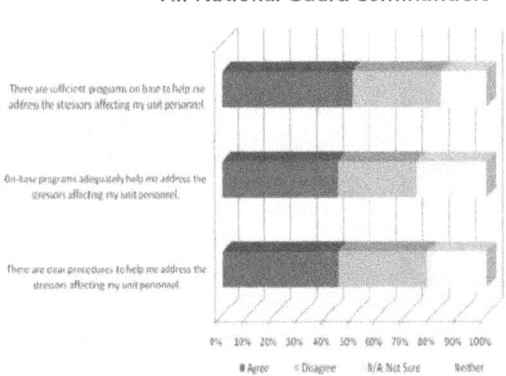

More ANG commanders <u>disagree</u> that programs/procedures to address unit personnel stressors are sufficient, adequate or clear

U.S. AIR FORCE

T

DS Staff

Col Joan Garbutt
Laura Miller, PhD
Lt Col John Giles
Lt Col Jason Knight
Maj Chad Schrecengost
Maj Tracy Maza
Capt Marissa Carlton
Capt Tracy Barnett
Capt Shane Blevins

HAF Teams

Risk Assessment and Prevention

Col Andy Huff
Col Belinda Morrone
Ms. Connie Wright
Lt Col James Bachinsky
Lt Col Mark Bell
Lt Col Mark DiCarlo
Lt Col Mark Formica
Lt Col Clifford Gyves
Maj Jason Knudsen
Maj Brian Musselman
Mr. Peter Koeppl, Contractor

Preparing the Force

Col Michael Hafer
Lt Col Lowell Sensintaffar
Lt Col Aaron Benson
Lt Col Mark DiCarlo
Lt Col Mark Formica
Lt Col Marshall S. Furr
Lt Col Gary Hayward
Lt Col Frederick Helmer
Lt Col Tara Morrison
Maj Jason Knudsen
Capt Carl Cook

Sharing Information

Col Keith Givens
Ms. Connie Wright
Lt Col Angel Olivares
Lt Col Bridgette Arnold
Lt Col Eric Obergfell
Lt Col Kevin Seeley
Maj Reid Novotny
Maj Renae Hilton

Developing the Force

Col James Miner
Lt Col Amy Asher
Ms. Ladonna McGrew
Lt Col Charles Motsinger
Maj Thomas Hoskins
Mr. Christopher Merlo
Chap (Maj) Abner Valenzuela
CMSgt Saint Carter
CMSgt Lawrence Chang
Ms. Pamela Friend

Leading the Force

Mr. Tom Kelly
Chap (Col) Jerry Pitts
Col Annette Sanks
Lt Col Mark Formica
Lt Col Janice Langer
Lt Col Roger Neumann
Lt Col Jeff Puckett
Mr. Mike Dickey
Ms. Carmen Livoti
Chap (Maj) Matthew Franke
Capt Thomas Oziemblowsky

Responding and Recovering

Col Elizabeth Arledge
Chap (Col) Jerry Pitts
Lt Col John Conaway
Lt Col Elizabeth Demmons
Mr. Mike Dickey
Lt Col Karl Kraan
Ms. Gretchen Shannon
Lt Col Tom Taylor
Maj Gary Byrd
Maj Dan Janning
Maj Scott Olech
Capt Ian Phillips
SA Brian Alexander

Other HAF Contributors

Mr. Jim Neighbors
Col Gregory Cate
Col James Byrne
Col John Forbes
Lt Col James DeLong
Mr. Gary Brisbane
Mr. Dan Stanton
Mr. Dan Cipra
Ms. Jessica Pezzaro
Ms. Ellen Campana
Ms. Mercedes Greene

Red Team

Col Dan Charchian
Frank Wondolowski, PhD
SA James Cangialosi

Reachback Advisor

Lt Gen Richard T. Swope, USAF (Ret.)

Major Command and Direct Reporting Unit Teams

ACC

Col Bob LaBrutta
Col Howard Stendahl
Col Alan Metzler
Col Victoria Bowens
Col David Crow
Col Mike Dwyer
Col Jeff Yocum
Lt Col Tim Wagoner
Lt Col Joseph Piasecki
Lt Col David Schobel
Lt Col Erik Fegenbush
Lt Col John D. Smith
Lt Col Mitzi Thomas-Lawson
Mr. Jean Michel
Ms. M. Eileen Jones
Mr. Michael Hassan
Maj Joel Fenlason
Ms. Jill Gibson
Mr. Mark Salisbury
Mr. Angelo Dart
Capt Justine Iacono
SMSgt Bryan Vibert

AETC

Col Bruce Lovely
Chap (Col) Bobby Page
Col Gerard Jolivette
Col Lee Pittman

Col Tal Metzgar
Col John Lopardi
Mr. Chip Manning
Ms. Bonnie Molina
Mr. Byron Cotton
Lt Col Christopher Alonzo
Lt Col Cheryl Scaglione
Lt Col Sonya Collins
Lt Col Kristine Blackwell
Lt Col Christopher Oleksa
Lt Col Matthew McConnell
Chap (Lt Col) Charles Cornelisse
Mr. Gerard Kinane
Mr. Charles Wyatt
Mr. David Smith
Capt Johanna Jaboneta
CMSgt William Dambacher
CMSgt Michael Young
SMSgt Ulanda Isaaks

AFDW

Mr. Steve Doss
Col June Gavron
Col David Timm
Col Brian Bellacicco
Col Wally Vaughn
Mr. Ryan Ferrell
Ms. Wanda Jones-Heath
Ms. Marsha Johnson

AFGSC

Brig Gen Ed Walker
Col Pete Ellis
Col Charles Campbell
Col Jon Stovall
Col Mike Kelly
Col Annette Foster
Col Jimmy Sterling
Col Ronald Grove
Col Lynden Skinner
Col Michael O'Connor
Col Dewey Little
Mr. Kelvin Bowen
Mr. John Good
Mr. Robert Thomson
Lt Col Lori LaVezzi
Lt Col Paul Cairney
Lt Col Paul Gardetto
Lt Col Michael Saylor
Lt Col John Thomas
Lt Col Carl Wright
Maj Adam Curtis
Maj Christopher Karns
Maj Ryan Wheeler
1Lt Daniel Minnocci
SMSgt Eric Hein
TSgt Carl Koester
SA Michael Allen
SA Melody Mitchell

AFMA

Col Brian Norman
Mr. Grover Lindsey
Ms. Bernadette Oncale
Mischell Navarro, PhD
Mr. Louis Datko

AFMC

Mr. David Taylor
Col Kenneth Andersen
Col Joan Cunningham
Col Rick Hyland
Col Steven Merrill
Lt Col David Dusseau
Lt Col Michael Miles
Lt Col Roger Scott
Maj Franklin Swayne
Mr. Bill Klosterman
Mr. Russell Kofoed
Mr. Jeff Kirklighter
Ms. Libby Van Hook
Jeff Paddock, PhD
Mr. Mike Hall
Ms. Sharon Williams

AFOTEC

Col Edgar Vaughan
Ms. JoAnn Stringfield
Lt Col Carolyn Patrick
Mr. Roderick Earl
Barron Oder, PhD
Mr. Douglas Miles
CMSgt Kelly Branscom
Mr. Gerald Trujillo
SMSgt Peter Padilla
Mr. Timoteo Torrez
Mr. William Horst
MSgt Lonnie Allen
Ms. Jessica Leisey

AFRC

Col Joseph Vivori
Col Mike Kozak
Col Connie Hutchinson
Col Max Mendoza
Col Allen Gilbar
Mr. Jefferey Ippolito

AFRI

Chris Cain, PhD
Mr. Robyn Read
Lt Col Kristal Alfonso

AFSPC

Brig Gen John Raymond
Col Gerald Curry
Col Mary Fleurquin
Col Thomas French
Mr. Jonathan Grammer
Col Bill Hampton
Col Dawn Harl
Col Beverly Plosa-Bowser
Col Susan Rhodes
Chap (Col) Gregory Tate
Col Ralph Thompson, Jr.
Col Stephen Whiting
Ms. Nancy Brewer
Chap (Lt Col) Michael Grubbs
Lt Col Mark McCullohs
Lt Col Alexis Sotomayor
Mr. Al Strait
Mr. Al Brodecki
Maj Scott Bullis
Ms. Kathy Latzke
Capt Joy Tredway
MSgt June Geter
SA Steven Aguilar

AFSOC

Col Brady Reitz
Lt Col Chris Simpson
Lt Col Bill Marsh
Lt Col Chris Holton
Maj Charles Love
Maj Roy Frierson
Mr. David Charitat
CMSgt William Posey
Ms. Jeanne Haun

AMC

Col Diane Ritter
Col Wilkins Urquhart
Col Frank Jones
Col Barbara Jacob
Col Steven Ehlenbeck
Chap (Col) Gary Linsky
Mr. Tony Joyner
Lt Col John Jorgensen
Mr. John Hoercher
Mr. Paul Zabbo
Ms. Patti Sizemore
Capt Jonathan Stock
Capt Sandra Bannan
Mr. Stephen Pak
MSgt Mark Miller
SA Kim Gaestel

NGB/ANG

Col Ronald Gionta
Lt Col Anthony Lanuzo
Mr. Jerry Bivins

PACAF

Col James Strickler
Col Steve Hatfield
Col Mark Kling
Col Judith Hughes
Mr. Jeff Allen
Mr. Cliff Hogue
Mr. Johnny Bland
Lt Col James Tims
Lt Col Wendy Sherman
Lt Col Ron Gray
Lt Col Marie Colasanti
Lt Col Robert Lilke
Maj Cotina Jenkins
SMSgt Charlie Johnson

USAFA

Col Rick LoCastro
Col Ronald Nelson
Lt Col Edward Werner
Mr. Paul Ceciliani
Mr. James Rowell
Mr. J. Lance Matzke

USAFE

Col Carla Gammon
Col Gus Green
Col Joseph Mastrianna
Col Mike Johnson
Col Robert Moriarty
Col David Hocking
Col Rod Dorsey
Col Pamela Moxley
Col John Jordan
Mr. Perry D. Sell
Mr. Billy Trevino
Mr. Roger Davis
Lt Col Aubrey Burkel
Lt Col Craig Hess
Lt Col Victor Moncrieffe
Lt Col David Klaus
Maj Catherine Gambold
Maj Steve Smith
Maj Debra Shock
Maj Kevin Mares
Capt Lorena Venegas
Capt Christopher Smith
MSgt Sam Miller

Appendix E ◆ Recommendations

1.1 Develop Air Force policy addressing how risk assessment tools can be used to improve care and overall force protection for Air Force members. (OPR: SAF/IG)

1.2 Develop a risk assessment reference available for all Air Force members. (OPR: AF/SG)

1.3 Partner with the FBI's Comprehensive Analysis of Military Offenders project to ensure that its research approach reflects Air Force concerns and its products are applicable to Air Force populations. (OPR: SAF/IG)

1.4 Continue to update assessment tools as the state of knowledge and policy develop and include appropriate courses of action and resources for active-duty, National Guard, Air Force Reserve, civilians, contractors, and dependents. (OPR: SAF/IG)

1.5 Sponsor research to develop long-term behavioral indicators that may point to progressive indicators of violence among Air Force personnel. (OPR: SAF/IG)

2.1 Coordinate with the Under Secretary of Defense for Personnel and Readiness to review and update DoDI 1325.06, *Handling Dissident and Protest Activities among Members of the Armed Forces*, to ensure guidance is actionable and includes behavior examples as well as guidance on how to respond to uncertain situations, and revise AFI 51-903 accordingly. (OPR: AF/JA, SAF/GC)

2.2 Revise AFI 51-903, via an Air Force Guidance Memorandum, to improve identification of potential threats and clarify how commanders may determine which activities, including group participation, are disruptive to good order and discipline. (OPR: AF/JA, SAF/GC)

2.3 Update *The Military Commander and the Law* by adding resources on addressing extremist behaviors, including information or actions that indicate personnel may be engaged in extremist or other prohibited activities. (OPR: AF/JA)

2.4 Ensure unit leaders are aware of DA PAM 600-15, *Extremist Activities*, and consider publishing a similar Air Force document and associated training material to improve current awareness of extremist and prohibited activities. (OPR: AF/JA, SAF/IG)

3.1 Update AFI 36-2903, *Dress and Personal Appearance of Air Force Personnel*, to address prohibited tattoos, brands, and body art and to reference acceptable tools for unit leaders and other Airmen to identify prohibited markings. (OPR: AF/A1)

3.2 Disseminate AFOSI's "Visual Iconography: Gang and Right-Wing Hate Group Affiliated Symbols and Body Art" to commanders as an initial reference tool, followed by the AFI update. (OPR: SAF/IG)

3.3 Establish a comprehensive reference tool of prohibited body markings for recruiters, trainers, commanders, and supervisors. (OPR: SAF/IG)

3.4 Develop a centralized tracking tool to inform commander decisions of previously approved body markings. (OPR: AF/A1)

4.1 Amend current Air Force policy and procedures contained in AFI 31-101, *Integrated Defense*, to govern privately owned weapons in all Air Force housing. In doing so, consider whether effective as well as constructive notice is provided to individuals who enter installations but do not live on them. (OPR: AF/A4/7)

4.2 Coordinate with the Under Secretary of Defense for Intelligence to prepare a department-wide interim guidance message and interim guidance that will be incorporated into a revision of DoD 5200.08-R, *Physical Security Program*. (OPR: AF/A4/7)

5.1 Revise AFI 31-101, *Integrated Defense*, to require individuals to sign DD Form 2760, *Qualification to Possess Firearms or Ammunition*, when firearms are registered in accordance with DoDI 6400.06 and 18 USC 922. (OPR: AF/A4/7)

6.1 Train health care providers who conduct pre- or post-deployment interviews to assess non-mental-health-related risks for violence (e.g., potential for radicalization, gang involvement). (OPR: AF/SG)

6.2 Expand deployment risk assessment methods to include reliable, accessible collateral information. (OPR: AF/SG)

6.3 Encourage Airmen to share with leadership or support service providers pre- and post-deployment concerns about themselves as well as others. (OPR: AF/SG)

6.4 Consider adopting a program similar to the Fort Lewis Soldier Wellness Assessment Program, which requires all deploying personnel to meet personally with credentialed mental health providers. (OPR: AF/SG)

7.1 Develop appropriate changes to policy, programs, and procedures to establish mental health consultancy to help unit leaders more effectively address the risks for violence, similar to the manner in which unit leaders consult with chaplains. (OPR: AF/SG)

8.1 Coordinate with DoD to develop workplace violence and internal threat prevention and response policies, programs, and procedures. (OPR: AF/A4/7)

9.1 Revise AFMAN 31-201, vol. 4, *High Risk Response*, to establish policy and procedures on reporting indicators of violence and enable swift and appropriate response to prevent escalation. (OPR: AF/A4/7)

9.2 Update AFI 44-154, *Suicide and Violence Prevention Education and Training*, to include internal threat exercise requirements. (OPR: AF/SG)

10.1   Coordinate with DoD to draft an instruction, followed by a 90- or 40-series AFI integrating the full spectrum of violence into a comprehensive prevention and response program. (OPR: AF/A1)

11.1   Coordinate with DoD to establish standard contract language regarding prohibited activities, inappropriate or high risk behavior related to violence in the DoD workplace. If feasible, the standard language should be required for inclusion in all DoD contracts and should parallel standards set for government civilian employees on potential indicators of violence in the workplace. (OPR: SAF/AQ)

12.1   Revise AFI 36-703, *Civilian Conduct and Responsibility*, to more clearly address violence in the workplace. (OPR: AF/A1)

13.1   Address personal resiliency and risk management through formalized programs that provide an overarching approach to identifying and managing stressors. (OPR: AF/A1)

14.1   Integrate information on internal threats and workplace violence into the Integrated Delivery System community outreach and prevention programs. (OPR: AF/A1)

15.1   Consolidate guidance related to religious accommodation (e.g., dress, religious observance, immunization) in a single 52-series AFI. (OPR: AF/HC)

15.2   Revise policy to recommend leaders consult chaplains and legal counsel when making decisions about religious accommodation requests and to guide leaders on the challenges of such decisions in joint environments. (OPR: AF/HC)

15.3   Revise AFI 52-101, *Planning and Organizing*, to include procedures for religious accommodation. After AFPD 52-1 coordination is complete, ensure that the prevention, identification, and response to religious-based disrespect, harassment, and discrimination are sufficiently addressed in relevant training (e.g., equal opportunity training, free exercise of religion training, Wingman training, and commander courses). (OPR: AF/HC)

16.1   Coordinate with the Deputy Under Secretary of Defense for Military Personnel Policy to develop procedures for investigative bodies to convey pertinent information to the Armed Forces Chaplains Board on religious organizations and their endorsing agents that may affect their status to endorse military chaplains. (OPR: AF/HC)

16.2   Following revisions to DoD policy, update AFPD 52-1, *Chaplain Service*, to reflect any revised roles and responsibilities of the Air Force Chief of Chaplains. (OPR: AF/HC)

17.1   Revise AFI 90-501, *Community Action Information Board and Integrated Delivery System*, to incorporate a forum geared to support Air Force members who need assistance or intervention to preclude more serious issues. (OPR: AF/A1)

17.2 Fund a full-time, installation-level civilian position to oversee and integrate community, family, individual support, and resiliency programs. (OPR: AF/A1)

18.1 Consider the feasibility of adapting current background investigation processes and techniques to improve identification of internal threats. (OPR: SAF/AA)

19.1 Coordinate with DoD, DoS, and combatant commands to ensure foreign nationals working on OCONUS installations are subject to stringent investigation standards and procedures. (OPR: SAF/IA)

20.1 Coordinate with the Department of Homeland Security to ensure that foreign nationals granted access to CONUS installations are subject to the most stringent investigation standards and procedures possible. (OPR: SAF/IA)

21.1 Adopt the DoD Military Accessions Vital to National Interests program expanding background checks to include national/intelligence agency checks, single scope background investigation (interviews), and automated continuous evaluation checks (ACES). (OPR: AF/A1)

22.1 Examine the feasibility of implementing ACES checks on AFRC and ANG members. (OPR: AFRC, NGB)

23.1 Coordinate with the OSD Military Personnel Records Information Management Task Force (MPRIMTF) study that focuses on what information is appropriate to maintain in military personnel records over the course of a career. (OPR: AF/A1)

23.2 Develop procedures for storing and transferring information that includes possible indicators of violent behavior. (OPR: AF/A1)

23.3 Consider developing a system similar to the Air Force Judge Advocate's Automated Military Justice Analysis and Management System to track information that may indicate a potential for violent behavior. (OPR: AF/A1)

24.1 Revise AFI 90-201, *Inspector General Activities*, to make assessment of force protection, internal threat prevention, and response mandatory inspection items. (OPR: SAF/IG)

24.2 Develop a Force Protection Response Bulletin to disseminate best practices identified by IG inspections related to force protection, internal threats, and suicides. (OPR: SAF/IG)

25.1 Review and incorporate findings of the ongoing MPRIMTF into Air Force policy. (OPR: AF/A1)

26.1 Integrate AFOSI Investigative Information Management System case file database into Defense Law Enforcement Exchange, the DoD consolidated criminal investigations database. (OPR: SAF/IG)

Appendix E ◆ Recommendations

27.1   Coordinate with the Under Secretary of Defense for Intelligence to review DoDI 5240.6, *Counterintelligence (CI) Awareness, Briefing, and Reporting Programs.* (OPR: SAF/IG)

28.1   Coordinate with the DoD and the other Services to define requirements for a common threat reporting system similar to the DoJ/FBI *eGuardian* system. (OPR: SAF/IG)

29.1   Continue participation in the Technical Support Working Group of the Combating Terrorism Technical Support Office to collaborate with other Services, government agencies, academia, and civilian organizations on threat detection, prevention, and management efforts. (OPR: AF/A4/7)

30.1   Continue participation in the Physical Security Equipment Action Group and the Defense Installation Access Control behavioral analysis study. (OPR: AF/A4/7)

31.1   Coordinate with DoD and the other Services to share vehicle registration, debarment lists, and other relevant information required to screen personnel, vehicles, and grant access. (OPR: AF/A4/7)

31.2   Update AFI 31-201, *Security Forces Standards and Procedures,* to govern how debarment information is shared. (OPR: AF/A4/7)

31.3   Revise Air Force policy to require installation commanders to enter debarment information into a central database and to review Air Force debarments when making decisions to grant individuals base access. (OPR: AF/A4/7)

31.4   Fully fund and continue to install Defense Biometric Identification System (DBIDS) at all Air Force installations to improve communications between installations. (OPR: AF/A4/7)

31.5   Modify the DBIDS database to reflect debarment actions. (OPR: AF/A4/7)

31.6   Support DoD-wide implementation of DBIDS. (OPR: AF/A4/7)

32.1   Coordinate with DoD to establish standardized contract procedures and practices for TRICARE providers to recognize and report, within legal limits, potential indicators of violent behavior for active duty, ANG, and Air Force Reserve members who receive treatment through TRICARE providers. (OPR: SAF/MR)

33.1   Coordinate with DoD to develop policies, programs, and procedures for military medical personnel, commanders, and supervisors to receive and review indicators of potentially violent behavior for ANG and Air Force Reserve members who seek care from civilian medical institutions when not on active duty orders. (OPR: SAF/MR)

33.2   Coordinate with DoD to develop policies and procedures for civilian health care providers to alert military leaders when they believe active duty, ANG, and Air

Force Reserve members whom they treat pose a threat to themselves or others. (OPR: SAF/MR)

34.1 Revise AFI 44-109, *Mental Health, Confidentiality and Military Law*, paragraph 6, to reference DTM 09-006, *Revising Command Notification Requirements to Dispel Stigma in Providing Mental Health Care to Military Personnel*, or follow-on DoDI guidance currently in coordination. (OPR: AF/SG)

34.2 Revise AFI 41-210, *Patient Administration Functions*, paragraph 2.5.6.2. to add exceptions for commanders establishing need for and obtaining concurrence with the SJA before obtaining patient information on a military member. (OPR: AF/SG)

34.3 AF/SG incorporate reporting guidance IAW AFI 44-109, *Mental Health, Confidentiality and Military Law*, and AFI 41-210, *Patient Administration Functions*, into all levels of health care provider training, beginning with medical school at the Uniformed Services University of the Health Sciences through the chief of medical staff. (OPR: AF/SG)

35.1 Continue deploying and expand the ANG directors of psychological health and AFRC regional psychological health advocates programs. (OPR: AFRC, NGB)

36.1 Publish derivative Air Force guidance upon release of DoDI 5420.xxx, *Counterintelligence Activities in Cyberspace*, to include when the coordinated offices involved in defense cyber activities should alert leaders to potential threats in their command. (OPR: SAF/IG)

37.1 Engage with the OSD to better define the term *force protection*. (OPR: AF/A3/5)

38.1 Coordinate with the DoD to identify a single executive agent to manage force protection-related common reporting systems. (OPR: SAF/IG)

39.1 Task the Force Protection Steering Group to develop options for appointing a HAF force protection lead. (OPR: AF/A4/7)

39.2 Develop an AFPD to establish and clarify roles and responsibilities within the HAF for the force protection mission. (OPR: AF/A4/7)

40.1 Participate in the Defense Science Board (DSB) multidisciplinary group to develop assessment programs for internal threats. (OPR: AF/A4/7)

40.2 Provide commanders with a multidisciplinary capability focused on detecting and neutralizing internal threats, based on recommendations from the DSB independent study. (OPR: AF/A4/7)

41.1 Revise AFI 10-206, *Operational Reporting*, to ensure incidents related to force protection within the CONUS are reported according to prescribed timelines to

Appendix E ◆ Recommendations

USNORTHCOM, AFNORTH, and appropriate Air Force and DoD agencies. (OPR: AF/A3/5)

41.2 Revise AFI 10-206, *Operational Reporting*, Attachment 2, to ensure AFNORTH and USNORTHCOM are notified for all incident types having force protection implications. (OPR: AF/A3/5)

42.1 Coordinate with DoD to develop standardized threat-reporting procedures and incorporate any new policies and procedures into existing AFIs as necessary. (OPR: SAF/IG)

43.1 Participate with the Joint Staff to explore and research technology to improve legacy OPREP-3 reporting systems. (OPR: AF/A3/5)

44.1 Ensure those involved in the installation reporting process (e.g., command post representatives, command chain, etc.) are properly trained and proficient in their tasks and have appropriate resources, tools, checklists, and guidance to accomplish them. (OPR: AF/A3/5)

44.2 Evaluate the need for command post controllers to be certified to monitor external information sources, approve, and submit initial voice reports on behalf of the installation commander. (OPR: AF/A3/5)

45.1 Coordinate with appropriate DoD, joint, and Service representatives to revise operational reporting policies to include specific examples of incident types that should trigger an OPREP-3 PINNACLE report. (OPR: AF/A3/5)

46.1 Coordinate with Joint Staff and USNORTHCOM representatives to revise CJCSM 3150.05C, *Joint Reporting Structure (JRS) Situation Monitoring Manual*, and US Northern Command Instruction 10-211, *Operational Reporting*, to include instructions on how to disseminate incident reports, including rapid horizontal notification. (OPR: AF/A3/5)

46.2 Revise AFI 10-206, *Operational Reporting*, to reflect Joint and GCC policies on disseminating information. (OPR: AF/A3/5)

47.1 Participate in DoD revision of MOUs governing participation in Joint Terrorism Task Forces (JTTF). (OPR: SAF/IG)

47.2 Coordinate with the FBI and the Director National Intelligence to determine the feasibility of expanding Air Force representation on priority JTTFs. (OPR: SAF/IG)

48.1 Establish an MOU with the National Counterterrorism Center/Defense Intelligence Unit to establish an Air Force intelligence analyst position and assign an Air Force liaison officer. (OPR: AF/A2)

49.1   Embed a national tactical integration element in the AFOSI Investigations, Collections, and Operations Nexus organization to ensure timely signals intelligence indications and warning support. (OPR: AF/A2)

50.1   Review requirements and coordinate with joint partners and the Defense Threat Reduction Agency for including tenant and joint organizations in base exercises and inspections. (OPR: AF/A4/7)

50.2   Update AFI 90-201, *Inspector General Activities*, to address inspections at joint base locations. (OPR: SAF/IG)

50.3   At joint base locations where the Air Force is lead, the joint base commander must include tenant units in emergency management exercises. (OPR: AF/A4/7)

50.4   At locations where the Air Force is supported by another Service, the senior Air Force commander should ensure Air Force personnel are aware of emergency management procedures and exercise accordingly. (OPR: AF/A4/7)

51.1   Annually review, validate, and disseminate Health Insurance Portability and Accountability Act (HIPAA) training resources to wing, group, and squadron commander courses. (OPR: AF/SG)

51.2   Revise AFI 41-210, *Patient Administration Functions*, paragraph 1.4.2.2, HIPAA Privacy Officer Responsibilities, Education, Training, and Communication, to provide commanders initial patient privacy orientation within 90 days of their assignment. (OPR: AF/SG)

52.1   Assess the requirements for, and implications of, conducting separate officer training courses within Officer Training School to ensure common military professionalism competencies among competitive categories. (OPR: AF/A1)

53.1   Revise AFI 16-109, *International Affairs Specialist (IAS) Program*, to include specific command oversight duties within SAF/IA and AU for members attending academic or PME programs in foreign countries. (OPR: SAF/IA)

54.1   Revise advanced chaplain and chaplain assistant training and refresher courses to include mass casualty and workplace violence response familiarization training. (OPR: AF/HC)

55.1   Revise AFI 52-104 to address training and provide guidance on the requirement for chaplains to provide spiritual support in response to incidents involving workplace violence. (OPR: AF/HC)

56.1   Air Force Chief of Chaplains and the Civil Air Patrol (CAP) should review and update Chaplain Corps Region Staff College training to ensure CAP chaplains are prepared to respond to the full range of emergencies, to include mass casualties. (OPR: AF/HC)

57.1 Evaluate training requirements and appropriately resource contracted clergy to provide support during mass casualty incidents on military installations. (OPR: AF/HC)

58.1 Incorporate provider-specific resiliency care in the ARP. (OPR: AF/A1)

59.1 Develop a process to collaborate with civilian entities in addressing resiliency issues. (OPR: AF/SG)

60.1 Coordinate with Assistant Secretary of Defense for Health Affairs to incorporate resiliency and readiness self-care skills into initial and follow-on training and education programs for military health care providers. (OPR: SAF/MR)

61.1 Reinstitute workplace violence prevention education and training as outlined in AFI 44-154, *Suicide and Violence Prevention Education and Training*, across the career-long continuum of learning. (OPR: AF/SG)

62.1 Revise AFI 10-245 to integrate response procedures for defending the Total Force against internal threats (e.g., active shooter) into existing training across the continuum of learning. (OPR: AF/A4/7)

63.1 Incorporate Sponsor Program guidance found in AFI 36-3009, *Airman and Family Readiness Centers*, into AFI 36-2103, *Individualized Newcomer Treatment and Orientation Program*, to consolidate Sponsor Program policy. Cross-reference consolidated policy appropriately. (OPR: AF/A1)

63.2 Require sponsors for all first-term Airmen and new officer accessions to support relocation to first duty stations, and update AFI 36-2103 accordingly. (OPR: AF/A1)

64.1 Incorporate forthcoming DoD electronic sponsorship application and training (e-SAT) into the Air Force Sponsor Program to standardize sponsor participation, training, and customer feedback available to commanders. (OPR: AF/A1)

64.2 Make feedback available to commanders from the forthcoming reports function of e-SAT to assist program effectiveness. (OPR: AF/A1)

65.1 Revise the SAF/IG inspection checklists to include Sponsor Program metrics. (OPR: SAF/IG)

66.1 Communicate the importance and value of the Wingman concept and development of Wingman Day through focused messages from senior Air Force leaders to all AF members (e.g., recommended strategic messages, themes, activities, and training templates that address a wide range of behaviors related to violence risk). (OPR: AF/A1)

66.2   Provide unit leaders statistics and background information that MAJCOMs can tailor for installation-level Wingman Days. (OPR: AF/A1)

66.3   Include strategies for executing Wingman Day events in appropriate PME, commanders' courses, and other training venues. (OPR: AF/A1)

66.4   Publish a "Knowing Your Airmen" guide for leaders' use on Wingman Day. (OPR: AF/A1)

67.1   Revise AFI 36-2406, *Officer and Enlisted Evaluation System*, via an Air Force Guidance Memorandum, to incorporate greater accountability and automation into the feedback process. (OPR: AF/A1)

68.1   Form an integrated process team to evaluate and refine officer, enlisted, and civilian feedback tools and processes. (OPR: AF/A1)

69.1   Modify AFI 36-3212, *Physical Evaluation for Retention, Retirement, and Separation*, to include Physical Evaluation Board liaison officers (PEBLO) duties to relay Medical Evaluation Board (MEB)/Physical Evaluation Board (PEB) processes and timely updates to affected Airmen and their commanders and first sergeants. (OPR: AF/SG)

69.2   Revise the *Disability Counseling Guide for Physical Evaluation Board Liaison Officers (PEBLO)* to incorporate material from the updated AFIs. (OPR: AF/SG)

70.1   Review Air Force Medical Service (AFMS) force management, and consider changes to compensation, quality-of-life factors, operations tempo, and deployment issues to sustain high-quality health care. (OPR: AF/SG)

71.1   None.

72.1   Coordinate with Office of the Under Secretary of Defense for Personnel and Readiness (OUSD[P&R]) to integrate existing policies and provide appropriate guidance to sustain high-quality care, as well as publish an anti-stigma DoDI based on DTM 09-006. (OPR: AF/SG)

72.2   Address health-care-specific stigma concerns as part of the ongoing biennial review process for AFI 44-109, *Mental Health, Confidentiality and Military Law*. (OPR: AF/SG)

72.3   Consolidate Air Force mental health guidance into a 40-series AFI. (OPR: AF/SG)

73.1   Augment chiefs of medical staff by continuing the current Senior Clinician Billet Program pilot project, and evaluate the program within six months of implementing the 2010 O-6 assignment plan. (OPR: AF/SG)

Appendix E ◆ Recommendations

74.1 Revise applicable professional military education and professional continuing education programs to include learning outcomes focused on authorities, procedures, and programs that support Total Force teaming and leadership. (OPR: AF/A1)

74.2 Revise reference materials for officer, enlisted, and civilian members to clarify authorities, procedures, and programs that support Total Force teaming and leadership. (OPR: AF/A1)

75.1 Establish and chair a HAF-level working group to synchronize Air Force Emergency Management policy and programs. (OPR: AF/A4/7)

76.1 Appoint the Director of Operations (AF/A3/5) as the OPR for the mass notification systems (MNS). (OPR: AF/A3/5)

76.2 Evaluate mass notification technologies and recommend viable, tailored solutions for installation use. (OPR: AF/A3/5)

77.1 Determine the appropriate HAF-level OPR for exercise evaluation team (EET) policies, programs, and procedures. (OPR: SAF/IG)

78.1 Include tenant units in installation emergency management exercises. (OPR: SAF/IG)

79.1 Ensure that installation exercises include situations requiring changes in the force protection condition (FPCON). (OPR: SAF/IG)

80.1 Revise the Air Force emergency management program to comply with the DoD's forthcoming installation emergency management program policy. (OPR: AF/A4/7)

81.1 Establish a formal acquisition program for MNS capabilities, including procurement and sustainment support. (OPR: AF/A3/5)

82.1 Develop policy to ensure effective emergency call routing. (OPR: AF/A4/7)

83.1 Designate a single Air Force office responsible for developing Air Force enhanced 9-1-1 (E9-1-1) policy. (OPR: SAF/CIO A6)

83.2 Update Air Force policy to comply with DoD E9-1-1 policy guidance. (OPR: SAF/CIO A6)

84.1 Ensure the emergency communications center (ECC) enabling concept approved in August 2009 is fully developed and funded. (OPR: AF/A4/7)

85.1 Evaluate the feasibility of providing an emergency medical dispatch (EMD) program on Air Force installations. (OPR: AF/SG, AF/A4/7)

86.1 Field a common operational picture (COP) as a mid- to long-term solution to support emergency-response capabilities. (OPR: AF/A4/7)

87.1 Installations review current COP capabilities and ensure that an interim solution is in place and is practiced as part of the installation emergency management program. (OPR: AF/A4/7)

88.1 Coordinate with DoD to develop minimum system requirements for a COP. (OPR: AF/A4/7)

89.1 Continue developing security forces and police-response procedures to high-risk situations through the use of tactics, techniques, and procedures (TTP). (OPR: AF/A4/7)

90.1 Incorporate active shooter response training into Air Force antiterrorism level-1 (AT-1) training. (OPR: AF/A4/7)

90.2 Incorporate best practices and TTPs for active shooter response into recurring training for military and civilian personnel. (OPR: AF/A4/7)

91.1 Incorporate a case study based on the Fort Hood shooting and similar incidents into wing, group, and incident commander training courses. (OPR: AF/A4/7)

92.1 Update Air Force policy to address the need to integrate, track, exercise, and inspect MAAs. (OPR: AF/A4/7)

93.1 Modify AFI 31-101, *Integrated Defense*, to require security forces squadrons (SFS) and AFOSI jointly to establish MOUs with civilian law enforcement agencies to include expectations for scope and timeliness. (OPR: AF/A4/7)

94.1 Synchronize Emergency Family Assistance Control Center (EFACC)-related AFIs to ensure awareness and participation of all pertinent agencies during EFACC execution and sustainment. (OPR: AF/A1)

95.1 Revise religious support policies to synchronize mass casualty response efforts. (OPR: AF/HC)

96.1 Align Air Force policy with DoD guidance to address memorial service attendance. (OPR: AF/A1)

96.2 Fund one civilian position and provide funding to support civilian family requests to attend memorial services. (OPR: AF/A1)

97.1 Coordinate with DoD to develop policies and procedures for casualty notification and mortuary support of fatalities involving private citizens on an Air Force installation. (OPR: AF/A1)

98.1 Revise Air Force traumatic stress response (TSR) policy to synchronize mental health support services in the aftermath of mass casualty incidents. (OPR: AF/SG)

99.1 Add hostage-negotiation consultation to TSR team capabilities outlined in AFI 44-153, *Traumatic Stress Response*. (OPR: AF/SG)

Executive Writing Team

Editor-in-Chief

Chris Cain, PhD

Co-Chiefs Content Integration

Capt Marissa Carlton
Capt Johanna Jaboneta

Editing Team

Col Joan Garbutt
Col Bruce Lovely
Lt Col Scott Peel
Maj Tracy Maza
Laura Miller, PhD
Mr. Jim Howard
Mr. Robyn Read

Technical Writers

Mr. Ben Bryant
Ms. Cheryl Hackley
Mr. Dale Hamby
Mr. Tom Zamberlan
Mr. Michael Arnone
Mr. Mike Ivey
Mr. Gilbert Mendez
Ms. Karen Roberts-Gaither
Mr. C. Boyd Norwood

Content Editors

Richard Bailey, PhD
Marvin Bassett, PhD
Mrs. Belinda Bazinet
Mr. Jerry Gantt
Ms. Demorah Hayes
Ms. Jeanne Shamburger

Technical Editors

Ms. Carolyn Burns
Mrs. Sandi Davis
Ms. Tammi Long
Ms. Catherine Parker
Mrs. Sherry Terrell
Mr. Andrew Thayer

Graphic Designers

Mr. Daniel Armstrong
Ms. Susan Fair

Printing Specialists

Ms. Ann Bailey
Mrs. Nedra Looney
Mrs. Vivian O'Neal